W9-BTF-216

FamilyCircle®

ANNUAL recipes 2011

CHICKEN VEGGIE
NOODLE BOWL,
PAGE 109

Meredith, Consumer Marketing
Des Moines, Iowa

RED VELVET CUPCAKES,
PAGE 99

WELCOME TO A YEAR'S WORTH OF FABULOUS *FAMILY CIRCLE*® RECIPES!

We all want to feed our families well—whether that's a quick weeknight meal before rushing off to the evening's activities or a once-a-year special occasion. When it comes to the things we consider most important in that endeavor, there are several attributes that make a recipe really appeal to us: speed and ease, healthfulness, affordability and, of course, great taste.

At *Family Circle,* our job as editors is to help make your life easier—and that's where *Family Circle Annual Recipes 2011* comes in. Each month, the Healthy Family Dinners feature presents great ideas for fast, fresh and delicious weeknight food. We also know how popular slow cookers are with busy cooks. Our regular Slow Cooker Suppers section provides innovative recipes for delicious dinners that are ready to eat when you walk through the door. And recipes featured in Eating Well on a Budget, a new department for us, help you watch your wallet while enjoying a fabulous homemade meal.

The other job we have as editors is to help make your life more inspired. Whatever is happening seasonally leads us to get creative in the kitchen—or outside of it. At the peak of grill season, try Classic Cheddar Sliders (page 160) or an elegant grilled Tuna "Burger" au Poivre (page 162). Spend a cold and snowy winter Saturday making Classic Cinnamon Buns (page 11). For Valentine's Day, express the intensity of your love with a rich, decadent Chocolate Walnut Torte (page 34).

We know that cooking isn't just about putting food on the table. It's about being together around the table with family and friends. Enjoy!

Linda

Linda Fears, Editor in Chief
Family Circle® Magazine

Family Circle® Annual Recipes 2011

Meredith® Corporation Consumer Marketing
Vice President, Consumer Marketing: Janet Donnelly
Consumer Product Marketing Director: Steve Swanson
Consumer Marketing Product Manager: Wendy Merical
Business Director: Ron Clingman
Senior Production Manager: George Susral

Waterbury Publications, Inc.
Editorial Director: Lisa Kingsley
Associate Editor: Tricia Bergman
Creative Director: Ken Carlson
Associate Design Director: Doug Samuelson
Contributing Copy Editors: Terri Fredrickson, Gretchen Kauffman
Contributing Indexer: Elizabeth T. Parson

Family Circle® **Magazine**
Editor in Chief: Linda Fears
Creative Director: Karmen Lizzul
Food Director: Regina Ragone, M.S., R.D.
Senior Food Editor: Julie Miltenberger
Associate Food Editor: Michael Tyrrell
Assistant Food Editor: Melissa Knific
Editorial Assistant: Megan Bingham

Meredith National Media Group
President: Tom Harty
Vice President, Production: Bruce Heston

Meredith Corporation
Chairman and Chief Executive Officer: Stephen M. Lacy

In Memoriam: E.T. Meredith III (1933–2003)

Copyright © 2011 by
Meredith Corporation.
Des Moines, Iowa.
First Edition.
Printed in the United States of America.
ISSN: 1942-7646
ISBN: 978-0-696-30093-6

All of us at Meredith® Consumer Marketing are
dedicated to providing you with information
and ideas to enhance your home. We welcome
your comments and suggestions. Write to us at:
Meredith Consumer Marketing, 1716 Locust St.,
Des Moines, IA 50309-3023.

LET'S EAT! Sitting down at your own table at the end of the day to enjoy a fresh, flavorful home-cooked meal soothes away the day's stresses and satisfies on so many levels. This compilation of recipes from the 2011 issues of *Family Circle* Magazine makes it simpler than ever to serve up delicious food you cook yourself—whether it's a quick weeknight dinner or a special evening with friends. Recipes are organized by month to take advantage of what's in season and to make it easy to find just the right recipe for any occasion. In addition to the hundreds of healthful, great-tasting recipes, you'll find dozens of tips, cooking tutorials and tantalizing photographs that will tempt you into the kitchen again and again.

Philly Cheesesteak Burger (shown below; recipe on page 161) is part of the Flipping Out feature in the July chapter. Flipping Out presents fresh and fun ideas for all kinds of grilled burgers—made with different types of ground meats, in varying sizes and with an array of flavor profiles to please everyone in the family.

**CHOCOLATE
ANGEL FOOD CAKE,
PAGE 34**

**CHOCOLATE DULCE
DE LECHE BARS,
PAGE 34**

CONTENTS

NEW ENGLAND CLAM
& CORN CHOWDER,
PAGE 15

PENNE WITH VODKA
SAUCE & VEGETABLES,
PAGE 17

INDIVIDUAL SWEET & SAVORY MEAT LOAF

MAKES 4 servings **PREP** 20 minutes **BAKE** at 350° for 45 minutes

1¼ pounds lean ground beef
⅔ cup rolled oats
½ cup sweetened applesauce
1 large summer squash, shredded
2 large carrots, peeled and shredded
3 tablespoons ketchup
1 egg
1½ teaspoons Italian seasoning
1 teaspoon garlic powder
1 teaspoon onion powder
½ plus ⅛ teaspoon salt
½ teaspoon black pepper
1½ pounds sweet potatoes, peeled and cut into ½-inch-thick half-moons
2 tablespoons olive oil
1 teaspoon smoked paprika
Steamed broccoli (optional)

① Heat oven to 350°. Coat 4 small loaf pans (5 x 3 x 2-inch) with nonstick cooking spray.

② In a large bowl, mix together beef, oats, applesauce, squash, carrots, ketchup, egg, Italian seasoning, garlic powder, onion powder, ½ teaspoon salt and black pepper. Spoon into prepared loaf pans. Bake at 350° for 45 minutes or until internal temperature registers 160° on an instant-read thermometer. Cool slightly before turning out.

③ Meanwhile, in a large bowl, toss together sweet potatoes, olive oil and smoked paprika. Place on baking sheet and bake with meat loaf for 45 minutes or until tender. Sprinkle with ⅛ teaspoon salt.

④ Serve meat loaf with the sweet potatoes. Accompany with steamed broccoli, if desired.

PER SERVING 454 calories; 13 g fat (4 g sat.); 37 g protein; 47 g carbohydrate; 7 g fiber; 667 mg sodium; 141 mg cholesterol

NEW ENGLAND CLAM & CORN CHOWDER

MAKES 4 servings **PREP** 15 minutes
COOK 17 minutes

- 1 tablespoon olive oil
- 1 small onion, finely chopped
- ½ cup dry white wine
- ¼ cup all-purpose flour
- 2 cups reduced-fat (2%) milk
- 1 cup low-sodium chicken broth
- 3 cans (6 ounces each) minced clams
- 1 pound small red-skinned potatoes, cut into ½-inch pieces
- 2 cups frozen corn, thawed
- 1 teaspoon low-sodium Old Bay seasoning
- ¼ teaspoon salt
- ¼ teaspoon black pepper
- 2 tablespoons chopped parsley
  Tossed salad, crusty bread (optional)

① Heat oil in a large saucepan over medium heat; add onion and cook 5 minutes, stirring occasionally. Stir in wine and cook 1 minute; sprinkle in flour and cook 1 minute.

② Gradually stir in milk and chicken broth. Drain liquid from clams into measuring cup. Add 1 cup of the clam juice to the pot and reserve the clams. Add potatoes; cover and simmer 10 minutes.

③ Add reserved clams, corn, Old Bay, salt and pepper. Bring to a simmer to heat through. Turn off heat and stir in parsley.

④ Serve with tossed salad and crusty bread, if desired.

PER SERVING 381 calories; 7 g fat (2 g sat.); 21 g protein; 56 g carbohydrate; 4 g fiber; 807 mg sodium; 38 mg cholesterol

GRILLED CHICKEN "FRANCESE-STYLE"

MAKES 4 servings **PREP** 15 minutes **GRILL** 10 minutes **COOK** 6 minutes

- 1½ pounds thinly sliced chicken cutlets
- 1½ teaspoons lemon pepper
- ½ package (18 ounces) prepared polenta, cut into ½-inch-thick slices
- 1 tablespoon olive oil
- 3 tablespoons chopped shallot
- ½ cup white wine
- 1 tablespoon all-purpose flour
- 1 cup low-sodium chicken broth
- 2 tablespoons lemon juice
- 2 tablespoons capers
- 2 tablespoons chopped parsley
- ¼ teaspoon salt
- ⅛ teaspoon black pepper
- 2 tablespoons unsalted butter
  Roasted carrots (optional)

① Heat a lightly greased grill pan over medium-high heat. Season the chicken with the lemon pepper. Grill 3 minutes per side or until internal temperature registers 160° on an instant-read thermometer. Remove and keep warm. Grill polenta slices 1 to 2 minutes per side until grill marks form. Set aside.

② In a medium-size saucepan, heat oil over medium-high heat. Add shallot and cook 3 minutes, stirring occasionally. Add wine and simmer 1 minute. Stir together flour and broth and add to saucepan; simmer 2 minutes, until thickened. Stir in lemon juice, capers, parsley, salt and pepper. Whisk in butter.

③ Serve chicken with the sauce and the grilled polenta. Accompany with roasted carrots, if desired.

PER SERVING 356 calories; 13 g fat (5 g sat.); 37 g protein; 16 g carbohydrate; 1 g fiber; 745 mg sodium; 109 mg cholesterol

PEANUT-CHIP COOKIES

MAKES 60 cookies   **PREP** 15 minutes   **REFRIGERATE** 15 minutes   **BAKE** at 350° for 12 minutes

1¾ cups all-purpose flour
1 teaspoon baking soda
¼ teaspoon salt
½ cup reduced-fat peanut butter
¼ cup (½ stick) unsalted butter, softened
½ cup packed light-brown sugar
¼ cup plus 1 tablespoon granulated sugar
¼ cup fat-free milk
1 egg
1 teaspoon vanilla extract
⅓ cup mini chocolate chips
¼ cup finely chopped peanuts

① Heat oven to 350°.

② In a medium-size bowl, whisk together flour, baking soda and salt. Set aside.

③ In a large bowl, beat peanut butter and butter on medium speed 2 minutes, until creamy. Add brown sugar and ¼ cup of the granulated sugar, and beat 2 minutes. Beat in milk, egg and vanilla. Beat in dry ingredients until just combined. Stir in chips and nuts. Chill dough 15 minutes.

④ For each cookie, roll 2 teaspoons of dough into a ball and place on baking sheets 2 inches apart. With fork, flatten each ball into a 1½-inch round, making a crosshatch pattern. Sprinkle a small amount of the remaining sugar over the top of each.

⑤ Bake at 350° for 10 to 12 minutes, until lightly browned around edges. Let cool on sheets 1 minute. Transfer to rack; let cool.

PER COOKIE 48 calories; 2 g fat (0 g sat.); 1 g protein; 7 g carbohydrate; 0 g fiber; 50 mg sodium; 4 mg cholesterol

PORK TERIYAKI

MAKES 4 servings **PREP** 20 minutes
MARINATE 2 hours **COOK** 12 minutes

PORK

2	tablespoons light teriyaki sauce
4	cloves garlic, chopped
	Juice and zest of 1 lime
1	pound pork tenderloin

SAUCE

1	can (14.5 ounces) low-sodium chicken broth
3	tablespoons light teriyaki sauce
4	teaspoons cornstarch
1	teaspoon sugar
¾	teaspoon hot sauce

VEGETABLES

2	tablespoons vegetable oil
1	large onion, peeled and thinly sliced
1	red pepper, seeded and sliced
8	ounces sliced mushrooms
1	bunch scallions, trimmed and cut into 1-inch pieces
1	bag (12 ounces) microwave-ready green beans, cooked following package instructions
3	cups cooked brown rice

① **Pork.** In a large resealable bag, combine teriyaki sauce, garlic, lime juice and zest. Add pork and marinate in refrigerator for 2 hours.

② **Sauce.** In a small bowl, combine chicken broth, teriyaki sauce, cornstarch, sugar and hot sauce. Set aside.

③ **Vegetables.** Remove pork from marinade and discard marinade. Cut pork into ½-inch slices. Heat 1 tablespoon oil in a large nonstick skillet over medium-high heat. Stir-fry pork for 3 minutes. Remove from skillet and keep warm.

④ Add remaining tablespoon oil to skillet. Add onion and cook 4 minutes; stir in red pepper, mushrooms and scallions. Cook 3 minutes. Stir in the green beans, broth mixture and pork. Simmer for 2 minutes, until thickened.

⑤ Serve the pork over cooked brown rice.

PER SERVING 501 calories; 13 g fat (2 g sat.); 33 g protein; 66 g carbohydrate; 9 g fiber; 746 mg sodium; 74 mg cholesterol

PENNE WITH VODKA SAUCE & VEGETABLES

MAKES 6 servings **PREP** 20 minutes
LET STAND 10 minutes **COOK** 16 minutes

1	box (14½ ounces) Barilla Plus Multigrain Penne
1	pound zucchini, cut into ½-inch quarter-moons
1	cup frozen peas
8	cups baby spinach
1	tablespoon olive oil
1	small onion, peeled and finely chopped
6	ounces sliced Canadian bacon, chopped
⅓	cup vodka
1	can (15 ounces) no-salt-added diced tomatoes
1	can (8 ounces) no-salt-added tomato sauce
½	teaspoon salt
⅛	to ¼ teaspoon red pepper flakes
½	cup fat-free half-and-half
½	cup shredded Parmesan cheese

① Bring a large pot of lightly salted water to a boil. Add penne and cook following package directions, 11 minutes. Add zucchini and peas during last 3 minutes. Stir in spinach. Drain and place back into the pot.

② Meanwhile, heat oil in a large nonstick skillet over medium-high heat. Add onion and cook 5 minutes, stirring occasionally; add Canadian bacon and vodka and cook 1 minute. Stir in tomatoes, tomato sauce, salt and red pepper. Reduce heat to medium-low and simmer, uncovered, for 10 minutes.

③ Stir half-and-half and ¼ cup cheese into the sauce. Toss with pasta and let stand for 10 minutes. Stir and spoon into serving bowl and top with remaining cheese.

PER SERVING 457 calories; 8 g fat (2 g sat.); 25 g protein; 63 g carbohydrate; 9 g fiber; 741 mg sodium; 24 mg cholesterol

Multigrain pasta mixed with lots of greens effortlessly ups your family's whole-grain and vegetable intake.

Slow Cooker Suppers

Come home on busy weeknights to a hearty, satisfying and ready-to-serve meal.

BEEF STROGANOFF

MAKES 6 servings **PREP** 15 minutes **SLOW COOK** 4½ hours on HIGH or 6½ hours on LOW

- 1½ pounds beef chuck steak, trimmed and cut into ½-inch cubes
- 1 package (14 ounces) white mushrooms, cleaned and quartered
- 2 onions, finely chopped
- 2 tablespoons tomato paste
- 1 cup low-sodium beef broth
- ½ cup white wine
- ¼ cup low-sodium soy sauce
- 1 cup reduced-fat sour cream
- 2 tablespoons cornstarch
- ¼ teaspoon black pepper
- 6 cups cooked egg noodles (optional)
- 3 tablespoons chopped parsley (optional)

① Combine beef, mushrooms, onions, tomato paste, broth, wine and 3 tablespoons of the soy sauce in slow cooker bowl. Cover and cook on HIGH for 4 hours or on LOW for 6 hours or until beef is tender.

② In a small bowl, stir together sour cream, remaining 1 tablespoon soy sauce, cornstarch and black pepper; whisk into slow cooker bowl and cook an additional 30 minutes or until sauce has thickened. Serve over egg noodles and sprinkle with parsley, if desired.

PER SERVING 246 calories; 8 g fat (3 g sat.); 26 g protein; 13 g carbohydrate; 1 g fiber; 373 mg sodium; 78 mg cholesterol

HEARTY MEATLESS SAUCE

MAKES 8 servings **PREP** 15 minutes
SLOW COOK 3½ hours on HIGH or 5 hours on LOW

- 1 large green pepper, seeded and finely chopped
- 1 large onion, chopped
- 3 cloves garlic, minced
- 2 cans (28 ounces each) whole plum tomatoes in puree
- 1 package (12 ounces) soy crumbles
- 2 tablespoons balsamic vinegar
- 1 teaspoon dried basil
- ½ teaspoon sugar
- ½ teaspoon salt
- 12 ounces uncooked spaghetti, broken into thirds
- ¼ cup chopped fresh basil
- 2 tablespoons chopped parsley

① Stir together pepper, onion, garlic, tomatoes, soy crumbles, vinegar, dried basil, sugar and salt in slow cooker, breaking up tomatoes with a wooden spoon. Cover and cook on HIGH for 2½ hours or on LOW for 4 hours.

② Stir in spaghetti, 1 cup boiling water, fresh basil and parsley and cover; cook for another hour or until pasta is tender.

PER SERVING 279 calories; 1 g fat (0 g sat.); 17 g protein; 49 g carbohydrate; 8 g fiber; 746 mg sodium; 0 mg cholesterol

HARVEST CHICKEN & POTATOES

MAKES 6 servings **PREP** 20 minutes **SLOW COOK** 5 hours on HIGH or 7 hours on LOW

- 1 pound boneless, skinless chicken breast, cut into 1-inch pieces
- 3 tablespoons flour
- ½ teaspoon salt
- ¼ teaspoon black pepper
- 12 ounces small new potatoes, scrubbed and halved
- 2 cups baby carrots, cut into thirds
- 2 celery stalks, cut into ½-inch pieces
- 1 large onion, chopped
- 1 can (4 ounces) sliced mushrooms, drained
- 2 cloves garlic, minced
- ¾ teaspoon dried thyme
- ½ teaspoon dried sage
- 1 cup low-sodium chicken broth
- 1 tablespoon unsalted butter, softened

① In a medium-size bowl, stir together chicken, 2 tablespoons of the flour, ¼ teaspoon of the salt and the pepper; add to slow cooker. Stir in potatoes, carrots, celery, onion, mushrooms, garlic, ½ teaspoon of the thyme, the sage and broth. Cover and cook on HIGH for 4 hours or on LOW for 6 hours.

② In a small bowl, stir together remaining 1 tablespoon flour and the butter until a paste forms. Push the chicken and veggies to one side and whisk paste, remaining ¼ teaspoon each salt and thyme into slow cooker bowl. Cook 1 more hour or until thickened.

PER SERVING 194 calories; 3 g fat (1 g sat.); 21 g protein; 21 g carbohydrate; 3 g fiber; 455 mg sodium; 50 mg cholesterol

Spice up your slow cooker suppers with recipes that celebrate global cuisine. Serve Indian-style chicken one night and Latin-style pork the next.

BLACK BEANS & PORK

MAKES 6 servings   **PREP** 15 minutes
SLOW COOK 4 hours on HIGH or 6 hours on LOW

- 1½ pounds boneless pork loin, trimmed and cut into ½-inch cubes
- 1 teaspoon chili powder
- 1 teaspoon ground coriander
- ¼ teaspoon salt
- ¼ teaspoon black pepper
- 1 onion, chopped
- 2 cans (15 ounces each) black beans, drained and rinsed
- 1 can (14.5 ounces) diced tomatoes with green chiles
- ¼ cup chopped cilantro
- 3 cups cooked white rice (optional)

① In a slow cooker bowl, toss together pork, chili powder, coriander, salt and pepper. Stir in onion, beans, tomatoes and 1¼ cups water. Cover and cook on HIGH for 4 hours or on LOW for 6 hours.

② Stir in cilantro. Using a potato masher, mash beans slightly until mixture is thickened. Serve bean mixture over rice, if desired.

PER SERVING 311 calories; 9 g fat (3 g sat.); 30 g protein; 25 g carbohydrate; 9 g fiber; 1,043 mg sodium; 56 mg cholesterol

INDIAN-SPICED CHICKEN THIGHS

MAKES 4 servings   **PREP** 15 minutes   **SLOW COOK** 3 hours, 15 minutes on HIGH or 5 hours, 15 minutes on LOW

- 3 pounds boneless, skinless chicken thighs
- 2 onions, thinly sliced
- 3 garlic cloves, minced
- ½ cup golden raisins
- 1¾ teaspoons garam masala
- ½ teaspoon salt
- ¼ teaspoon black pepper
- 1 cup low-sodium chicken broth
- ½ cup plain yogurt
- 2 tablespoons cornstarch
- ⅓ cup toasted slivered almonds
- 2 cups cooked basmati rice (optional)

① Combine chicken, onions, garlic, raisins, 1 teaspoon of the garam masala, ¼ teaspoon of the salt, the pepper and broth in slow cooker bowl. Cover and cook for 3 hours on HIGH or 5 hours on LOW.

② In a small bowl, stir together the remaining ¾ teaspoon garam masala, remaining ¼ teaspoon salt, the yogurt and cornstarch. Remove chicken to a platter and keep warm.

③ Whisk yogurt mixture into slow cooker bowl and cover; cook an additional 15 minutes or until sauce has thickened. Stir in almonds and serve sauce with chicken over rice, if desired.

PER SERVING 621 calories; 24 g fat (5 g sat.); 73 g protein; 33 g carbohydrate; 3 g fiber; 717 mg sodium; 333 mg cholesterol

BLACK BEANS & PORK

**CHOCOLATE WALNUT
TORTE, PAGE 34**

FEBRUARY

26

41

Game On

Our healthy Super Bowl party playbook offers a home-field advantage.

MINI STUFFED POTATOES, PAGE 29

TWO-WAY NACHOS,
PAGE 29

SAUSAGE & PEPPER HEROES

MAKES 8 servings **PREP** 15 minutes **BAKE** at 450° for 50 minutes

- 1 pound all-purpose potatoes, peeled and cut into ½-inch cubes
- 3 large green bell peppers, cored, seeds removed and cut into ½-inch slices
- 2 large onions, peeled and cut into ½-inch slices
- 1 package (12 ounces) fully cooked Italian-flavored chicken sausage, cut into coins
- 3 tablespoons olive oil
- ½ teaspoon salt
- ½ teaspoon dried Italian seasoning
- ¼ teaspoon red pepper flakes
- 1 package (12 ounces) Arnold wholewheat Fill 'ems Sandwich Thins

① Heat oven to 450°.

② In a large bowl, toss together potatoes, peppers, onions, sausage and olive oil. Season with salt, Italian seasoning and red pepper. Evenly distribute between 2 rimmed baking sheets.

③ Bake at 450° for 45 to 50 minutes or until vegetables are tender. Stir sausage and vegetables and rotate pans after 25 minutes.

④ Spoon sausage and pepper mixture into the Fill 'ems and serve.

PER SERVING 309 calories; 13 g fat (3 g sat.); 13 g protein; 41 g carbohydrate; 8 g fiber; 696 mg sodium; 38 mg cholesterol

CHEESY CRAB DIP

MAKES 12 servings **PREP** 15 minutes
BAKE at 350° for 30 minutes

8   ounces reduced-fat cream cheese, softened
⅓   cup light mayonnaise
⅓   cup fat-free milk
2   tablespoons chopped fresh dill, plus more sprigs, to garnish
1   teaspoon Worcestershire sauce
¼   teaspoon garlic salt
¾   pound imitation crabmeat (surimi), coarsely chopped
6   tablespoons grated Parmesan cheese
    Sliced carrot, celery, cucumber and radishes, for dipping

① Heat oven to 350°. Coat a 9-inch pie plate with nonstick cooking spray.

② In a large bowl, combine cream cheese, mayonnaise, milk, dill, Worcestershire sauce and garlic salt. Fold in imitation crabmeat. Spoon mixture evenly into prepared pie plate. Sprinkle Parmesan cheese evenly over top.

③ Bake at 350° for 25 to 30 minutes until lightly browned. Cool slightly.

④ Garnish with dill sprigs and serve with sliced vegetables.

PER SERVING 114 calories; 8 g fat (4 g sat.); 6 g protein; 5 g carbohydrate; 0 g fiber; 464 mg sodium; 25 mg cholesterol

BUTTERNUT SQUASH CINCINNATI-STYLE CHILI

MAKES 8 servings **PREP** 20 minutes **BAKE** at 400° for 30 minutes **COOK** 28 minutes

½   of a large butternut squash, seeds removed, cut into ½-inch cubes
2   tablespoons olive oil
¾   teaspoon salt
2   large onions, peeled and chopped
2   large green bell peppers, cored, seeds removed and chopped
4   cloves garlic, chopped
2   cans (14½ ounces each) no-salt-added diced tomatoes
¼   cup chili powder
1   teaspoon ground cinnamon
1   teaspoon sugar
½   teaspoon ground allspice
2   cans (15½ ounces each) pinto beans, drained and rinsed
1   box (14 ounces) whole-wheat spaghetti, cooked following package directions
1   cup shredded reduced-fat cheddar cheese
1   cup reduced-sodium oyster crackers
4   large scallions, trimmed and thinly sliced

① Heat oven to 400°. Place squash in a large rimmed baking pan and toss with 1 tablespoon of the oil and ¼ teaspoon of the salt. Bake at 400° for 30 minutes. Set aside.

② In a large pot, heat remaining tablespoon oil over medium-high heat. Add onions, peppers and garlic. Cook 8 minutes, stirring occasionally. Add tomatoes, chili powder, cinnamon, sugar, allspice and remaining ½ teaspoon salt. Simmer 15 minutes over medium-low heat, with lid ajar. Stir occasionally.

③ Stir in cooked squash and beans. Simmer 5 minutes.

④ Serve chili over cooked spaghetti. Scatter cheese, oyster crackers and scallions over the top.

PER SERVING 456 calories; 9 g fat (2 g sat.); 20 g protein; 79 g carbohydrate; 18 g fiber; 542 mg sodium; 3 mg cholesterol

ROCKY ROAD BROWNIES

For a slightly more decadent dessert, serve with a small scoop of frozen yogurt, which adds only 50 calories.

ROCKY ROAD BROWNIES

MAKES 25 brownie squares **PREP** 15 minutes
BAKE at 350° for 30 minutes

⅔ cup unsweetened cocoa powder
⅓ cup all-purpose flour
½ teaspoon baking powder
⅛ teaspoon salt
⅓ cup canola oil
⅓ cup granulated sugar
⅓ cup packed light-brown sugar
4 egg whites, lightly beaten
2 teaspoons vanilla extract
½ cup finely chopped walnuts
¼ cup mini chocolate chips
½ cup mini marshmallows

① Heat oven to 350°. Line an 8 x 8-inch baking pan with nonstick foil, overhanging ends of pan.

② In medium-size bowl, combine cocoa powder, flour, baking powder and salt. Set aside.

③ In a large bowl, whisk together oil, sugars, egg whites and vanilla. Stir in cocoa mixture. Spoon batter evenly into prepared pan. Sprinkle walnuts over batter. Bake at 350° for 25 minutes. Scatter the chips and marshmallows over the top and bake for an additional 5 minutes. Remove from oven and cool completely.

④ To slice, coat a sharp chef's knife with cooking spray and cut into 25 squares, using a rocking motion. Respray knife frequently.

PER SQUARE 97 calories; 5 g fat (1 g sat.); 2 g protein; 11 g carbohydrate; 1 g fiber; 20 mg sodium; 0 mg cholesterol

MINI STUFFED POTATOES

MAKES 12 potatoes **PREP** 20 minutes
BAKE at 400° for 30 minutes

12 small potatoes, about 2 inches in diameter (1½ pounds total)
1 tablespoon vegetable oil
¼ plus ⅛ teaspoon salt
6 tablespoons reduced-fat sour cream
2 ounces crumbled Gorgonzola cheese
1 bunch chives, snipped
4 slices turkey bacon, cooked and finely chopped

① Heat oven to 400°.

② Trim a small amount off one side of each potato so they lie flat. Toss potatoes with oil and place on a baking sheet, cut-side down. Sprinkle with ¼ teaspoon of the salt. Bake at 400° for 25 to 30 minutes or until tender. Cool slightly.

③ In a small bowl, blend remaining ⅛ teaspoon salt, sour cream, Gorgonzola and half the chives.

④ Slice off top of each potato and scoop out about 1 tablespoon of the flesh, reserving for another use. Stuff each potato with a generous tablespoon of the sour cream mixture. Sprinkle bacon pieces and remaining chives over the tops. Serve slightly warm or at room temperature.

PER POTATO 77 calories; 4 g fat (2 g sat.); 3 g protein; 7 g carbohydrate; 1 g fiber; 202 mg sodium; 12 mg cholesterol

TWO-WAY NACHOS

MAKES 6 servings **PREP** 10 minutes
BAKE at 350° for 15 minutes

6 ounces baked tortilla chips
2 cups (8 ounces) cooked shredded chicken
1 can (15 ounces) black beans, drained and rinsed
1 cup jarred salsa
1 cup shredded reduced-fat Mexican cheese blend
4 scallions, trimmed and thinly sliced

① Heat oven to 350°. Line bottom and sides of a 13 x 9 x 2-inch baking dish with tortilla chips. Scatter chicken and beans over the chips. Spoon salsa over the beans and top with cheese and scallions.

② Bake at 350° for 15 minutes until heated through and cheese is melted. Serve immediately.

PER SERVING 282 calories; 6 g fat (2 g sat.); 19 g protein; 37 g carbohydrate; 6 g fiber; 686 mg sodium; 35 mg cholesterol

Variation: Replace chicken and beans with ½ pound coarsely chopped cooked shrimp and 1 can (8 ounces) drained crushed pineapple.

PER SERVING 230 calories; 5 g fat (2 g sat.); 13 g protein; 33 g carbohydrate; 3 g fiber; 597 mg sodium; 70 mg cholesterol

Dark Victory

Tame your sweet tooth (and your sweetie) with these elegant cocoa confections.

CHOCOLATE DULCE DE LECHE BARS, PAGE 34

CHOCOLATE WALNUT
TORTE, PAGE 34

MOCHA SHORTBREAD

MAKES 16 servings **PREP** 15 minutes
CHILL 2 hours **BAKE** at 350° for 30 minutes

1   cup flour
¼   teaspoon kosher salt
4   ounces bittersweet chocolate, finely
    chopped
2   teaspoons espresso powder
½   cup (1 stick) unsalted butter,
    softened
¼   cup granulated sugar
    Confectioners' sugar, for dusting
    (optional)

① Whisk together flour and salt; transfer
flour mixture to food processor with chopped
chocolate and process for 1 minute or until
chocolate is finely ground; set aside.

② Stir together espresso powder and
2 teaspoons hot water until espresso
dissolves; set aside. Beat butter for 3 minutes.
Add granulated sugar and beat 2 minutes
or until well blended. Beat in espresso
mixture. Reduce speed to low and gradually
beat in flour mixture.

③ Press dough into a 9-inch round fluted
nonstick tart pan. Score into 16 pie-shape
wedges without cutting completely through
dough. Cover with plastic wrap and chill at
least 2 hours.

④ Heat oven to 350°. Uncover shortbread
and bake at 350° for 30 minutes. Remove
to a wire rack and remove side of pan. Dust
with confectioners' sugar, if desired. Cut
through score marks before serving.

PER SERVING 122 calories; 9 g fat (5 g sat.);
1 g protein; 12 g carbohydrate; 1 g fiber;
31 mg sodium; 15 mg cholesterol

FRUITY CHOCOLATE CLUSTERS

MAKES 40 clusters **PREP** 15 minutes
MICROWAVE 1 minute **CHILL** 15 minutes

1½   cups dried cranberries
1½   cups toasted slivered almonds
2   cups broken-up pretzel stick pieces
8   ounces bittersweet chocolate,
     chopped

① Line a baking sheet with waxed paper;
set aside.

② In a medium-size bowl, stir together
cranberries, almonds and pretzel pieces.

③ Place chocolate in a medium-size
microwave-safe bowl and microwave for
1 minute, stirring halfway through;
microwave another 15 seconds if necessary
and stir until smooth.

④ Stir cranberry mixture into chocolate
until completely coated. Place 1 heaping
tablespoonful of chocolate mixture onto
prepared baking sheet, shaping into a
mound. Repeat with remaining mixture.
Chill for 15 minutes before serving.

PER CLUSTER 74 calories; 4 g fat (1 g sat.);
1 g protein; 9 g carbohydrate; 1 g fiber;
40 mg sodium; 0 mg cholesterol

DOUBLE CHOCOLATE COOKIES

MAKES about 3 dozen cookies
PREP 15 minutes **MICROWAVE** 1 minute
BAKE at 375° for 11 minutes

2	**cups all-purpose flour**
½	**cup cocoa powder**
1	**teaspoon baking soda**
½	**teaspoon salt**
12	**ounces milk chocolate**
¾	**cup (1½ sticks) unsalted butter**
¾	**cup packed light-brown sugar**
½	**cup granulated sugar**
2	**large eggs**
2	**teaspoons vanilla extract**

① Heat oven to 375°. Whisk together the flour, cocoa powder, baking soda and salt in a medium-size bowl.

② Coarsely chop 6 ounces of the chocolate, and finely chop the remaining 6 ounces. Microwave coarsely chopped chocolate with butter for 1 minute, stirring halfway through. Microwave an additional 15 seconds if necessary; stir until smooth.

③ Transfer chocolate mixture to a large mixing bowl. Add sugars, eggs and vanilla; beat with an electric mixer on medium speed until well combined. Reduce speed to low and gradually beat in flour mixture. Stir in remaining finely chopped chocolate pieces.

④ Drop heaping tablespoonfuls of dough onto ungreased baking sheets, about 2 inches apart.

⑤ Bake at 375° for 9 to 11 minutes or until set. Let the cookies cool on baking sheet on a wire rack for 2 minutes. Transfer the cookies to rack; let cool completely.

PER COOKIE 140 calories; 7 g fat (4 g sat.); 2 g protein; 18 g carbohydrate; 1 g fiber; 80 mg sodium; 24 mg cholesterol

CHOCOLATE WALNUT TORTE

MAKES 16 servings **PREP** 15 minutes
MICROWAVE 1 minute **BAKE** at 350° for
65 minutes

1   cup flour
¼   teaspoon salt
¼   teaspoon baking soda
8   ounces semisweet chocolate
¾   cup (1½ sticks) unsalted butter,
     softened
1   cup sugar
1   teaspoon vanilla extract
3   eggs
½   cup buttermilk
1   cup chopped toasted walnuts

GLAZE
4   ounces semisweet chocolate, chopped
½   cup heavy cream

① Heat oven to 350°. Coat an 8-inch cake pan with nonstick cooking spray. Line bottom with waxed paper; spray paper.

② In small bowl, whisk together flour, salt and baking soda; set aside.

③ Microwave chocolate and butter in a medium-size microwave-safe bowl for 1 minute, stirring halfway through; microwave another 15 seconds if necessary and stir until smooth. Whisk in sugar and vanilla, then stir in eggs, buttermilk and ⅔ cup of the walnuts until well blended. Stir in flour mixture until just combined.

④ Pour batter into prepared pan. Bake at 350° for 60 to 65 minutes or until a toothpick inserted in the center tests clean. Remove to a wire rack and cool in pan 5 minutes, then invert pan onto wire rack and cool completely. Remove and discard wax paper.

⑤ **Glaze.** Place chocolate in small bowl. Heat cream in a saucepan over medium heat until just simmering. Pour over chocolate. Let stand 4 minutes to melt; stir until smooth.

⑥ Place cake on wire rack over baking sheet. Pour glaze over cake; use spatula to smooth over top and sides. Pat remaining ⅓ cup walnuts around top. When glaze is firm, remove cake to a platter and serve.

PER SERVING 332 calories; 24 g fat (12 g sat.); 4 g protein; 29 g carbohydrate; 2 g fiber; 80 mg sodium; 73 mg cholesterol

CHOCOLATE ANGEL FOOD CAKE

MAKES 16 servings **PREP** 20 minutes
BAKE at 350° for 40 minutes

1½ cups sugar
¾   cup cake flour (not self-rising)
⅓   cup cocoa powder
¾   teaspoon baking soda
¼   teaspoon salt
2   ounces semisweet chocolate, chopped
12 egg whites
1   teaspoon cream of tartar
1   teaspoon vanilla extract

CHOCOLATE SAUCE
4   ounces bittersweet chocolate,
     chopped
½   cup heavy cream

① Heat oven to 350°. Lightly coat bottom of a 10-inch angel food cake pan with nonstick cooking spray. Whisk together ¾ cup of the sugar, the flour, cocoa powder, baking soda and salt. Stir in chocolate.

② Whisk egg whites and cream of tartar on high speed for 2 to 3 minutes or until soft peaks form. Add remaining ¾ cup sugar to bowl and beat for 3 minutes or until stiff, glossy peaks form. Beat in vanilla.

③ Gently fold flour mixture into egg whites until fully combined. Pour batter into prepared pan and smooth top. Gently tap on counter to remove any air bubbles. Bake at 350° for 35 to 40 minutes or until toothpick inserted in center tests clean. Remove from oven; invert over wire rack until completely cool. Run a thin knife around edges and center to release cake from pan, if necessary.

④ **Chocolate Sauce.** Place chocolate in small bowl. Heat cream in saucepan over medium heat until just simmering. Pour over chocolate. Let stand 4 minutes to melt. Stir until smooth. Serve with cake.

PER SERVING 165 calories; 7 g fat (4 g sat.); 4 g protein; 26 g carbohydrate; 1 g fiber; 140 mg sodium; 10 mg cholesterol

CHOCOLATE DULCE DE LECHE BARS

MAKES 16 servings **PREP** 15 minutes
CHILL 3 hours, 15 minutes **BAKE** at 350° for
25 minutes **COOK** 2 minutes
MICROWAVE 1 minute

CRUST
18 graham cracker boards, crushed
4   tablespoons sugar
½   teaspoon salt
½   cup (1 stick) unsalted butter, melted

FILLING & TOPPING
3   tablespoons cornstarch
2   tablespoons milk
2   cans (14 ounces each) sweetened
     condensed milk
4   tablespoons unsalted butter, softened
2   tablespoons light corn syrup
8   ounces milk chocolate, chopped
1   teaspoon vegetable shortening

① Heat oven to 350°. Line a 13 x 9 x 2-inch baking pan with nonstick foil; overhang short ends slightly.

② **Crust.** Stir the graham cracker crumbs, sugar, salt and butter in a bowl until evenly moistened. Transfer crumb mixture to prepared baking pan; press crumb mixture evenly over the bottom of the pan. Refrigerate 30 minutes.

③ Bake the crust at 350° for 17 minutes or until lightly browned. Remove to a rack and cool completely.

④ **Filling & Topping.** Stir together cornstarch and milk. Bring condensed milk, butter and corn syrup to a boil over medium-high heat in a small saucepan, stirring constantly to prevent burning. Whisk in cornstarch mixture; cook 2 minutes, whisking, or until thickened. Pour over crust, spreading level. Bake at 350° for 8 minutes or until topping starts to bubble. Remove to a rack; refrigerate for 2 hours or until cool.

⑤ Microwave chocolate and shortening for 1 minute or until melted, stirring halfway. Stir until smooth. Spread evenly over filling and refrigerate for at least 45 minutes or until set. Use foil to lift bar from pan to a cutting board. Cut into 16 bars.

PER SERVING 456 calories; 20 g fat (12 g sat.); 7 g protein; 63 g carbohydrate; 1 g fiber; 269 mg sodium; 50 mg cholesterol

CHOCOLATE
ANGEL FOOD CAKE

CHOCOLATE DULCE
DE LECHE BARS

Take Comfort

A bowl of homemade soup, chili or stew is a surefire way to take the chill out of winter.

**RED PEPPER-TOMATO SOUP,
PAGE 38**

COUNTRY DIJON
BEEF STEW,
PAGE 41

With a salad and some crusty bread, even a meatless, vegetable-rich soup becomes a hearty, satisfying—and healthful—meal.

RED PEPPER-TOMATO SOUP

MAKES 6 servings **PREP** 15 minutes
COOK 8 minutes

1   jar (12 ounces) roasted red peppers in brine, drained
1   can (14.5 ounces) diced tomatoes
1   tablespoon olive oil
1   can (28 ounces) tomato puree
1   cup low-sodium and fat-free chicken broth
1   tablespoon sugar
½   teaspoon salt
¼   teaspoon pepper
1   cup heavy cream
     Croutons, for serving

① Combine drained peppers and diced tomatoes in a blender. Puree until smooth.

② Heat oil in a large soup pot over medium heat. Add pepper-tomato mixture, tomato puree, chicken broth, sugar, salt and pepper. Heat just to simmering, about 8 minutes. Remove from heat and whisk in heavy cream. Return to stove and heat through. Ladle soup into bowls; top each with a few croutons.

PER SERVING 236 calories; 17 g fat (10 g sat.); 5 g protein; 17 g carbohydrate; 1 g fiber; 694 mg sodium; 54 mg cholesterol

WINTER VEGGIE BISQUE

MAKES 6 servings **PREP** 15 minutes
COOK 12 minutes

1   large onion, peeled and halved
1   Granny Smith apple, peeled and cored
3   carrots, trimmed and peeled
2   tablespoons unsalted butter
2   packages (12 ounces each) frozen cooked winter squash, thawed
3   cups vegetable broth
2   tablespoons sugar
1   teaspoon ground ginger
¾   teaspoon salt
½   teaspoon ground cinnamon
⅛   teaspoon cayenne
½   cup heavy cream

① Shred onion, apple and carrots either with a box grater or with a shredding blade in a food processor. Heat butter in a large pot over medium heat. Add shredded onion, apple and carrot. Cook 7 minutes, until softened.

② Stir in squash, broth, sugar, ginger, salt, cinnamon and cayenne. Bring to a boil over high heat. Reduce heat to medium-low and simmer 5 minutes.

③ Transfer mixture to food processor fitted with chopping blade or to blender. Puree until smooth (do this in batches, if necessary). Return to pot and stir in heavy cream. Gently heat through.

PER SERVING 210 calories; 11 g fat (7 g sat.); 1 g protein; 27 g carbohydrate; 4 g fiber; 800 mg sodium; 37 mg cholesterol

TRADITIONAL BEEF & BEAN CHILI

MAKES 10 servings **PREP** 15 minutes
COOK 20 minutes

2   pounds ground round
1   large onion, diced
1   sweet red pepper, cored and diced
4   cloves garlic, sliced
6   tablespoons chili powder
½   teaspoon dried oregano
½   teaspoon ground cumin
¼   teaspoon cayenne
1   can (28 ounces) fire-roasted diced tomatoes
1   can (15 ounces) tomato sauce
1   tablespoon sugar
1   tablespoon tomato paste
½   teaspoon salt
2   cans (15 ounces each) dark kidney beans, drained and rinsed
     Sour cream and chopped scallions, for serving (optional)

① Coat a large heavy-bottomed pot with nonstick cooking spray. Add ground beef and cook over medium-high heat, stirring, for 5 minutes. Add onion, pepper and garlic and cook 4 minutes. Stir in chili powder, oregano, cumin and cayenne. Cook 1 minute.

② Stir in diced tomatoes, tomato sauce, sugar, tomato paste and salt. Cover and cook over medium heat for 10 minutes, stirring occasionally. Uncover and stir in beans. Heat through, then serve garnished with sour cream and scallions, if desired.

PER SERVING 329 calories; 15 g fat (5 g sat.); 24 g protein; 27 g carbohydrate; 7 g fiber; 789 mg sodium; 62 mg cholesterol

TRADITIONAL BEEF & BEAN CHILI

WINTER VEGGIE BISQUE

CHICKEN & CORN CHILI

MAKES 8 servings **PREP** 15 minutes **COOK** 16 minutes

2   tablespoons olive oil
1   large onion, chopped
1   green bell pepper, cored and chopped
1   teaspoon ground cumin
½   teaspoon ground coriander
½   teaspoon chili powder
1   can (14.5 ounces) low-sodium chicken broth
1   can (14.5 ounces) diced tomatoes, drained
1¼ pounds boneless, skinless chicken breasts, cut into bite-size pieces
1   box (10 ounces) frozen corn, thawed
2   cans (15 ounces each) cannellini beans, drained and rinsed
¾   teaspoon salt
    Shredded cheddar cheese

① Heat oil in large pot over medium heat. Add onion and green pepper. Cook, stirring, 5 minutes. Stir in cumin, coriander and chili powder; cook 1 minute.

② Stir in chicken broth and tomatoes. Bring to a simmer. Add chicken. Cover and simmer over low heat for 10 minutes or until chicken is cooked through.

③ Stir corn, beans and salt into pot. Heat through. Spoon into bowls and top with shredded cheese.

PER SERVING 276 calories; 8 g fat (2 g sat.); 25 g protein; 28 g carbohydrate; 6 g fiber; 706 mg sodium; 48 mg cholesterol

COUNTRY DIJON BEEF STEW

MAKES 6 servings **PREP** 15 minutes
COOK 1 hour, 12 minutes

- 1 tablespoon unsalted butter
- 1 small onion, chopped
- 8 ounces (about 2 cups) mushrooms, cleaned, trimmed and quartered
- 2 pounds boneless beef chuck, trimmed and cut into 1-inch chunks
- 4 tablespoons all-purpose flour
- 2 tablespoons olive oil
- 1 can (14.5 ounces) low-sodium beef broth
- 1 tablespoon Worcestershire sauce
- 1 tablespoon country-style grainy Dijon mustard
- 3 carrots, peeled and cut into ½-inch coins
- 1 teaspoon chopped fresh rosemary
- ¼ teaspoon salt
- ¼ teaspoon black pepper
  Cooked egg noodles (optional)

① Heat butter in a large pot over medium heat. Add onion and mushrooms and cook 5 minutes. Transfer to a bowl.

② Meanwhile, toss beef with 3 tablespoons of the flour. Add 1 tablespoon of the oil to the pot and increase heat to medium-high. Add half the beef and cook 2 minutes, browning on all sides. Transfer to bowl with onions and mushrooms. Add remaining tablespoon oil and second half of beef to pot. Cook 2 minutes, browning on all sides. Transfer to bowl; reduce heat to medium.

③ Add ¾ cup of the beef broth to the pot. Whisk in Worcestershire and mustard, scraping up any brown bits on bottom of the pan. Add mixture from bowl back to the pot along with the remaining beef broth. Cover and simmer on low for 15 minutes.

④ Uncover and stir in carrots. Cover and cook an additional 45 minutes.

⑤ In small bowl, stir together 2 tablespoons water, the remaining tablespoon flour, rosemary, salt and pepper. Stir into stew and cook 3 minutes, until thickened. Serve with noodles, if desired.

PER SERVING 307 calories; 13 g fat (4 g sat.); 34 g protein; 11 g carbohydrate; 2 g fiber; 396 mg sodium; 69 mg cholesterol

PASTA FAGIOLI

MAKES 8 servings **PREP** 15 minutes **COOK** 16 minutes

- 2 tablespoons olive oil
- 1 onion, diced
- 3 cloves garlic, chopped
- 1 can (14.5 ounces) diced tomatoes with basil, garlic and oregano
- 2 cans (14.5 ounces each) reduced-sodium chicken broth
- 8 ounces (about 2 cups) small pasta shells
- 1 teaspoon Italian seasoning
- 1 bunch fresh kale, tough stems discarded, cut into 1-inch pieces and washed
- 2 cans small white beans, drained and rinsed
- 1 tablespoon tomato paste
- ½ teaspoon salt
- ¼ teaspoon pepper
  Grated Parmesan, for serving

① Heat oil in a large pot over medium heat. Add onion and cook 5 minutes. Add garlic; cook 1 minute.

② Stir in tomatoes, broth and 3 cups water. Bring to a simmer over high heat. Add pasta and Italian seasoning. Cook, stirring, 5 minutes.

③ Stir in kale; cook 5 minutes more. Reduce heat to medium and stir in beans, tomato paste, salt and pepper. Heat through.

④ Ladle into bowls; garnish with Parmesan.

PER SERVING 260 calories; 5 g fat (1 g sat.); 13 g protein; 48 g carbohydrate; 8 g fiber; 791 mg sodium; 0 mg cholesterol

Slow Cooker Suppers

Mac & cheese, pot roast and pot pie—classic comfort food made simple.

Yes, you can make yummy macaroni and cheese in the slow cooker! A last-minute topping of buttered, toasted bread crumbs makes it taste oven-baked.

MAC & CHEESE

MAKES 8 servings **PREP** 15 minutes
SLOW COOK on HIGH for 3 hours or LOW for 4 hours **COOK** 2 minutes

- 10 ounces (about 2¼ cups) dry elbow macaroni
- 1 cup shredded cheddar cheese
- 1 cup shredded Gruyère cheese
- 8 ounces American cheese, thinly sliced and roughly chopped
- 1½ cups milk
- 1 can (12 ounces) evaporated milk
- 1½ teaspoons Worcestershire sauce
- ¾ teaspoon dry mustard
- ¼ teaspoon salt
- ¼ teaspoon black pepper
- 1 tablespoon unsalted butter
- ½ cup panko bread crumbs

① Coat inside of slow cooker bowl with nonstick cooking spray.

② Combine macaroni, cheddar, Gruyère and American cheeses, milk and evaporated milk in slow cooker bowl; stir well and cover; cook on HIGH for 3 hours or LOW for 4 hours.

③ When there is 30 minutes of cook time remaining, stir in Worcestershire, mustard, salt and pepper.

④ Melt butter in a small nonstick skillet over medium-high heat. Stir in panko and cook, stirring often, for 2 minutes or until toasted and golden. Sprinkle over Mac & Cheese and serve immediately.

PER SERVING 452 calories; 25 g fat (17 g sat.); 24 g protein; 35 g carbohydrate; 1 g fiber; 646 mg sodium; 71 mg cholesterol

POT ROAST WITH ROOT VEGETABLES

MAKES 8 servings **PREP** 15 minutes **SLOW COOK** on LOW for 10 hours **COOK** 3 minutes

- 4 pounds boneless chuck roast, trimmed
- ½ teaspoon salt
- ¼ teaspoon black pepper
- 4 large carrots, peeled and cut into 3-inch lengths
- 4 parsnips, peeled, quartered lengthwise and cut into 3-inch pieces
- 2 ribs celery, finely chopped
- 1 large onion, finely chopped
- 2 bay leaves
- 1 can low-sodium beef broth
- ½ cup red wine
- 3 tablespoons flour
- 3 tablespoons unsalted butter, softened

① Place the roast in the slow cooker and sprinkle with salt and pepper. Add the carrots, parsnips, celery, onion and bay leaves around the roast and pour the broth and wine over the meat and vegetables. Cover and cook on LOW for 10 hours.

② Mash together the flour and butter to form a paste. Transfer the meat and vegetables to a platter and keep warm. Whisk flour paste into liquid in slow cooker; strain liquid into a medium-size saucepan. Place saucepan over medium-high heat and bring to a boil; boil for 3 minutes or until liquid thickens. Remove bay leaves and serve sauce with pot roast and vegetables.

PER SERVING 436 calories; 16 g fat (7 g sat.); 52 g protein; 17 g carbohydrate; 4 g fiber; 292 mg sodium; 134 mg cholesterol

SLOW COOKER CHICKEN POT PIE

MAKES 8 servings **PREP** 20 minutes
COOK 11 minutes **SLOW COOK** on HIGH for
4 hours or LOW for 7 hours

⅓ cup all-purpose flour
1¾ teaspoons poultry seasoning
1¾ teaspoons dried thyme
½ teaspoon salt
¼ teaspoon black pepper
2 pounds boneless, skinless chicken
thighs and breasts, cut into 1-inch
pieces
2 tablespoons vegetable oil
2 large carrots, peeled and cut into
half-moons
2 celery ribs, sliced
2 red-skin potatoes, scrubbed and cut
into ½-inch pieces
8 white mushrooms, thinly sliced
1 large onion, chopped
1½ cups low-sodium chicken broth
2¼ cups biscuit mix
⅔ cup milk

① Combine flour, poultry seasoning,
1 teaspoon of the thyme, salt and pepper in
a large resealable bag; add chicken pieces
to bag and toss to coat.

② Heat 1 tablespoon oil in a large
nonstick skillet over medium-high heat.
Remove chicken from bag with a slotted
spoon, shaking off excess flour. Set
remaining flour mixture aside and add
chicken to skillet. Cook for 5 minutes,
stirring occasionally, or until browned;
place in slow cooker.

③ Add remaining 1 tablespoon oil to
skillet and stir in carrots, celery, potatoes,
mushrooms and onion; cook, stirring often,
for 5 minutes. Stir remaining flour mixture
into skillet and cook 1 minute. Add broth
to skillet and bring to a boil. Pour skillet
contents into slow cooker bowl. Cover
and cook on HIGH for 4 hours or LOW for
7 hours.

④ When there is 1 hour cook time
remaining, stir together biscuit mix, milk
and remaining ¾ teaspoon thyme. Drop
biscuit mix by the tablespoonful over top
of chicken mixture. Cover slow cooker
bowl with a cotton dish towel and place lid
over top. Continue cooking until biscuits
are cooked through.

PER SERVING 388 calories; 13 g fat (3 g sat.);
30 g protein; 38 g carbohydrate; 3 g fiber;
801 mg sodium; 91 mg cholesterol

SWEET SPICED SHORT RIBS

MAKES 8 servings **PREP** 15 minutes **SLOW COOK** on LOW for 9 hours

1 medium-size onion, finely chopped
2 garlic cloves, minced
1 teaspoon cinnamon
1 can (8 ounces) tomato sauce
1 tablespoon plus 2 teaspoons red
wine vinegar
1 tablespoon plus 1 teaspoon
light-brown sugar
¼ teaspoon salt
¼ teaspoon black pepper
4 pounds beef short ribs
3 cups cooked egg noodles (optional)

① Blend onion, garlic, cinnamon, tomato
sauce, 1 tablespoon vinegar, 1 tablespoon

brown sugar, salt and pepper in a bowl.
Place ribs in slow cooker bowl and pour
sauce over top. Cover and cook on LOW
for 9 hours.

② Transfer ribs to a platter. Skim and
discard excess fat from liquid. Stir in
remaining 2 teaspoons vinegar and
1 teaspoon brown sugar. Top ribs with
sauce. Serve with cooked noodles, if desired.

PER SERVING 416 calories; 23 g fat (10 g sat.);
44 g protein; 6 g carbohydrate; 1 g fiber;
371 mg sodium; 134 mg cholesterol

SLOW COOKER
CHICKEN POT PIE

CIDER-GLAZED CHICKEN,
PAGE 51

MARCH

52

62

66

Pantry Raid

A stash of nutritious, quick-cook ingredients means you can whip up dinner in no time flat.

**BALSAMIC PORK CUTLETS,
PAGE 55**

**LEMONY PENNE &
BROCCOLI, PAGE 52**

CIDER-GLAZED CHICKEN

CIDER-GLAZED CHICKEN

MAKES 4 servings **PREP** 20 minutes
BAKE at 450° for 35 minutes **COOK** 13 minutes

VEGETABLES

- ¾ pound parsnips, peeled and cut into ½-inch pieces
- ¾ pound carrots, peeled and cut into ½-inch pieces
- ¾ pound red-skinned potatoes, scrubbed and cut into ½-inch pieces
- 2 tablespoons olive oil
- ½ teaspoon salt
- ¼ teaspoon black pepper
- 1 tablespoon fresh rosemary

CHICKEN

- 2 tablespoons olive oil
- 1¼ pounds thin-cut boneless, skinless chicken breasts
- ¼ cup Wondra flour
- 1 cup apple cider
- 2 teaspoons grainy Dijon mustard
- ½ teaspoon dried thyme
- ¼ teaspoon salt
- ¼ teaspoon black pepper

① Heat oven to 450°. Coat a large baking pan with cooking spray.

② **Vegetables.** Place parsnips, carrots and potatoes in a large bowl. Toss with olive oil, salt, pepper and rosemary. Spoon into the prepared pan and roast at 450° for 35 minutes, turning after 15 minutes.

③ **Chicken.** Heat a large nonstick skillet over medium-high heat. Add 1 tablespoon oil. Coat chicken in flour and add half to skillet. Cook 2 minutes per side. Remove to a plate and repeat with remaining tablespoon oil and chicken. Remove chicken to plate.

④ Reduce heat to medium and pour cider into skillet. Cook 1 minute, scraping up any browned bits from pan. Stir in mustard, thyme, salt and pepper. Add chicken and simmer on medium-low, covered, for 4 minutes.

⑤ Spoon sauce over chicken. Serve with the roasted vegetables.

PER SERVING 489 calories; 16 g fat (3 g sat.); 37 g protein; 48 g carbohydrate; 8 g fiber; 681 mg sodium; 82 mg cholesterol

CHICKEN TAGINE STEW

MAKES 4 servings **PREP** 20 minutes **COOK** 31 minutes

- 1 tablespoon olive oil
- ¾ pound boneless, skinless chicken thighs, cut into bite-size pieces
- 1 large onion, peeled and chopped
- ¾ pound small potatoes, scrubbed and cut into ½-inch pieces
- ½ pound carrots, peeled and cut into ¼-inch coins
- 1 can (14.5 ounces) reduced-sodium chicken broth
- 1½ teaspoons ground cinnamon
- 1 teaspoon ground cumin
- ¼ teaspoon cayenne pepper
- 1 pound zucchini, cut into bite-size cubes
- 1 can (15 ounces) chickpeas, drained and rinsed
- ¼ plus ⅛ teaspoon salt
- 2 cups cooked couscous

① Heat oil in a large, heavy-bottomed pot over medium-high heat. Add chicken and cook for 2 minutes per side, until browned. Remove to a plate and reserve.

② Add onion and cook for 3 minutes, stirring occasionally. Reduce heat if onions start to burn. Stir in potatoes, carrots, broth, cinnamon, cumin and cayenne. Simmer, covered, on medium heat for 10 minutes. Add zucchini, chickpeas, ¼ teaspoon of the salt and reserved chicken. Simmer, covered, for an additional 12 to 14 minutes or until vegetables are tender. Stir occasionally.

③ Serve stew over cooked couscous. Sprinkle ⅛ teaspoon salt over top before serving.

PER SERVING 507 calories; 10 g fat (2 g sat.); 32 g protein; 73 g carbohydrate; 12 g fiber; 666 mg sodium; 83 mg cholesterol

Add a few fresh green ingredients—broccoli, spinach or zucchini—to pantry staples and a quick, healthful dinner is done.

CHEESY-CHIPOTLE FLOUNDER

MAKES 4 servings **PREP** 15 minutes
COOK 35 minutes **BAKE** at 450° for 20 minutes

1	cup brown rice
1	can (14½ ounces) diced tomatoes with jalapeños
½	teaspoon chili powder
½	teaspoon dried oregano
¼	teaspoon ground cumin
1	lemon
¼	cup chipotle mayonnaise (such as Kraft)
¼	cup reduced-fat cheddar cheese
4	flounder fillets, about 6 ounces each
½	pound spinach, steamed

① Heat oven to 450°. Coat a 13 x 9 x 2-inch baking dish with nonstick cooking spray.

② In a medium-size pot, bring 2¼ cups water to a boil. Stir in rice and simmer, covered, on low for 20 minutes. Stir in tomatoes, chili powder, oregano and cumin. Simmer an additional 15 minutes or until rice is tender.

③ Meanwhile, fold fish in half skinned-side down and place in prepared dish. Cut lemon in half. Squeeze ½ of the lemon over inside and outside of fish. Mix together the mayo and cheese and spread evenly over the top of the fish. Bake at 450° for 15 to 20 minutes or until fish flakes easily with a fork.

④ Serve fish with brown rice and spinach. Garnish with remaining lemon, sliced.

PER SERVING 443 calories; 9 g fat (2 g sat.); 40 g protein; 49 g carbohydrate; 7 g fiber; 795 mg sodium; 92 mg cholesterol

LEMONY PENNE & BROCCOLI

MAKES 4 servings **PREP** 10 minutes **COOK** 10 minutes

8	ounces whole-wheat penne
4	tablespoons olive oil
6	cloves garlic, sliced
1	pound broccoli florets
1	can (19 ounces) cannellini beans, drained and rinsed
	Juice and zest of 1 lemon
¼	teaspoon salt
¼	teaspoon red pepper flakes
½	cup fresh basil leaves
¼	cup grated Parmesan cheese
	Tossed salad (optional)

① Cook penne following package directions, about 10 minutes. Drain, reserving 1 cup of the cooking liquid. Transfer pasta to large serving bowl.

② While pasta is cooking, heat 2 tablespoons of the oil in a large nonstick skillet over medium-high heat. Add garlic and cook for 1 to 2 minutes, until golden. Add broccoli and ⅓ cup water to skillet and cook, covered, stirring occasionally, for 5 minutes or until tender.

③ Stir beans into skillet and heat through. Add lemon juice, zest, salt and red pepper. Add contents of skillet to pasta. Stir in the remaining 2 tablespoons oil and enough reserved cooking liquid to create a sauce. Tear in the basil. Serve immediately with the cheese on the side. Accompany with a tossed salad, if desired.

PER SERVING 497 calories; 18 g fat (3 g sat.); 24 g protein; 70 g carbohydrate; 12 g fiber; 767 mg sodium; 4 mg cholesterol

CHEESY-CHIPOTLE FLOUNDER

PECAN STREUSEL
COFFEE CAKE

PECAN STREUSEL COFFEE CAKE

MAKES 16 servings **PREP** 15 minutes
BAKE at 350° for 55 minutes

½   cup chopped pecans
⅓   cup light-brown sugar
1¼ teaspoons ground cinnamon
2½ cups all-purpose flour
1½ teaspoons baking powder
1½ teaspoons baking soda
¼   teaspoon salt
6   tablespoons unsalted butter, softened
½   cup Splenda for Baking
2   eggs
4   egg whites
1½ teaspoons vanilla extract
2   containers (6 ounces each) fat-free plain yogurt

① Heat oven to 350°. Coat a 10-inch tube pan with nonstick cooking spray.

② Combine pecans, brown sugar and cinnamon in small bowl. Set aside.

③ In a large bowl, whisk together flour, baking powder, baking soda and salt.

④ In a second large bowl, beat butter and Splenda on medium speed until fluffy. Add eggs and egg whites, one at a time, beating well after each addition. Beat in vanilla.

⑤ Reduce speed to low and alternately beat in flour mixture and yogurt, beginning and ending with flour mixture.

⑥ Spread half of the batter into prepared pan and sprinkle evenly with half of pecan mixture. Carefully spread remaining batter over top and sprinkle with remaining pecan mixture.

⑦ Bake at 350° for 50 to 55 minutes or until a toothpick inserted in cake comes out clean. Cool on a wire rack for 20 minutes. Gently remove side from pan. Run a small sharp knife around bottom and center and cool completely before removing from pan.

PER SERVING 206 calories; 8 g fat (3 g sat.); 5 g protein; 28 g carbohydrate; 1 g fiber; 230 mg sodium; 38 mg cholesterol

BALSAMIC PORK CUTLETS

MAKES 4 servings **PREP** 15 minutes **COOK** 16 minutes

4   boneless pork chops, about 5 ounces each, pounded to ½-inch thickness
¼   cup Wondra flour
1   tablespoon olive oil
½   cup chopped onion
1   small red sweet pepper, seeds removed and chopped
2   cloves garlic, chopped
1   can (14.5 ounces) beef broth
1   can (6.5 ounces) mushroom pieces, drained
3   tablespoons balsamic vinegar
1   teaspoon dried parsley
½   teaspoon dried basil
¼   teaspoon black pepper
⅛   teaspoon salt
1   cup orzo, cooked following package directions

① Coat pork chops in Wondra flour. Reserve unused flour. Heat oil in a large nonstick skillet over medium-high heat. Add pork and cook 2 minutes per side. Remove to a plate.

② Add onion to skillet and cook 1 minute, stirring so onion doesn't burn. Add red pepper and garlic and cook 1 minute. Stir 1 tablespoon of the reserved flour into broth and add to skillet; stir in mushrooms, vinegar, parsley, basil, black pepper and salt. Bring to simmer.

③ Add pork; cover and simmer on medium-low heat for 10 minutes, turning after 5 minutes.

④ Serve pork with the cooked orzo and Garlic String Beans (recipe below). Serve extra sauce on the side.

PER SERVING 505 calories; 15 g fat (3 g sat.); 41 g protein; 53 g carbohydrate; 6 g fiber; 736 mg sodium; 88 mg cholesterol

GARLIC STRING BEANS

Bring a large pot of lightly salted water to a boil. Add 1 pound green beans, trimmed, and cook 5 minutes. Drain. In same pot heat 1 tablespoon olive oil; add 4 cloves smashed garlic and cook until golden. Add string beans and ⅛ teaspoon salt. Stir to heat through and coat with oil.

Meatball Madness

After years of simmering on the back burner, meatballs are making the rounds again.

AUSTRIAN MEATBALLS
& SPAETZLE, PAGE 63

MEATBALL POPS WITH ROASTED RED PEPPER–FETA DIP, PAGE 62

SWEET & SOUR MEATBALL SLIDERS, PAGE 62

MEATBALL HEROES,
PAGE 63

MINI MEATBALL SOUP

MAKES 8 servings **PREP** 15 minutes **COOK** 17 minutes

MEATBALLS

1 pound ground chicken
¼ cup seasoned bread crumbs
1 large egg
2 scallions, chopped
2 tablespoons grated Parmesan cheese
½ teaspoon fresh thyme leaves, chopped

SOUP

2 tablespoons canola oil
2 large carrots, peeled and chopped
3 medium parsnips, peeled and chopped
4 scallions, chopped
1 large can (48 ounces) light and
   fat-free chicken broth

2 sprigs fresh thyme
1 head escarole, trimmed, cleaned and
   chopped
1 cup Israeli couscous
2 tablespoons grated Parmesan
½ teaspoon salt
¼ teaspoon black pepper

① **Meatballs.** In large bowl, combine ground chicken, bread crumbs, egg, scallions, Parmesan and chopped thyme. Stir until evenly blended. With wet hands, form into 1-inch meatballs, about 40 total. Set aside.

② **Soup.** In large stock pot, heat oil over medium heat. Add carrots, parsnips and scallions. Cook 5 minutes, to soften. Add broth, thyme sprigs and 4 cups water; increase heat to high and bring to a simmer.

③ Gently drop meatballs into simmering broth mixture. Reduce heat to medium and cook 4 minutes. Add escarole in 2 batches, and the couscous. Cook 8 more minutes, then stir in Parmesan, salt and pepper. Serve warm.

PER SERVING 270 calories; 10 g fat (2 g sat.); 19 g protein; 27 g carbohydrate; 5 g fiber; 615 mg sodium; 66 mg cholesterol

There's a surprise inside this version of the most famous meatball of all—a gooey, melty piece of cheese.

SPAGHETTI & MEATBALLS

MAKES 8 servings **PREP** 25 minutes **COOK** 22 minutes **BAKE** at 325° for 17 minutes

MEATBALLS

1½ pounds meatloaf mix (or ½ pound each ground beef, pork and veal)
1 small onion, minced
¼ cup seasoned bread crumbs
2 cloves garlic, minced
2 tablespoons chopped fresh parsley
2 tablespoons grated Parmesan
1 large egg
2½ ounces (2½ pieces) string cheese, halved lengthwise, then cut into ½-inch pieces
1 tablespoon olive oil

SPAGHETTI AND SAUCE

1 pound thick spaghetti
2 cloves garlic, sliced
1 can (28 ounces) crushed tomatoes with basil
1 can (15 ounces) diced tomatoes with garlic and onion
2 tablespoons tomato paste
2 teaspoons sugar
¼ teaspoon each salt and pepper
¼ cup fresh basil, sliced

① **Meatballs.** Heat oven to 325°. In a large bowl, combine meatloaf mix, onion, bread crumbs, garlic, parsley, Parmesan and egg. Mix until ingredients are evenly blended. Form about 1 tablespoon meat mixture around a piece of string cheese. Shape into a ball. Repeat with remaining mixture and cheese, for a total of 40 meatballs.

② Heat oil in a large nonstick skillet over medium to medium-high heat. Brown meatballs in two batches, 3 minutes per batch, turning once. Transfer to a rimmed baking sheet. Remove skillet from heat. Bake meatballs at 325° for 17 minutes. Keep warm.

③ **Spaghetti and Sauce.** Meanwhile, bring a large pot of water to boiling. Add spaghetti and cook 12 minutes, according to package directions. Drain and transfer to platter.

④ While pasta boils, return skillet to medium heat. Add sliced garlic and cook 1 minute. Add crushed tomatoes, diced tomatoes, tomato paste, sugar, salt and pepper. Simmer on medium-low, stirring occasionally, 15 minutes. Remove from heat and stir in basil and meatballs.

⑤ To serve, transfer spaghetti to a platter or individual bowls and top with meatballs and sauce.

PER SERVING 488 calories; 14 g fat (5 g sat.); 30 g protein; 56 g carbohydrate; 4 g fiber; 529 mg sodium; 93 mg cholesterol

MEATBALL POPS WITH ROASTED RED PEPPER-FETA DIP

MAKES 12 appetizer servings **PREP** 20 minutes **SOAK** 1 minute **BAKE** at 375° for 20 minutes

MEATBALLS

- 2 slices whole-wheat bread, crusts removed
- 3 tablespoons milk
- 1 pound ground beef
- 1 pound ground lamb
- 3 scallions, chopped
- 3 tablespoons chopped fresh mint
- 2 tablespoons fresh oregano, chopped
- 2 teaspoons lemon zest
- 3 cloves garlic, minced
- 1 large egg
- ½ teaspoon salt
- ¼ teaspoon black pepper

DIP

- 4 ounces feta cheese
- ½ cup roasted red peppers, drained
- 1 container (7 ounces) 2% plain Greek yogurt
- 2 tablespoons lemon juice
- 2 cloves garlic
- 1 tablespoon milk
- ⅛ teaspoon salt

① Heat oven to 375°. Place a wire rack in a rimmed baking sheet. Coat rack with nonstick cooking spray.

② **Meatballs.** Crumble bread into a large bowl. Add milk and soak 1 minute. Add beef, lamb, scallions, mint, oregano, lemon zest, garlic, egg, salt and pepper. Shape into 36 meatballs, then thread each meatball onto a 6- or 8-inch skewer. Transfer to prepared rack, overlapping skewers as necessary.

③ Bake meatballs at 375° for 20 minutes. Meanwhile, prepare **Dip.** Combine feta, red peppers, yogurt, lemon juice, garlic, milk and salt in food processor or blender. Pulse until fairly smooth. Serve skewers with dip.

PER POP PLUS DIP 219 calories; 13 g fat (6 g sat.); 19 g protein; 5 g carbohydrate; 1 g fiber; 348 mg sodium; 73 mg cholesterol

SWEET & SOUR MEATBALL SLIDERS

MAKES 12 sliders **PREP** 15 minutes **COOK** 31 minutes

- ½ green bell pepper, cored and finely chopped
- 1 tablespoon onion flakes
- 1 can (15 ounces) tomato sauce
- ¾ teaspoon garlic salt
- ¼ teaspoon black pepper
- 2 pounds ground pork
- 2 large eggs
- ⅓ cup corn flake crumbs
- 1 tablespoon olive oil
- 1 medium onion, sliced
- ¼ cup sugar
- ¼ cup cider vinegar
- 1 package soft dinner rolls (12 per package)

① Coat a small nonstick skillet with nonstick cooking spray. Heat over medium heat.

② Add green pepper to skillet; cook 4 minutes. Stir in onion flakes, 3 tablespoons of the tomato sauce, ½ teaspoon of the garlic salt and the pepper. Remove from heat.

③ Place pork in a large bowl. Stir in eggs, corn flake crumbs and green pepper mixture until evenly blended. Shape into 12 meatballs, a generous ⅓ cup for each.

④ Heat oil in a large, lidded nonstick skillet over medium heat. Add onion; cook 7 minutes, stirring. Add remaining tomato sauce, remaining ¼ teaspoon garlic salt, the sugar and vinegar. Add meatballs to skillet and cover. Reduce heat to medium-low and simmer 17 to 20 minutes or until cooked through, turning halfway.

⑤ Spoon 1 meatball and some onion sauce onto a roll. Repeat with all meatballs, most of the sauce and the rolls.

PER SLIDER 333 calories; 20 g fat (7 g sat.); 17 g protein; 22 g carbohydrate; 1 g fiber; 453 mg sodium; 91 mg cholesterol

AUSTRIAN MEATBALLS & SPAETZLE

MAKES 8 servings **PREP** 15 minutes
COOK 25 minutes

- 1 box (10.5 ounces) spaetzle
- 1 package (10 ounces) brown mushrooms, trimmed and cleaned
- 2 shallots, peeled
- 2 cloves garlic, peeled
- 1 pound ground beef
- 1 pound ground pork
- ⅓ cup plain bread crumbs
- 1 large egg
- 1 teaspoon dried sage
- ½ teaspoon salt
- ¼ teaspoon black pepper
- 2 tablespoons olive oil
- 1 can (14.5 ounces) light and low-sodium beef broth
- 2 tablespoons all-purpose flour

① Heat a large pot of lightly salted water to boiling. Add spaetzle and cook 25 minutes, following package directions.

② Meanwhile, combine 1 cup of the mushrooms, the shallots and garlic in a food processor or mini chopper. Pulse to finely chop. Transfer to a large bowl and add ground beef and pork, bread crumbs, egg, dried sage, salt and pepper. Mix just until combined. Shape into 32 meatballs, using 2 tablespoons mixture for each.

③ Heat oil in large, lidded nonstick skillet over medium-high heat. Add meatballs to skillet; it will be a tight fit. Brown meatballs, turning occasionally. Slice remaining mushrooms and add to skillet with all but ¼ cup of the beef broth. Cover skillet; reduce heat to medium-low. Simmer 15 minutes.

④ Mix flour into reserved broth. With a slotted spoon, remove meatballs from skillet. Stir flour mixture into skillet. Simmer 3 minutes, until thickened. Drain spaetzle. Transfer to a platter. Stir meatballs back into sauce in skillet, then spoon over spaetzle and serve.

PER SERVING 491 calories; 20 g fat (7 g sat.); 31 g protein; 36 g carbohydrate; 2 g fiber; 361 mg sodium; 131 mg cholesterol

MEATBALL HEROES

MAKES 5 sandwiches **PREP** 15 minutes **COOK** 17 minutes **BROIL** 2 minutes

MEATBALLS

- 1 package (about 20 ounces) Italian-flavored or plain ground turkey (such as Honeysuckle White)
- ½ cup ricotta cheese
- 3 tablespoons chopped fresh parsley
- 2 tablespoons plain bread crumbs
- 2 tablespoons milk
- 1 large egg
- 1 tablespoon olive oil

SAUCE, BREAD AND CHEESE

- 2 cups jarred marinara
- 2 tablespoons olive oil
- 1 tablespoon garlic paste
- 5 hero rolls, or 2 small Italian loaves, each cut into thirds (save 1 piece for another use)
- 5 slices provolone

① Heat oven to broil. **Meatballs.** Combine seasoned turkey (see **Note**), ricotta, parsley, bread crumbs, milk and egg in a large bowl. Mix gently to combine. Shape into 15 meatballs, 3 tablespoons mixture for each.

② Heat oil in a large, lidded nonstick skillet over medium heat. Brown meatballs, 2 minutes per side. **Sauce.** Reduce heat to medium and add marinara. Cover and gently simmer on medium-low for 13 minutes or until cooked through. Spoon sauce over meatballs halfway through.

③ **Bread and Cheese.** In a small bowl, blend 2 tablespoons oil and the garlic paste. Slice rolls or bread and brush insides with garlic oil. Broil 2 minutes to toast rolls.

④ Once meatballs are cooked, tuck 3 meatballs with some sauce on a roll. Top with a slice of cheese and return to oven to melt cheese. Repeat with all meatballs, rolls and cheese.

Note. If using plain ground turkey, season with ½ teaspoon salt, 1 teaspoon Italian seasoning and ⅛ teaspoon black pepper.

PER HERO 600 calories; 31 g fat (10 g sat.); 39 g protein; 42 g carbohydrate; 4 g fiber; 1,098 mg sodium; 128 mg cholesterol

BUTTERSCOTCH PUDDING CAKE

MAKES 8 servings **PREP** 15 minutes **SLOW COOK** 2½ hours on HIGH

- 1 cup all-purpose flour
- 1 package (3 ounces) cook-and-serve butterscotch pudding mix
- ¼ cup sugar
- 2 teaspoons baking powder
- ¼ teaspoon salt
- ¾ cup milk
- 2 tablespoons canola oil
- 1 tablespoon vanilla extract
- ½ cup butterscotch chips

TOPPING
- 3 tablespoons butterscotch sauce
- ½ cup sugar

- 1⅓ cups boiling water
  Whipped cream (optional)

① Coat slow cooker bowl with nonstick cooking spray.

② In medium-size bowl, whisk together the flour, pudding mix, sugar, baking powder and salt. Make a well in the center and add milk, canola oil and vanilla. Gently stir until batter is smooth. Stir in butterscotch chips. Pour evenly into slow cooker bowl.

③ **Topping.** In a small bowl, stir the butterscotch sauce and the sugar together; pour in the 1⅓ cups boiling water and stir until smooth. Pour over batter in slow cooker. Cover and cook on HIGH for about 2½ hours or until cake is puffed and top layer is set. Let stand, covered, 30 minutes before serving. Serve with whipped cream, if desired.

PER SERVING 319 calories; 8 g fat (4 g sat.); 3 g protein; 56 g carbohydrate; 1 g fiber; 277 mg sodium; 2 mg cholesterol

PB&J BREAD PUDDING

MAKES 10 servings **PREP** 15 minutes
SLOW COOK 3 hours on HIGH

10	cups diced Italian or French bread
4	eggs
1	cup creamy peanut butter
2½	cups milk
¾	cup sugar
1	tablespoon vanilla extract
¼	teaspoon salt
1	cup strawberry jam

① Generously coat slow cooker bowl with nonstick cooking spray. Place bread in slow cooker bowl.

② In a large bowl, lightly whisk eggs, then whisk in peanut butter until well blended. Whisk in milk, sugar, vanilla and salt. Pour over bread in slow cooker bowl. Press down bread until submerged in liquid. Place spoonfuls of the jam in and around the bread mixture, pushing them in with a spoon. Cover and cook on HIGH for about 2¾ hours or until internal temperature reaches 160° on an instant-read thermometer.

③ Remove lid and cook an additional 15 minutes. Cool slightly before serving.

PER SERVING 511 calories; 18 g fat (5 g sat.); 17 g protein; 74 g carbohydrate; 4 g fiber; 500 mg sodium; 88 mg cholesterol

BAKED APPLES

MAKES 6 servings **PREP** 15 minutes **SLOW COOK** 3 hours on HIGH

6	small McIntosh apples (about 2 pounds)
¼	cup brown sugar
¼	cup chopped walnuts
2	tablespoons raisins
1	tablespoon dried cranberries
1	teaspoon lemon zest
¾	teaspoon cinnamon
¼	teaspoon nutmeg
2	tablespoons unsalted butter, cut into small pieces
¼	cup orange juice

① Core apples, leaving bottoms intact and using a paring knife to enlarge holes. Peel skin from around top of apples. Place apples in single layer in oval slow cooker bowl (if you have a round slow cooker, you can cook only 5 apples).

② Stir together sugar, walnuts, raisins, cranberries, zest, cinnamon and nutmeg. Place 1½ tablespoons raisin mixture in each apple; divide butter and place on top of apple filling. Pour orange juice and ¼ cup water over top of apples. Cover and cook on HIGH for about 3 hours.

③ Place apples in individual bowls and spoon remaining sauce over top.

PER SERVING 193 calories; 7 g fat (3 g sat.); 1 g protein; 34 g carbohydrate; 4 g fiber; 6 mg sodium; 10 mg cholesterol

When baking a cake in a slow cooker, place a couple paper towels across the top of the cooker before you put the lid on to catch drips and to prevent a soggy cake.

FRUIT CRUMBLE

MAKES 8 servings **PREP** 15 minutes
SLOW COOK 3½ hours on HIGH

3   pears (about 1½ pounds), peeled, cored and sliced
2   Granny Smith apples (about ¾ pound), peeled, cored and sliced
1   cup frozen cherries
1   cup dried cranberries
½   cup granulated sugar
2   tablespoons cornstarch
1   teaspoon vanilla extract
½   teaspoon cinnamon

TOPPING
1   cup flour
½   cup quick-cooking rolled oats
¾   cup light-brown sugar
½   teaspoon cinnamon
½   cup (1 stick) cold, unsalted butter, cut into pieces
    Vanilla ice cream (optional)

① Coat slow cooker bowl with nonstick cooking spray. Place pears, apples, cherries and cranberries in slow cooker and mix together with sugar, cornstarch, vanilla and cinnamon until well blended. Cover and cook on HIGH for 30 minutes.

② **Topping.** Meanwhile, mix together flour, oats, brown sugar and cinnamon. Cut in the butter with a pastry blender or fingers and mix until mixture resembles coarse crumbs. Lift lid and spread topping evenly over fruit.

③ Replace cover and cook on HIGH for 3 hours more or until fruit is very tender. Let cool for 10 minutes before serving. Serve with ice cream, if desired.

PER SERVING 441 calories; 12 g fat (7 g sat.); 3 g protein; 83 g carbohydrate; 6 g fiber; 12 mg sodium; 30 mg cholesterol

STEAMED LEMON CAKE

MAKES 8 servings **PREP** 15 minutes **SLOW COOK** 4 hours on HIGH

1   package (16 ounces) pound cake mix
¾   cup buttermilk
3   tablespoons unsalted butter, softened
2   large eggs
¼   cup lemon juice
½   teaspoon lemon zest

FROSTING
2   cups confectioners' sugar
¼   cup (½ stick) unsalted butter, softened
2   tablespoons milk
½   teaspoon lemon extract

① Coat an 8-cup soufflé dish with nonstick cooking spray. Line bottom with wax paper; spray paper.

② Beat together the pound cake mix, buttermilk, butter, eggs, lemon juice and zest on low speed for 30 seconds; increase speed to medium and beat for 2 to 3 minutes or until well blended and smooth. Spread batter into prepared dish. Cover dish tightly with foil and place in a 5-quart oval slow cooker bowl. Add 4 cups boiling water around soufflé dish. Cover and cook on HIGH for 4 hours. Cake is done when a toothpick inserted in the center tests clean and cake springs back when touched.

③ Remove dish to a rack and cool uncovered for 10 minutes. Run a thin knife around edge of cake and invert onto wire rack; turn right side up to cool completely.

④ **Frosting.** In medium-size bowl, beat confectioners' sugar, butter, milk and lemon extract until smooth. Spread over cake.

PER SERVING 491 calories; 20 g fat (9 g sat.); 4 g protein; 74 g carbohydrate; 1 g fiber; 347 mg sodium; 81 mg cholesterol

FRUIT CRUMBLE

SHREDDED BEEF TACOS,
PAGE 91

APRIL

76

80

99

The beautiful shape of a Bundt cake is so pretty, the cake needs very little additional adornment. This simple spring cake—flavored with lemon and topped with icing and fresh berries—is perfect for any spring celebration.

LEMON BUNDT CAKE

MAKES 12 servings **PREP** 15 minutes **BAKE** at 325° for 1 hour

CAKE

- 4 **cups cake flour (not self-rising)**
- 1 **tablespoon baking powder**
- ¾ **teaspoon salt**
- 1 **cup (2 sticks) unsalted butter, softened**
- 1½ **cups sugar**
- 4 **eggs**
- 2 **teaspoons vanilla extract**
- ¼ **cup lemon juice**

DRIZZLE AND FILLING

- 1 **cup confectioners' sugar**
- ¼ **teaspoon lemon extract**
- 1 **package (4 ounces) fresh blueberries**
- 1 **package (6 ounces) fresh raspberries**
- 1 **tablespoon strawberry jelly or seedless raspberry jam, melted**

① Heat oven to 325°. Generously coat a 10-cup kugelhopf or Bundt pan with nonstick baking spray, making sure to get into all the ridges.

② **Cake.** In medium-size bowl, combine flour, baking powder and salt. Set aside.

③ In large bowl, beat butter until smooth. Beat in sugar until fluffy. Add eggs one at a time, beating well after each addition. Beat in vanilla. On low, beat in flour mixture, alternating with 1 cup water and the lemon juice. Scrape into prepared pan.

④ Bake cake at 325° for 1 hour or until toothpick inserted in cake comes out clean. Cool in pan on wire rack for 15 minutes. Carefully trim cake level, run thin knife around cake edge and invert directly onto rack to remove pan. Cool completely.

⑤ **Drizzle and Filling.** In medium bowl, blend confectioners' sugar, 2 tablespoons water and lemon extract. Whisk until blended and smooth. Drizzle over cake, allowing to drip down side.

⑥ In small bowl, toss together blueberries, raspberries and melted jelly or jam. Fill center of cake with as much of the berry mixture as possible. Serve remaining berries alongside slices of cake.

PER SERVING 445 calories; 17 g fat (10 g sat.); 5 g protein; 68 g carbohydrate; 2 g fiber; 272 mg sodium; 111 mg cholesterol

Sea Change

Get off the hook at dinnertime with these five ways to prepare heart-healthy fish.

TUNA WITH FRESH CHERRY TOMATO SAUCE, PAGE 76

**SCALLOP-QUINOA
PAELLA, PAGE 76**

PANKO FISH NUGGETS

M
B:
1
5
3
1
2 ... potatoes (about
10 ounces each), scrubbed and
each cut into 8 wedges

1 tablespoon olive oil
¼ teaspoon salt
½ cup all-purpose flour
4 egg whites
1 tablespoon Dijon mustard
1½ cups panko bread crumbs
1½ pounds cod, cut into 1½-inch pieces

① Heat oven to 450°. Place a large rack over a baking sheet and coat with nonstick cooking spray. Set aside.

② In a small bowl, stir together the wasabi powder and 1 tablespoon water. Whisk in sour cream, mayonnaise and scallion. Refrigerate.

③ Place potatoes on a baking sheet and toss with olive oil and salt. Bake at 450° for 30 minutes or until tender, turning after 20 minutes.

④ Meanwhile, place flour in a shallow glass dish. In a second dish, whisk together egg whites and mustard. Place panko on a separate plate. Coat cod with flour, dip in egg mixture and coat with panko. Place fish pieces on prepared baking rack. Add pan to oven after potatoes have baked for 15 minutes. Bake fish for 15 minutes.

⑤ Serve cod with potato wedges and wasabi sauce on the side.

PER SERVING 478 calories; 12 g fat (4 g sat.); 45 g protein; 48 g carbohydrate; 2 g fiber; 525 mg sodium; 98 mg cholesterol

Count Your Chickens

Five delicious recipes to spice up everyone's favorite bird—fast.

**CHICKEN À LA CALABRESE,
PAGE 81**

**TANDOORI CHICKEN
THIGHS, PAGE 82**

SWEET & SOUR ASIAN WRAPS

MAKES 4 servings **PREP** 20 minutes **COOK** 5 minutes

DIPPING SAUCE
- 2 tablespoons light soy sauce
- 2 tablespoons rice vinegar
- 2 teaspoons sugar
- 1 teaspoon fish sauce
- ¼ teaspoon Sriracha (Thai hot sauce)

WRAPS
- 1 tablespoon canola oil
- 1 pound ground chicken
- 1 small red sweet pepper, cored, seeds removed and chopped
- 1 teaspoon sugar
- ½ teaspoon garlic powder
- ½ teaspoon ground ginger
- ¼ teaspoon Sriracha
- 2 scallions, chopped

- 1 tablespoon light soy sauce
- 16 large Bibb lettuce leaves (about 2 heads)
  Sliced cucumber, scallions, mint, lime, for serving
- 3 cups cooked brown rice

① **Dipping Sauce.** In a small bowl, stir together soy sauce, vinegar, sugar, fish sauce, sriracha and 1 tablespoon water. Set aside.

② **Wraps.** Heat oil in a large nonstick skillet over medium-high heat. Crumble in chicken and cook 2 minutes, breaking up large pieces with a wooden spoon. Stir in red pepper, sugar, garlic powder, ginger and Sriracha. Cook 3 minutes, until no longer pink, stirring occasionally. Take off heat and stir in scallions and soy sauce.

③ To serve, spoon ¼ cup chicken mixture into each lettuce leaf and top with cucumber, scallions, mint and a squeeze of lime. Serve with Dipping Sauce and brown rice.

PER SERVING 427 calories; 17 g fat (5 g sat.); 26 g protein; 44 g carbohydrate; 5 g fiber; 723 mg sodium; 137 mg cholesterol

CHICKEN À LA CALABRESE

MAKES 8 servings **PREP** 20 minutes
COOK 15 minutes **BAKE** at 450° for 15 minutes,
then at 350° for 25 minutes

- 1 whole chicken (3½ to 4 pounds), cut into 8 pieces, skin removed, wings reserved for another use
- 1 tablespoon olive oil
- 1 large onion, peeled and sliced
- 2 large sweet peppers, cored, seeded and sliced
- 3 cloves garlic, smashed
- 1 can (28 ounces) whole tomatoes in puree
- ½ cup white wine
- ½ teaspoon salt
- ¼ teaspoon black pepper
- ¼ teaspoon red pepper flakes
- ¼ cup fresh parsley leaves
- ¼ cup fresh mint leaves
- 1 sprig fresh oregano
- 1 sprig fresh thyme
- ¾ pound whole-grain penne, cooked following package directions
- ¼ cup grated Romano cheese

① Heat oven to 450°. Place chicken pieces in a lightly greased lidded casserole (or large open casserole dish); roast, uncovered, at 450° for 15 minutes.

② Meanwhile, heat oil in a large nonstick skillet over medium-high heat. Add onion, peppers and garlic and cook 5 minutes, stirring occasionally. Add tomatoes, wine, salt, pepper and red pepper flakes, breaking up tomatoes with a wooden spoon. Simmer, uncovered, 10 minutes, stirring occasionally. Stir in parsley, mint, oregano and thyme.

③ Pour sauce over chicken. Cover and reduce heat to 350°. Bake for an additional 25 minutes or until internal temperature registers 170° on an instant-read thermometer.

④ Serve chicken and sauce over cooked pasta. Garnish with grated Romano cheese.

PER SERVING 475 calories; 10 g fat (2 g sat.); 49 g protein; 44 g carbohydrate; 6 g fiber; 508 mg sodium; 123 mg cholesterol

CHICKEN PARMESAN

MAKES 4 servings **PREP** 15 minutes **COOK** 13 minutes **BAKE** at 350° for 15 minutes

- ½ cup whole-wheat bread crumbs
- ⅓ cup all-purpose flour
- 2 eggs, slightly beaten
- 4 thinly sliced boneless, skinless chicken breasts (about 4 ounces each)
- 2 tablespoons, plus 1 teaspoon olive oil
- 1 cup marinara sauce
- ¾ cup shredded reduced-fat mozzarella cheese
- ¾ cup low-sodium chicken broth
- 4 cloves smashed garlic
- 1½ pounds green beans
- ½ pound sliced mushrooms
- ⅛ teaspoon salt
- ⅛ teaspoon black pepper

① Heat oven to 350°.

② Place bread crumbs and flour separately in two shallow dishes and the eggs in a shallow bowl. Coat chicken in flour and dip in egg, shaking off excess. Coat with bread crumbs and place on a plate.

③ In a large nonstick skillet, heat 2 tablespoons of the oil over medium-high heat. Sauté chicken 2 to 3 minutes per side, until browned.

④ In the bottom of a baking dish, mix ¼ cup of the marinara sauce with 2 tablespoons water. Place chicken in dish and top each with 3 tablespoons sauce and 3 tablespoons cheese. Bake at 350°, covered, for 15 minutes.

⑤ Meanwhile, in a large skillet, simmer broth and garlic, covered, 2 minutes. Add the green beans and mushrooms and simmer, covered, for 5 minutes, until tender. Drain and toss with the remaining teaspoon olive oil and season with salt and pepper. Serve with chicken.

PER SERVING 453 calories; 18 g fat (5 g sat.); 38 g protein; 34 g carbohydrate; 6 g fiber; 787 mg sodium; 156 mg cholesterol

Mild and juicy, chicken is so versatile it takes on a world of flavors and preparations to please any palate.

TANDOORI CHICKEN THIGHS

MAKES 4 servings **PREP** 15 minutes **BAKE** at 400° for 40 minutes **COOK** 20 minutes

CHICKEN

1   tablespoon chopped gingerroot
1   tablespoon lemon juice
1   teaspoon curry powder
2   cloves garlic, chopped
¼   teaspoon salt
⅛   teaspoon ground cinnamon
⅛   teaspoon cayenne pepper
4   large bone-in chicken thighs (about 1½ pounds), skin removed

LENTILS

1   tablespoon olive oil
1   medium onion, peeled and chopped
3   cloves garlic, chopped
1   cup yellow lentils
1   tablespoon chopped gingerroot
1   teaspoon curry powder
½   teaspoon salt
1   pound red Swiss chard, cut into 1-inch slices, tough stems removed

① Heat oven to 400°.

② **Chicken.** In a small bowl, stir together ginger, lemon juice, curry, garlic, salt, cinnamon and cayenne. Place chicken in a baking dish, flesh-side up; rub ginger-curry mixture over top of each piece. Bake at 400° for 40 minutes or until internal temperature registers 170° on an instant-read thermometer.

③ Meanwhile, make **Lentils.** In a large pot, heat oil over medium-high heat. Add onion and garlic and cook 5 minutes, stirring occasionally. Stir in 2 cups water, lentils, ginger, curry and salt. Simmer, covered, over medium heat 10 minutes, stirring occasionally. Stir in chard and simmer 5 minutes.

④ Serve chicken with lentils, and Easy Chutney and Mint Raita (see recipes, below), if desired.

PER SERVING 451 calories; 13 g fat (3 g sat.); 48 g protein; 39 g carbohydrate; 14 g fiber; 747 mg sodium; 166 mg cholesterol

EASY CHUTNEY

Heat 2 teaspoons oil in a medium-size saucepan; add ½ cup each chopped red onion and chopped green pepper and cook 5 minutes. Stir in 1 teaspoon hot curry powder, ¼ cup peach preserves, 2 tablespoons cider vinegar, ¼ teaspoon salt and 2 chopped ripe mangoes. Cook, covered, 5 minutes. Cool.

MINT RAITA

Combine ½ cup reduced-fat plain yogurt; ½ cucumber, peeled, seeded and chopped; 2 tablespoons chopped mint; a squeeze of lemon juice; and pinch of salt. Refrigerate.

CHICKEN CUTLET SALAD

MAKES 4 servings **PREP** 15 minutes **COOK** 7 minutes

1½ pounds chicken cutlets (about 6 ounces each)
5   tablespoons balsamic vinegar
1   teaspoon dried oregano
¾   teaspoon salt
¼   teaspoon black pepper
4   tablespoons olive oil
1   pound plum tomatoes, chopped
1   large head of escarole, washed, dried and cut into bite-size pieces
1   head romaine lettuce, washed, dried and cut into bite-size pieces
1   small red onion, peeled and thinly sliced
    Fresh basil, for garnish

① Brush chicken with 1 tablespoon of the vinegar and season with the oregano, ¼ teaspoon of the salt and ⅛ teaspoon of the pepper. Heat 1 tablespoon of the oil in a large nonstick skillet over medium-high heat. Cook chicken 3 minutes per side. Remove to plate; keep warm.

② Add remaining 4 tablespoons vinegar, ½ teaspoon salt, ⅛ teaspoon black pepper, 3 tablespoons olive oil and the plum tomatoes to skillet. Scrape up any browned bits from bottom of skillet and gently heat through, about 1 minute.

③ Toss together escarole, romaine lettuce and red onion. Slice chicken and serve over salad and spoon warm tomato vinaigrette over the top. Garnish with fresh basil.

PER SERVING 378 calories; 18 g fat (3 g sat.); 38 g protein; 16 g carbohydrate; 7 g fiber; 558 mg sodium; 94 mg cholesterol

CHICKEN CUTLET SALAD

Loco for Tacos

A delicious Mexican-inspired dinner is just four steps away: Stuff. Fold. Eat. Repeat.

GRILLED CHICKEN TACOS

MAKES 8 soft tacos **PREP** 15 minutes
GRILL 12 minutes

1½ pounds boneless, skinless chicken
     breast cutlets
1   teaspoon adobo seasoning salt
     (such as Goya)
1   package small flour tortillas
     (8 per package)
     Fresh Salsa, shredded lettuce,
     shredded cheese, sour cream and
     Guacamole, for serving

① If needed, pound chicken to even
thickness. Sprinkle adobo seasoning salt
onto both sides of the chicken.

② Heat grill or grill pan to medium-high
heat. Lightly coat grill rack with oil.
For broiler method, see **Note**, below.
Grill chicken until cooked through, 5 to
6 minutes per side. Transfer to a
cutting board.

③ Cut chicken crossways into thin strips.
To serve, spoon about ¼ cup chicken
strips onto a tortilla. Add Fresh Salsa,
shredded lettuce, shredded cheese, sour
cream and Guacamole.

Note. Heat broiler to high. Broil chicken
until cooked through, about 6 or 7 minutes
per side.

PER TACO 355 calories; 13 g fat (2 g sat.);
26 g protein; 34 g carbohydrate; 4 g fiber;
611 mg sodium; 49 mg cholesterol

FRESH SALSA

In a medium bowl, combine 1 pound
tomatoes, cored and chopped; 1 medium-
size red onion, finely chopped; ¼ cup fresh
cilantro, chopped; 3 cloves garlic, chopped;
1 jalapeño chile, seeded and finely chopped;
¼ teaspoon salt; ¼ teaspoon black pepper;
3 tablespoons lime juice; and 1 tablespoon
olive oil.

GUACAMOLE

Peel, pit and mash 2 avocados. Stir in
½ cup Fresh Salsa and ⅛ teaspoon salt.

**SHREDDED BEEF TACOS,
PAGE 91**

BAJA-STYLE SHRIMP
TACOS, PAGE 91

PORK CARNITAS

Corn or flour tortillas; soft shell or hard shell; pork, beef, veggie or shrimp filling? There's a taco for every taste.

PORK CARNITAS

MAKES 10 servings **PREP** 15 minutes
SLOW COOKER 3 hours on HIGH or 6 hours on LOW

- 2 pounds pork loin, trimmed and cut into 1-inch pieces
- 4 garlic cloves, minced
- ⅓ cup cilantro leaves plus ¼ cup chopped cilantro
- 1 large onion, chopped
- 1½ teaspoons dried oregano
- 1 teaspoon orange zest
- ¾ teaspoon salt
- ¼ teaspoon red pepper flakes
- 1 can (14.5 ounces) low-sodium chicken broth
  Zest and juice of 1 lime
- 1 package (7.5 ounces) soft corn tortillas
  Shredded romaine lettuce, sour cream and salsa (optional)

① Combine pork, garlic, ⅓ cup cilantro leaves, onion, oregano, orange zest, salt and red pepper flakes in slow cooker bowl and pour broth over top so pork is mostly submerged. Cover and cook on HIGH for 3 hours or LOW for 6 hours or until pork is very tender.

② Remove pork from slow cooker using a slotted spoon and let cool slightly. When cool, shred pork and stir together with ¼ cup cilantro, lime zest and juice, and ½ cup cooking liquid. Serve in warmed tortillas with lettuce, sour cream and salsa, if desired.

PER TACO 204 calories; 6 g fat (2 g sat.); 22 g protein; 16 g carbohydrate; 3 g fiber; 524 mg sodium; 50 mg cholesterol

GROUND BEEF TACOS SUPREME

MAKES 12 tacos **PREP** 15 minutes **COOK** 10 minutes **MICROWAVE** 45 seconds

- 1½ pounds 90% lean ground beef
- 2 tablespoons onion flakes
- 1 tablespoon chili powder
- 1 teaspoon garlic powder
- ½ teaspoon salt
- ¼ teaspoon ground cumin
- ¼ teaspoon black pepper
- 3 tablespoons tomato paste
- 1 package (4.6 ounces) hard taco shells
  Shredded lettuce, diced tomato, grated pepper-Jack cheese and sour cream (optional)

① Heat a large nonstick skillet over medium-high heat. Crumble in beef and cook 5 minutes, stirring occasionally with wooden spoon to break up meat.

② Add onion flakes, chili powder, garlic powder, salt, cumin and pepper. Cook 3 minutes.

③ Whisk tomato paste together with ⅓ cup water. Add to skillet. Cook 2 minutes, until thickened.

④ Meanwhile, heat taco shells in microwave for 45 seconds, as per package directions. Spoon ground beef filling into taco shells and serve with lettuce, tomato, cheese and sour cream, if desired.

PER TACO 147 calories; 5 g fat (2 g sat.); 14 g protein; 11 g carbohydrate; 1 g fiber; 239 mg sodium; 35 mg cholesterol

VEGGIE TACOS

MAKES 12 hard tacos **PREP** 10 minutes **COOK** 10 minutes **MICROWAVE** 45 seconds

- 2 tablespoons olive oil
- ¾ pound zucchini, trimmed and diced
- 3 scallions, trimmed and sliced
- 2 teaspoons chili powder
- ¼ teaspoon ground cumin
- ¼ teaspoon dried oregano
- ¼ teaspoon salt
- ¼ teaspoon pepper
- 1 can (14.5 ounces) pinto beans, drained and rinsed
- 1 can (8¾ ounces) corn, drained and rinsed
- 2 cups baby spinach, chopped
- ¾ cup salsa verde (tomatillo salsa)
- 1 package (4.6 ounces) hard taco shells
- ⅔ cup crumbled farmer cheese or queso blanco
- Lime wedges

① Heat oil in large nonstick skillet over medium to medium-high heat. Add zucchini and scallions and cook 5 minutes. Add chili powder, cumin, oregano, salt and pepper. Cook 1 minute.

② Stir in beans, corn, spinach and salsa. Cook 3 to 4 minutes or until spinach is wilted.

③ Meanwhile, heat taco shells in microwave for 45 seconds, as per package directions. Spoon about ⅓ cup veggie mixture into a taco shell and sprinkle with a little cheese. Add a squeeze of lime and serve.

PER TACO 160 calories; 7 g fat (2 g sat.); 5 g protein; 22 g carbohydrate; 4 g fiber; 458 mg sodium; 4 mg cholesterol

SHREDDED BEEF TACOS

MAKES 12 soft tacos **PREP** 15 minutes
COOK 26 minutes **PRESSURE COOK** 42 minutes
(see Note)

2 tablespoons canola oil
1 flank steak (about 1½ pounds)
1 medium onion, chopped
1 green bell pepper, seeded and chopped
1 sweet red pepper, seeded and chopped
2 teaspoons chili powder
½ teaspoon ground cumin
½ teaspoon salt
½ teaspoon pepper
3 cloves garlic, chopped
½ teaspoon dried oregano
1 can (14.5 ounces) fire-roasted diced tomatoes
½ cup reduced-sodium 99% fat-free beef broth
1 package (7.5 ounces) soft corn tortillas
   Lettuce, diced red onion, shredded cheese (optional)

① Heat 1 tablespoon of oil over medium-high heat in pot of a pressure cooker. Brown steak 5 to 6 minutes, turning once. Remove to a plate.

② Reduce heat to medium and add remaining tablespoon oil to pot. Stir in onion, peppers, chili powder, cumin, salt and pepper. Cook 3 minutes, stirring occasionally. Stir in garlic and oregano; cook 2 minutes more.

③ Return steak to pot with any drippings, and top with tomatoes and beef broth. Lock lid in place. Over high heat, bring up to pressure, about 7 minutes. Lower heat to maintain pressure; cook 35 minutes.

④ Quick-release pressure by setting under cool running water. Open lid away from you, letting any excess steam escape.

⑤ Remove steak to a cutting board and cut across grain into 2-inch strips. Return sauce in cooker to medium heat and simmer, uncovered, 15 minutes. Meanwhile, shred meat with two forks and return to pot. Serve shredded beef and sauce on corn tortillas. Top with lettuce, diced red onion and cheese, if desired.

Note. For traditional stove-top method, use a 4-quart heavy lidded pot and proceed with recipe through beginning of step 3. After adding steak, tomatoes and beef broth to pot, cover and cook over low heat for 1½ hours. Continue with recipe at step 5.

PER TACO 122 calories; 6 g fat (2 g sat.);
13 g protein; 4 g carbohydrate; 1 g fiber;
230 mg sodium; 24 mg cholesterol

BAJA-STYLE SHRIMP TACOS

MAKES 8 tacos **PREP** 15 minutes
MARINATE 10 minutes **BROIL** 7 minutes

MARINADE AND DRESSING
⅓ cup cilantro leaves, finely chopped
¼ cup fresh lime juice
¼ cup olive oil
1 tablespoon honey
½ teaspoon chili powder
½ teaspoon salt
¼ teaspoon ground cumin
¼ teaspoon pepper
TACOS
1 pound cleaned medium shrimp (35-40 count)
4 cups finely shredded coleslaw mix (or green and red cabbage)
1 package taco-size flour tortillas (8 per package)
1 cup prepared guacamole

① **Marinade and Dressing.** In a small bowl, whisk together cilantro, lime juice, oil, honey, chili powder, salt, cumin and pepper.

② **Tacos.** Heat broiler to high. In medium-size bowl, combine ¼ cup of the marinade and the shrimp. In second medium-size bowl, combine remaining marinade and the coleslaw mix. Let both marinate for 10 minutes.

③ Transfer shrimp to a broiler pan. Broil, 2 to 3 inches from heat, for 6 to 7 minutes, turning once.

④ Spread a tortilla with about 2 tablespoons guacamole. Top with 4 or 5 shrimp and ¼ cup slaw. Repeat with all ingredients.

PER TACO 285 calories; 15 g fat (4 g sat.);
7 g protein; 34 g carbohydrate; 1 g fiber;
656 mg sodium; 10 mg cholesterol

Smaller shrimp—35 to 40 per pound—work best in these shrimp tacos.

Sweet Charity

Rake in the dough and join Share Our Strength's fight to end childhood hunger.

$ 100, each

WHOOPIE PIES, PAGE 97

**RED VELVET CUPCAKES,
PAGE 99**

$ 1 00/each

CHOCOLATE-CHERRY
FUDGE BROWNIES,
PAGE 97

PINK LEMONADE CRUMB BARS

MAKES 18 bars **PREP** 15 minutes **BAKE** at 350° for 55 minutes

CRUST AND CRUMBS

2	cups plus 2 tablespoons all-purpose flour
½	cup sugar
½	cup blanched slivered almonds
⅛	teaspoon salt
1	cup (2 sticks) unsalted butter, melted
1	teaspoon vanilla extract

FILLING

1½	cups sugar
¼	cup all-purpose flour
5	large eggs
½	cup seedless raspberry jam, stirred to loosen up
½	cup fresh lemon juice (about 2 lemons)
	Grated zest of 1 lemon (about 1½ teaspoons)

① Heat oven to 350°. Line a 13 x 9 x 2-inch metal baking pan with nonstick foil.

② **Crust and Crumbs.** Combine 2 cups of the flour, the sugar, almonds and salt in a food processor. Pulse to finely grind almonds and blend ingredients. While processor is running, add butter and vanilla. Reserve ⅔ cup crumbs mixture and press rest into bottom of prepared pan. Bake at 350° for 25 minutes. Meanwhile, with your hands, blend remaining 2 tablespoons flour into reserved crumbs.

③ **Filling.** In a medium-size bowl, whisk sugar and flour. Whisk in eggs, then raspberry jam. Whisk in lemon juice and zest.

④ Remove crust from oven and pour filling over crust. Return to oven and bake 15 minutes. Sprinkle crumbs over top of bar and bake an additional 15 minutes. Cool in pan on rack. Chill before cutting into bars. Refrigerate until packaging or serving.

PER BAR 269 calories; 12 g fat (6 g sat.); 4 g protein; 37 g carbohydrate; 1 g fiber; 35 mg sodium; 77 mg cholesterol

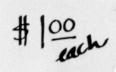

JUMBO KITCHEN SINK COOKIES, PAGE 99

WHITE CHOCOLATE CEREAL CLUSTERS

MAKES 48 clusters **PREP** 15 minutes **COOK** 3 minutes **LET STAND** 25 minutes

2½ cups Cinnamon Chex cereal
2½ cups Golden Grahams cereal
1   cup mini marshmallows
1   cup golden raisins
3   cups white chocolate morsels

① Line 3 large baking sheets with waxed paper. Pour cereals into a colander; sift out small pieces.

② In a large bowl, combine cereals, marshmallows and raisins.

③ Heat a medium saucepan of water to simmering. Place white chocolate morsels in a glass or metal bowl and place over simmering water. Heat, stirring, until melted, about 3 minutes. Cool slightly.

④ Pour white chocolate over mixture in bowl; stir until all dry pieces are coated. Working quickly, drop by heaping spoonfuls onto prepared sheets. Let stand at room temperature until dry to the touch, about 25 minutes.

PER CLUSTER 88 calories; 4 g fat (2 g sat.); 1 g protein; 13 g carbohydrate; 0 g fiber; 42 mg sodium; 1 mg cholesterol

CHOCOLATE-CHERRY FUDGE BROWNIES

MAKES 24 brownies **PREP** 10 minutes
SOAK 5 minutes **MICROWAVE** 2 minutes
BAKE at 350° for 25 minutes

- 1 cup dried tart cherries, coarsely chopped
- 1 cup (2 sticks) unsalted butter
- 4 squares (1 ounce each) unsweetened baking chocolate, coarsely chopped
- 2 cups sugar
- 4 large eggs
- 1½ cups all-purpose flour
- 2 teaspoons vanilla extract
- ¼ teaspoon salt
- 1 cup semisweet mini chocolate chips

① Heat oven to 350°. Line a 15 x 10 x 1-inch jelly-roll pan with nonstick foil.

② Combine cherries and 1 cup hot water in a bowl. Soak 5 minutes.

③ Meanwhile, combine butter and chopped chocolate in a large microwave-safe bowl. Microwave 1 minute; whisk to slightly blend. Microwave another minute; whisk until smooth.

④ Whisk in sugar. Whisk in eggs, one at a time. Whisk in flour, vanilla and salt. Drain softened cherries and stir into batter, along with ¾ cup of the mini chips. Spread into foil-lined pan. Sprinkle with remaining ¼ cup mini chips.

⑤ Bake brownie at 350° for 25 minutes. Cool completely in pan on wire rack. Use foil to lift brownie from pan; cut into 24 squares.

PER BROWNIE 261 calories; 14 g fat (8 g sat.); 3 g protein; 34 g carbohydrate; 3 g fiber; 40 mg sodium; 55 mg cholesterol

WHOOPIE PIES

MAKES 18 whoopie pies **PREP** 5 minutes **BAKE** at 350° for 12 minutes

CAKES
- 1 box (18.25 ounces) devil's food cake mix
- 3 large eggs
- ½ cup vegetable oil
- ½ teaspoon baking powder

FILLING
- 1 stick unsalted butter, softened
- 2 cups confectioners' sugar
- ½ teaspoon vanilla extract

① Heat oven to 350°. Coat 3 large cookie sheets with nonstick cooking spray.

② **Cakes.** In large bowl, combine cake mix, eggs, oil, 3 tablespoons water and baking powder. Beat on low speed for 30 seconds, then on medium for 2 minutes; batter will be thick. Drop by heaping tablespoonfuls onto prepared sheets, spacing about 2 inches apart, for a total of 36 mounds.

③ Bake at 350° for 12 minutes, rotating sheets halfway through. Let cookies stand on sheets for 2 minutes, then use a thin metal spatula to quickly transfer cakes to wire racks to cool. Repeat with remaining batter.

④ While cakes are cooling, prepare **Filling.** In a medium-size bowl, beat butter until smooth. Add confectioners' sugar, vanilla and 1½ tablespoons water. Beat on low speed until blended, then increase speed to medium-high and beat until smooth. Spread a heaping tablespoon Filling onto a cake. Sandwich with a second cake. Repeat.

PER WHOOPIE PIE 250 calories; 15 g fat (5 g sat.); 3 g protein; 27 g carbohydrate; 1 g fiber; 187 mg sodium; 64 mg cholesterol

Red velvet—an old-fashioned favorite—is very much in style again. These cupcakes topped with rich cream cheese frosting will fly off the bake-sale table.

RED VELVET CUPCAKES

MAKES 24 cupcakes **PREP** 20 minutes
BAKE at 350° for 23 minutes

CUPCAKES

- 2¾ cups all-purpose flour
- ¼ cup unsweetened cocoa powder
- 1½ teaspoons baking powder
- ½ teaspoon baking soda
- ¼ teaspoon salt
- ¾ cup (1½ sticks) unsalted butter, softened
- 1½ cups granulated sugar
- ¾ cup reduced-fat sour cream
- 2 large eggs
- 1 bottle (1 ounce) red food coloring
- ½ cup 2% milk

FROSTING

- 1 package (8 ounces) Neufchâtel (reduced-fat cream cheese), softened
- ¼ cup (½ stick) unsalted butter, softened
- 1 box (16 ounces) confectioners' sugar
- 1 teaspoon vanilla extract

① Heat oven to 350°. Line 2 standard-size muffin pans with 24 cupcake liners.

② **Cupcakes.** In bowl, mix flour, cocoa, baking powder, baking soda and salt. In second bowl, beat butter and sugar on medium-high until smooth. Beat in sour cream. Beat in eggs, one at a time. On low speed, beat in flour mixture and food coloring, alternating with milk. Spoon into cupcake liners, filling each about ⅔ full.

③ Bake at 350° for 23 minutes or until toothpick inserted in centers of cupcakes comes out clean. Remove from pan; cool completely on wire rack.

④ Prepare **Frosting.** Beat Neufchâtel and butter until smooth. On low, beat in confectioners' sugar, then vanilla. Spread or pipe onto cupcakes.

PER CUPCAKE 287 calories; 11 g fat (7 g sat.); 4 g protein; 44 g carbohydrate; 1 g fiber; 130 mg sodium; 49 mg cholesterol

JUMBO KITCHEN SINK COOKIES

MAKES about 24 cookies **PREP** 15 minutes **BAKE** at 350° for 25 minutes

- 1 cup (2 sticks) unsalted butter, softened
- 1 cup granulated sugar
- 1 cup packed light-brown sugar
- 2 large eggs
- 1 teaspoon vanilla extract
- 2 cups all-purpose flour
- 2 teaspoons baking powder
- 1 teaspoon cinnamon
- ½ teaspoon salt
- ¼ teaspoon nutmeg
- 1 package (12 ounces) semisweet chocolate morsels
- 2 cups shredded coconut
- 1½ cups old-fashioned oats
- 1½ cups mixed jumbo raisins

① Heat oven to 350°.

② In a large bowl, beat butter, granulated sugar and brown sugar on medium speed. Beat in eggs, one at a time. Beat in vanilla. On low speed, beat in flour, baking powder, cinnamon, salt and nutmeg.

③ Stir in chocolate morsels, coconut, oats and raisins. Drop batter by ¼-cupfuls onto ungreased cookie sheets, about 2 inches apart. Press to flatten. Bake at 350° for 25 minutes or until light brown around edges. Transfer to wire racks to cool completely.

PER COOKIE 302 calories; 13 g fat (8 g sat.); 4 g protein; 45 g carbohydrate; 2 g fiber; 103 mg sodium; 35 mg cholesterol

INDIAN-SPICED
CAULIFLOWER,
POTATO &
CHICKPEAS,
PAGE 106

MAY

103

115

121

This recipe comes from *Family Circle* reader Megan Henson of Springfield, Ohio, who says her family has been making this fast, easy dessert for years. "It's perfect for casual get-togethers as well as festive occasions," she says.

FOUR STACK PIE

MAKES 12 servings **PREP** 15 minutes **BAKE** at 350° for 18 minutes **CHILL** 1 hour

- 1 large box (5.9 ounces) instant chocolate pudding
- 3 cups milk
- 1½ cups flour
- ½ cup (1 stick) unsalted butter, softened
- ½ cup chopped pecans
- 3 tablespoons granulated sugar
- 1 package (8 ounces) cream cheese, softened
- 1 cup confectioners' sugar
- 1½ cups frozen whipped topping, thawed

① Heat oven to 350°. Whisk together chocolate pudding mix and milk for 2 minutes or until thickened. Cover with plastic wrap; refrigerate.

② Using your hands or a pastry blender, mix together flour, butter, pecans and granulated sugar until well combined and crumbly. Press into bottom and side of a 9-inch deep dish pie plate. Bake crust at 350° for 18 minutes, until very lightly browned. Remove to a wire rack and cool completely.

③ Beat together cream cheese and confectioners' sugar on medium-high speed until completely smooth. Spread cream cheese mixture evenly over cooled crust. Top with chocolate pudding, then spread whipped topping over pudding. Chill for at least 1 hour or until set.

PER SERVING 377 calories; 20 g fat (11 g sat.); 5 g protein; 44 g carbohydrate; 1 g fiber; 293 mg sodium; 46 mg cholesterol

Eat Your Veggies

Not because your mom said so—but because they're hearty and satisfying.

TURKEY-VEGETABLE
FAJITAS, PAGE 109

GRILLED PORK
MEDALLIONS WITH
ROASTED CABBAGE SLAW,
PAGE 107

INDIAN-SPICED CAULIFLOWER, POTATOES & CHICKPEAS

MAKES 6 servings **PREP** 20 minutes **COOK** 28 minutes, 30 seconds

2 tablespoons vegetable oil
2 large onions, peeled and thinly sliced
4 teaspoons garam masala
2 cans (14.5 ounces each) no-salt-added diced tomatoes
¾ pound small red-skinned potatoes, cut into 1-inch pieces
1 medium cauliflower, about 2 pounds, core removed, cut into florets
½ cup golden raisins
¾ teaspoon salt
2 cans (15.5 ounces each) chickpeas, drained and rinsed
1 bag (6 ounces) baby spinach
⅔ cup brown basmati rice, cooked following package instructions
⅓ cup unsalted cashews, chopped
1 lemon, cut into wedges (optional)

① Heat oil in a large, lidded nonstick 8-quart pot over medium-high heat. Add onions and cook, stirring occasionally, for 6 minutes, until nicely browned.

② Stir in garam masala and cook for 30 seconds. Add tomatoes with their juice and potatoes; simmer, covered, on medium heat 7 minutes. Stir in cauliflower, raisins, salt and chickpeas; simmer, covered, 12 to 15 minutes, stirring occasionally, or until potatoes and cauliflower are tender.

③ Gradually stir in spinach until wilted. Serve over rice and top with nuts. Squeeze lemon over each serving, if desired.

PER SERVING 476 calories; 11 g fat (2 g sat.); 16 g protein; 81 g carbohydrate; 16 g fiber; 704 mg sodium; 0 mg cholesterol

GRILLED PORK MEDALLIONS WITH ROASTED CABBAGE SLAW

MAKES 4 servings **PREP** 15 minutes
BAKE at 450° for 35 minutes **GRILL** 4 minutes

1   small head green cabbage (about 2 pounds), core removed, cut into 8 wedges
1   large red onion, peeled and cut into 8 wedges
1   bag (1 pound) baby carrots
3   tablespoons olive oil
¾   teaspoon salt
¼   teaspoon black pepper
2   tablespoons apple cider vinegar
1¼ pounds thin-sliced boneless pork chops
    Juice of 1 lemon (optional)

① Heat oven to 450°. Coat 2 baking sheets with nonstick cooking spray.

② Place cabbage on 1 prepared baking sheet, and onion and carrots on the second baking sheet. Brush with olive oil and season with ½ teaspoon of the salt and ⅛ teaspoon of the pepper. Roast vegetables at 450° for 20 minutes; rotate pans and roast for an additional 15 minutes. Drizzle with vinegar during last minute of cooking.

③ Meanwhile, heat a grill pan over medium-high heat. Season the pork with the remaining ¼ teaspoon salt and ⅛ teaspoon pepper and grill for 2 minutes per side or until cooked through.

④ To serve, place the pork on individual plates and arrange vegetables over the top. Squeeze lemon over servings, if desired.

PER SERVING 413 calories; 17 g fat (4 g sat.); 34 g protein; 30 g carbohydrate; 9 g fiber; 605 mg sodium; 88 mg cholesterol

GRILLED SCALLOPS & SPRING VEGETABLES

MAKES 4 servings **PREP** 20 minutes **COOK** 7 minutes **GRILL** 4 minutes

1   can (14.5 ounces) reduced-sodium chicken broth
6   cloves garlic, coarsely chopped
1   pound sugar snap peas, strings removed
2   pounds asparagus, cut into 2-inch pieces, woody ends removed
1   large leek, rinsed and sliced
2   red sweet peppers, diced
1   teaspoon fresh thyme
2   teaspoons garlic-pepper seasoning, plus more for serving
½   teaspoon salt
1   pound sea scallops
2   tablespoons olive oil
¾   cup orzo, cooked

① In a large 8-quart pot, bring broth to a simmer; add garlic and simmer for 1 minute. Add snap peas, asparagus and leek. Cook on medium-high heat for 5 minutes, covered, stirring occasionally. Stir in red peppers, thyme, 1 teaspoon of the garlic-pepper and ¼ teaspoon of the salt. Cook, covered, 1 minute. Remove from heat.

② Heat a large nonstick grill pan over medium-high heat. Brush both sides of scallops with olive oil and season with 1 teaspoon garlic-pepper and ¼ teaspoon salt. Grill 2 minutes per side or until cooked through. Remove from heat.

③ Serve scallops with orzo and vegetables. Spoon some of the cooking liquid over the orzo, if desired. Sprinkle each serving with additional garlic-pepper, if desired.

PER SERVING 497 calories; 8 g fat (1 g sat.); 35 g protein; 61 g carbohydrate; 13 g fiber; 723 mg sodium; 168 mg cholesterol

CHICKEN VEGGIE NOODLE BOWL

CHICKEN VEGGIE NOODLE BOWL

MAKES 4 servings **PREP** 20 minutes
COOK 12 minutes

- 1 cup reduced-sodium chicken broth
- 2 tablespoons light soy sauce
- 2 tablespoons cornstarch
- 1 tablespoon hoisin sauce
- 1 tablespoon rice vinegar
- 1 teaspoon Sriracha (chili-garlic sauce)
- 2 tablespoons vegetable oil
- ¾ pound uncooked chicken tenders, each cut into 3 strips
- 1¼ pounds bok choy, trimmed, rinsed and cut into 1-inch slices
- 1 large onion, peeled and sliced
- 3 cloves garlic, peeled and sliced
- 1 pound snow peas, strings removed
- 3 sweet peppers, cored, seeds removed and cut into ½-inch strips
- 6 ounces soba noodles, cooked following package directions
- 2 teaspoons sesame oil
- ¼ cup sliced scallions

① In a medium bowl, whisk together broth, soy sauce, cornstarch, hoisin, vinegar and Sriracha sauce. Set aside.

② Heat a large nonstick skillet or wok over medium-high heat. Add 1 tablespoon oil and stir-fry chicken for 3 minutes or until no longer pink inside. Remove to a plate and reserve.

③ Add remaining tablespoon oil to skillet along with bok choy, onion and garlic; stir-fry 3 minutes. Add snow peas and peppers and stir-fry 4 minutes or until vegetables are crisp-tender. Cover part of the time.

④ Stir in reserved sauce and chicken. Bring to a simmer and cook until sauce starts to thicken, about 2 minutes. Turn off heat.

⑤ Transfer to a large serving bowl and stir in the cooked noodles and sesame oil. To serve, spoon into individual bowls and garnish with scallions.

PER SERVING 472 calories; 13 g fat (2 g sat.); 29 g protein; 58 g carbohydrate; 9 g fiber; 697 mg sodium; 47 mg cholesterol

TURKEY-VEGETABLE FAJITAS

MAKES 4 servings **PREP** 25 minutes **MARINATE** 2 hours **COOK** 15 minutes

MARINADE
- ¼ cup lime juice
- 1 teaspoon ancho chile powder
- 1 teaspoon ground cumin
- ¼ teaspoon salt
- ¼ cup orange juice

TURKEY AND VEGETABLES
- 1 pound turkey cutlets, cut into long, thin strips
- 2 tablespoons canola oil
- 1 large sweet onion, peeled and sliced
- 2 green bell peppers, cored, seeded and sliced
- 1 cup shredded carrots
- 4 cloves garlic, coarsely chopped
- 1 pound zucchini, cut into ¼-inch-thick matchsticks
- ½ pound sliced mushrooms
- ½ teaspoon salt
- ½ cup cilantro leaves
- ¼ cup shredded reduced-fat Mexican cheese blend
- 4 scallions, sliced
- 8 corn tortillas, gently warmed

  Easy Avocado & Tomato Salsa (optional)

① **Marinade.** Mix together lime juice, chile powder, cumin and salt. Set aside 2 tablespoons of the mixture; place remainder in a resealable plastic bag and add the orange juice.

② **Turkey and Vegetables.** Add turkey to marinade in bag. Marinate in refrigerator for 2 hours.

③ Heat 1 tablespoon oil in a large nonstick skillet over medium-high heat. Remove turkey from marinade and add to skillet. Discard marinade. Cook 4 minutes, turning halfway through cooking time. Remove to a plate and keep warm.

④ Add remaining tablespoon oil to skillet. Stir in onion, green peppers, carrots and garlic. Cook, uncovered, 5 minutes, stirring occasionally. Add zucchini and mushrooms and cook an additional 5 minutes, stirring. Stir in turkey, reserved 2 tablespoons marinade and the salt; cook 1 minute.

⑤ Serve turkey and vegetables with cilantro, cheese, scallions and tortillas. If desired, accompany with Easy Avocado & Tomato Salsa (recipe, below).

PER SERVING 406 calories; 12 g fat (2 g sat.); 37 g protein; 42 g carbohydrate; 8 g fiber; 665 mg sodium; 50 mg cholesterol

EASY AVOCADO & TOMATO SALSA

Mix together 4 chopped plum tomatoes, ¼ cup chopped red onion, 2 tablespoons chopped cilantro, 1 tablespoon each olive oil and lime juice and ¼ teaspoon salt. Dice the flesh of 1 ripe avocado and gently fold in. For a zestier salsa, add a finely chopped jalapeño.

Prime Beef

Only the leanest, healthiest meats make the cut for these delicious dinners.

SIRLOIN OVER
FETTUCCINE ALFREDO,
PAGE 115

BEEF & CHEDDAR SLIDERS,
PAGE 115

FRENCH DIP SANDWICH

FRENCH DIP SANDWICH

MAKES 6 servings **PREP** 10 minutes
COOK 11 minutes **ROAST** at 450° for 25 minutes
BROIL 2 minutes

2   tablespoons unsalted butter
1   medium-large onion, sliced
1   cup lager beer
1   can (14.5 ounces) fat-free, lower-sodium beef broth
1   teaspoon sugar
¼   teaspoon salt
¼   teaspoon black pepper
1   boneless lean top round steak (about 1¼ pounds)
½   teaspoon Montreal steak seasoning
6   split-top rolls

① Heat oven to 450°. In large nonstick skillet, melt butter over medium to medium-high heat. Add onion and cook, stirring, 5 minutes.

② Pour beer and 1 cup of the beef broth into skillet. Stir in sugar, salt and pepper and bring to a simmer. Cook 3 minutes. Pour mixture into an oven-proof baking dish.

③ Return skillet to medium-high heat. Sprinkle steak with Montreal seasoning. Add to skillet and brown on both sides, 3 minutes total. Add remaining beef broth to skillet, scraping up any brown bits from pan. Transfer steak to baking dish; pour skillet contents over steak.

④ Cover dish with foil and roast at 450° for 25 minutes. Remove from oven and increase heat to broil. Open rolls slightly and toast under broiler for 1 to 2 minutes.

⑤ Thinly slice steak against the grain and return to baking dish. Divide meat and onions among rolls, spooning sauce over each. Serve sandwiches with additional sauce for dipping alongside.

PER SERVING 387 calories; 12 g fat (5 g sat.); 36 g protein; 30 g carbohydrate; 2 g fiber; 594 mg sodium; 72 mg cholesterol

STEAK & CAESAR SALAD

MAKES 6 servings **PREP** 15 minutes **GRILL** 12 minutes

⅓   cup light mayonnaise
¼   cup fresh lemon juice
¼   cup grated Parmesan
2   cloves garlic, peeled
1   tablespoon anchovy paste
½   teaspoon salt
½   teaspoon black pepper
2   tablespoons olive oil
4   beef tenderloin or eye round steaks (about 1¼ pounds total)
1   package (18 ounces) romaine hearts, cleaned and leaves separated

① In blender or mini chopper, combine mayonnaise, lemon juice, Parmesan, garlic, anchovy paste and ¼ teaspoon each of the salt and pepper. Cover blender and run until mixture is smooth and garlic is pureed. With blender running, add olive oil in a thin stream. Set aside.

② Season beef with remaining ¼ teaspoon each salt and pepper. Heat cast-iron skillet or grill pan over medium-high heat.

③ Toss romaine leaves with dressing in large bowl (do in batches, if necessary). Grill or pan-roast beef for 4 to 6 minutes per side, depending on thickness, until meat registers 135° on instant-read thermometer for medium-rare. Grill another minute per side for medium. Remove to cutting board and cover with foil.

④ Divide lettuce among plates. Slice steak and place alongside salad.

PER SERVING 276 calories; 18 g fat (5 g sat.); 23 g protein; 5 g carbohydrate; 1 g fiber; 435 mg sodium; 47 mg cholesterol

STEAK ARRACHERA

STEAK ARRACHERA

MAKES 6 servings **PREP** 10 minutes
MARINATE 48 hours **GRILL** peppers for
10 minutes, steak for 31 minutes

MARINADE

- ¾   cup inexpensive red wine
- 1   medium onion, sliced
- ¼   cup Worcestershire sauce
- 1   teaspoon ground coriander

STEAK AND PEPPERS

- 1   flat beef brisket (about 2 pounds)
- 2   green bell peppers, seeded and cut into pieces
- 1   sweet red pepper, seeded and cut into pieces
- 1   yellow pepper, seeded and cut into pieces
- 1   orange pepper, seeded and cut into pieces
- 2   teaspoons olive oil
     Sprinkle of salt and pepper

① **Marinade.** In a resealable plastic bag, combine wine, onion, Worcestershire and coriander. **Steak and Peppers.** Add brisket and seal bag. Marinate, refrigerated, for 48 hours (or as long as possible).

② Heat grill to medium to medium-high heat. While grill is heating, remove brisket from marinade. Strain marinade into a large bowl; add pepper pieces.

③ Grill peppers 5 minutes, then turn over and grill an additional 5 minutes. Transfer to a platter, drizzle with olive oil and sprinkle with some salt and pepper. Cover to keep warm.

④ Place brisket fat-side down on grill. Cook 13 minutes; reduce heat to medium if getting too browned. Turn meat over and continue to cook 16 to 18 minutes more or until meat registers 145° on an instant-read thermometer. Add meat to platter with peppers; cover with foil. Let rest 5 minutes and slice.

PER SERVING 250 calories; 8 g fat (3 g sat.); 34 g protein; 9 g carbohydrate; 2 g fiber; 132 mg sodium; 65 mg cholesterol

SIRLOIN OVER FETTUCCINE ALFREDO

MAKES 6 servings **PREP** 10 minutes
COOK pasta for 12 minutes, sauce for 8 minutes, steak for 6 minutes

- 1   box (12 ounces) roasted garlic or florentine fettuccine
- 1   cup frozen peas, thawed
- 2   tablespoons unsalted butter
- 2   tablespoons all-purpose flour
- 2   cups fat-free half-and-half
- ¾   teaspoon salt
- ¼   teaspoon ground nutmeg
- 1   pound grass-fed sirloin steak (about ¾ inch thick)
- ¼   teaspoon black pepper
- 1   tablespoon olive oil
- ½   cup shredded Parmesan cheese

① Bring a large pot of lightly salted water to boil over high heat. Cook pasta following package directions, 11 to 12 minutes. Add peas during last 1 minute of cook time. Drain and return to pasta pot.

② Meanwhile, prepare sauce. Melt butter in medium-size saucepan over medium heat. Whisk in flour, then slowly whisk in half-and-half. Season with ½ teaspoon of the salt and ⅛ teaspoon of the nutmeg. Bring just to boiling, stirring frequently, 8 minutes.

③ While the sauce cooks, season sirloin with remaining ¼ teaspoon salt, ⅛ teaspoon nutmeg and ¼ teaspoon pepper. Heat oil in a large nonstick skillet over medium-high heat. Add steak and cook 3 minutes.

④ Remove sauce from heat; whisk in Parmesan. Turn steak and cook another 3 minutes or until desired doneness. Pour sauce over pasta; toss to combine. Transfer to a platter. Slice steak; fan over fettuccine.

PER SERVING 447 calories; 12 g fat (5 g sat.); 29 g protein; 53 g carbohydrate; 4 g fiber; 440 mg sodium; 43 mg cholesterol

BEEF & CHEDDAR SLIDERS

MAKES 12 mini burgers **PREP** 10 minutes
GRILL over medium-high heat for 9 minutes

- 1½ pounds organic ground beef (90% lean)
- 1   tablespoon dried minced onion
- 1   tablespoon spicy brown mustard
- ¾   teaspoon garlic salt
- ½   teaspoon Italian seasoning
- ¼   teaspoon black pepper
- 12 very thin slices 2% cheddar cheese (about 3 ounces total)
- 12 small round dinner or potato rolls
- 1   large plum tomato sliced into 12 thin slices

① Heat gas grill to medium-high or prepare charcoal grill with medium-hot coals. In a large bowl, mix together the ground beef, dried onion, mustard, garlic salt, Italian seasoning and black pepper. Mix until well combined.

② Shape seasoned beef into 12 small patties, about ¼ cup mixture for each, forming patties that are 2½ inches across and ½ inch thick.

③ Transfer hamburger patties to the grill and cook 4 minutes. Flip and cook 4 additional minutes. Top burgers with cheese. Slice should be roughly the size of the burger; if not, cut or fold it to fit. Grill until slightly melted, 1 minute.

④ Slice buns in half horizontally and transfer burgers to buns. Place a plum tomato slice on each. Serve warm.

PER SLIDER 205 calories; 8 g fat (3 g sat.); 17 g protein; 16 g carbohydrate; 1 g fiber; 322 mg sodium; 40 mg cholesterol

Slow Cooker Suppers

Easy-on-the-cook chicken dinners for busy days.

STUFFED PEPPERS

The traditional filling of ground beef and rice is swapped for lean ground chicken and savory herb dressing in these slow-cooked stuffed peppers.

STUFFED PEPPERS

MAKES 5 peppers **PREP** 15 minutes
MICROWAVE 2½ minutes **SLOW COOK** for 6 hours on LOW

1½	tablespoons unsalted butter
1½	cups herb stuffing mix
2	ribs celery, diced
2	plum tomatoes, cored, seeded and diced (about 1 cup)
1	package (1 pound) ground chicken
¾	teaspoon salt
5	red or green bell peppers, tops removed and reserved, cored

① Combine butter and ¾ cup water in medium-size microwavable bowl. Microwave for 1 minute. Add stuffing mix and cover bowl, venting one side. Microwave an additional 1½ minutes. Stir with fork.

② In large bowl, combine celery, tomatoes and ground chicken. Stir until blended. Add stuffing and salt. Stir to combine.

③ Divide stuffing evenly among peppers. Replace pepper tops, fit into slow cooker (see Note) and add 1 cup hot water. Cover and slow cook for 6 hours on LOW. Remove with tongs and serve.

Note. An oval slow cooker works best for these; if you have a round cooker, you may only be able to fit 4 peppers. Divide extra filling among the peppers, mounding slightly.

PER PEPPER 292 calories; 15 g fat (6 g sat.); 19 g protein; 23 g carbohydrate; 4 g fiber; 695 mg sodium; 118 mg cholesterol

SPINACH, CHICKEN & FETA QUICHE

MAKES 8 servings **PREP** 10 minutes **SLOW COOK** for 6 hours on LOW

1	package (1 pound) ground chicken
1	package (10 ounces) frozen chopped spinach, thawed and squeezed dry
6	ounces feta cheese, crumbled (about 1¼ cups)
⅓	cup fresh dill, chopped
2	tablespoons onion flakes
6	large eggs
1	can (12 ounces) evaporated milk
½	teaspoon salt
¼	teaspoon pepper
1	cup Heart-Healthy Bisquick

① Coat a 5- or 6-quart slow cooker bowl with nonstick cooking spray.

② In a large bowl, combine chicken, spinach, feta, dill and onion flakes. Stir until evenly blended.

③ In medium-size bowl, whisk eggs, milk, salt and pepper. Stir into chicken mixture. Fold in Bisquick. Pour into prepared slow cooker. Cook for 6 hours on LOW. Remove slow cooker insert to wire rack, cut quiche into wedges and serve.

PER SERVING 394 calories; 21 g fat (8 g sat.); 31 g protein; 22 g carbohydrate; 2 g fiber; 950 mg sodium; 326 mg cholesterol

**CHICKEN PAPRIKASH,
PAGE 121**

WHITE CHICKEN CHILI,
PAGE 121

CHICKEN & RICE SOUP

On cool spring evenings, a veggie-packed chicken soup or slow-cooked chicken stew still hits the spot.

CHICKEN & RICE SOUP

MAKES 8 servings **PREP** 15 minutes
SLOW COOK for 6 hours on HIGH or 8 hours on LOW

1   cup wild rice and grain blend or all wild rice
1   medium onion, chopped
4   carrots, peeled and chopped
3   ribs celery, trimmed and chopped
1   package cremini mushrooms, cleaned and quartered (large ones cut in sixths)
1   whole chicken (3 or 4 pounds), cut up, wings reserved for another use
2   cans (14.5 ounces each) low-sodium chicken broth
2   teaspoons dried poultry seasoning
1   teaspoon salt
¼   teaspoon pepper

① Sprinkle rice into bottom of slow cooker. Add onion, carrots, celery and mushrooms. Remove skin from chicken pieces and trim rib bones from the breastbone. Place chicken pieces over vegetables; add broth and 4 cups water. Add poultry seasoning, ¼ teaspoon of the salt and the pepper.

② Cover and slow cook for 6 hours on HIGH or 8 hours on LOW. Carefully remove chicken to a cutting board; discard bones. Shred or chop chicken; return to slow cooker and add remaining ¾ teaspoon salt. Serve warm.

PER SERVING 230 calories; 4 g fat (1 g sat.); 25 g protein; 25 g carbohydrate; 3 g fiber; 384 mg sodium; 68 mg cholesterol

CHICKEN PAPRIKASH

MAKES 6 servings **PREP** 15 minutes
SLOW COOK for 4 hours on HIGH or 6½ hours on LOW

1½ pounds boneless, skinless chicken thighs, cut into 1-inch pieces
2   tablespoons all-purpose flour
½   pound fresh green beans, trimmed and cut into 2-inch pieces
1   cup frozen pearl onions, thawed
2   cans (8 ounces each) tomato sauce
3   tablespoons paprika
¼   teaspoon salt
¼   teaspoon pepper
¾   cup reduced-fat sour cream
    Cooked egg noodles, for serving

① Coat slow cooker bowl with nonstick cooking spray. In medium-size bowl, toss the chicken thighs with flour. Combine in slow cooker with green beans, onions, tomato sauce and 1 cup water. Stir to blend, then add 1 tablespoon of the paprika, the salt and pepper.

② Cover slow cooker and cook for 4 hours on HIGH or 6½ hours on LOW.

③ In a small bowl, whisk sour cream with remaining 2 tablespoons paprika. Scoop ½ cup sauce from slow cooker and gradually whisk into sour cream. Slowly stir sour cream mixture into slow cooker. Serve paprikash over noodles.

PER SERVING 366 calories; 16 g fat (6 g sat.); 39 g protein; 21 g carbohydrate; 6 g fiber; 896 mg sodium; 189 mg cholesterol

WHITE CHICKEN CHILI

MAKES 8 servings **PREP** 15 minutes
SLOW COOK for 6 hours on HIGH or 8 hours on LOW

2   pounds boneless, skinless chicken thighs
1   large green pepper, seeded and chopped
1   small onion, chopped
1   can (14.5 ounces) low-sodium chicken broth
1½ cups tomatillo salsa (salsa verde)
2   cans (15.5 ounces each) Great Northern beans
½   teaspoon ground cumin
¼   teaspoon black pepper
1   package (10 ounces) frozen corn kernels, thawed
¼   cup fresh cilantro, coarsely chopped
    Tortilla chips (optional)

① Place chicken thighs in slow cooker and top with green pepper and onion. In blender, combine chicken broth, salsa and 1 can of the beans (drained and rinsed). Puree until smooth. Add to slow cooker, along with cumin and black pepper.

② Cover and slow cook for 6 hours on HIGH or 8 hours on LOW. Uncover, and remove chicken thighs to cutting board. Stir corn, remaining can of beans (drained and rinsed) and cilantro into slow cooker. Shred chicken and return to slow cooker. Serve with tortilla chips, if desired.

PER SERVING 330 calories; 7 g fat (2 g sat.); 33 g protein; 36 g carbohydrate; 9 g fiber; 460 mg sodium; 110 mg cholesterol

STICKY TOFFEE
PUDDING,
PAGE 143

JUNE

132

135

145

Suppers with Sizzle

These 10 delicious, grill-ready recipes make it easy to get fired up any day of the week.

MIXED GRILL
KABOBS,
PAGE 135

**PULL-APART RIBS,
PAGE 137**

Skirt steak—so called because it comes from the lower midsection of the animal—is the traditional cut for fajitas. This Greek-style recipe is inspired by that Mexican dish but subs in Mediterranean ingredients.

SKIRT STEAK PITAS

MAKES 4 servings **PREP** 15 minutes **MARINATE** at least 1 hour **GRILL** 10 minutes

3   tablespoons olive oil
3   tablespoons red wine vinegar
1   tablespoon Dijon mustard
2   teaspoons dried Greek seasoning
1   teaspoon brown sugar
1   pound skirt steak
1   container (7 ounces) 2% Greek yogurt
2   ounces reduced-fat feta cheese, crumbled
4   Roma tomatoes, about 1 pound total, cut in half from top to bottom
1   large red onion, peeled and cut into ½-inch slices
4   whole-wheat pitas
1   cup shredded lettuce

① In a small bowl, blend olive oil, vinegar, mustard, 1 teaspoon of the Greek seasoning and brown sugar. Reserve 3 tablespoons of the mixture. Place the remainder in a large resealable plastic bag. Add the steak and marinate in the refrigerator for 1 to 4 hours.

② In a second small bowl, mix together the yogurt and feta; cover and refrigerate until ready to use.

③ Heat gas grill to medium-high or coals in charcoal grill to medium hot. Lightly coat grill rack with oil or cooking spray.

④ Brush tomatoes and onion with some of the reserved oil and wine mixture. Place tomatoes on grill, cut side down, along with onion slices. Grill for 3 minutes; turn, brush with remaining oil mixture and grill tomatoes for additional 2 minutes and onions for 3 minutes, until tender. Remove to a plate and keep warm.

⑤ Remove steak from resealable bag and grill about 2 minutes per side or until internal temperature reaches 130° on an instant-read thermometer for medium-rare. Remove from grill and allow to stand 2 minutes before thinly slicing.

⑥ Serve pita slightly warmed and layer with lettuce, yogurt mixture and sliced steak. Accompany with grilled tomatoes and onion.

PER SERVING 555 calories; 25 g fat (8 g sat.); 37 g protein; 48 g carbohydrate; 7 g fiber; 876 mg sodium; 62 mg cholesterol

**SEA BASS
WITH CREAMY
HERB SAUCE**

SEA BASS WITH CREAMY HERB SAUCE

MAKES 4 servings **PREP** 15 minutes
GRILL 10 minutes

SAUCE

½   cup reduced-fat sour cream
¼   cup reduced-fat mayonnaise
2   scallions, trimmed and chopped
1   tablespoon red wine vinegar
1   teaspoon Mrs. Dash Garlic & Herb salt-free seasoning blend
⅛   teaspoon salt
⅛   teaspoon black pepper

VEGETABLES & FISH

1   pound asparagus, trimmed
2   large red sweet peppers, cored, seeds removed and cut into ½-inch strips
2   large summer squash, ends trimmed and cut into ¼-inch planks
1½   pounds sea bass
2   tablespoons olive oil
2   tablespoons Mrs. Dash Garlic & Herb salt-free seasoning blend
⅛   teaspoon salt

① Sauce. In a medium-size bowl, stir together sour cream, mayonnaise, scallions, vinegar, seasoning blend, salt and black pepper. Cover and refrigerate until ready to serve.

② Vegetables & Fish. Heat gas grill to medium-high or coals in charcoal grill to medium hot. Lightly coat grill rack with oil or cooking spray.

③ Brush asparagus, peppers, squash and fish with oil. Sprinkle all sides with the seasoning blend. Grill vegetables about 8 to 10 minutes, turning as needed so vegetables do not burn. Grill fish flesh-side down 5 minutes. Turn and grill additional 3 minutes or until cooked through.

④ Sprinkle fish and vegetables with ⅛ teaspoon salt and serve with sauce.

PER SERVING 375 calories; 17 g fat (4 g sat.); 38 g protein; 36 g carbohydrate; 5 g fiber; 419 mg sodium; 89 mg cholesterol

PORK CHOPS & COLA SAUCE

MAKES 4 servings **PREP** 10 minutes **COOK** 20 minutes **GRILL** 12 minutes

1   can (12 ounces) cola (not diet)
1   cup ketchup
¼   cup cider vinegar
½   teaspoon onion powder
½   teaspoon garlic powder
½   teaspoon black pepper
4   bone-in pork chops (about 6 ounces each)
1   pound sweet potatoes, scrubbed and cut into ½-inch-thick slices

① Place cola, ketchup, vinegar, onion powder, garlic powder and black pepper in a medium-size saucepan. Simmer until sauce is reduced to 1 cup, about 20 minutes. Take off heat and reserve.

② Heat gas grill to medium-high or coals in charcoal grill to medium-hot. Lightly coat grill rack with oil or cooking spray.

③ Grill pork chops and sweet potatoes 4 minutes per side; generously brush both sides with ¾ cup of cola sauce and grill additional 2 minutes per side.

④ Serve pork chops and sweet potatoes with remaining sauce, if desired.

PER SERVING 424 calories; 8 g fat (3 g sat.); 38 g protein; 50 g carbohydrate; 3 g fiber; 672 mg sodium; 106 mg cholesterol

SPICE-RUBBED PORK TENDERLOIN

MAKES 4 servings **PREP** 15 minutes **MARINATE** at least 2 hours or overnight
GRILL 15 minutes **COOK** 3 minutes

1   teaspoon garlic powder
1   teaspoon onion powder
¾   teaspoon salt
½   teaspoon black pepper
½   teaspoon ground cinnamon
½   teaspoon ground cumin
1¼ pounds pork tenderloin
1   can (14½ ounces) reduced-sodium chicken broth
1   small onion, peeled and chopped
½   cup pomegranate-infused dried cranberries
1   cup uncooked couscous
½   cup toasted pine nuts

① In a small bowl, mix together garlic powder, onion powder, ½ teaspoon of the salt, black pepper, cinnamon and cumin. Reserve 1 teaspoon of the spice blend. Rub the remainder over the pork tenderloin and place in a resealable plastic bag. Refrigerate for at least 2 hours or overnight.

② Heat gas grill to medium-high or coals in charcoal grill to medium hot. Lightly coat grill rack with oil or cooking spray. Grill 14 to 15 minutes, turning twice, or until internal temperature registers 150° on an instant-read thermometer. Remove from grill and let rest 5 minutes before slicing.

③ Place chicken broth and onion in a saucepan. Bring to a boil; simmer 3 minutes. Stir in reserved rub, remaining ¼ teaspoon salt, cranberries and couscous; cover and let stand 5 minutes. Fluff with fork, garnish with pine nuts and serve with pork.

PER SERVING 455 calories; 11 g fat (2 g sat.); 37 g protein; 50 g carbohydrate; 4 g fiber; 717 mg sodium; 92 mg cholesterol

APRICOT-GLAZED TURKEY BREAST

MAKES 6 servings **PREP** 15 minutes
GRILL 50 minutes

POTATOES
6   Idaho baking potatoes (6 ounces each), scrubbed
1   cup chopped onion
6   tablespoons unsalted butter
½   teaspoon salt
⅛   teaspoon black pepper

TURKEY
⅓   cup apricot preserves
1   tablespoon Dijon mustard
1   tablespoon low-sodium soy sauce
½   teaspoon ground ginger
1   boneless, skinless turkey breast half (about 2½ pounds)
1   tablespoon olive oil
½   teaspoon salt
½   teaspoon black pepper

① Heat half of a gas grill to medium-high or coals in charcoal grill to medium-hot with coals stacked to one side for indirect grilling. Lightly coat grill rack with cooking oil or cooking spray.

② **Potatoes.** Cut potatoes in half lengthwise, almost all the way through so they will open like a book. Place an equal amount of onion in each and a pat of butter. Season with salt and pepper. Press closed and wrap tightly in foil. Place on the grill over direct heat. Grill with lid closed for 35 to 45 minutes.

③ **Turkey.** In a medium-size bowl, stir together preserves, mustard, soy sauce and ginger. Reserve ¼ cup for serving.

④ Brush turkey breast with olive oil and season with salt and pepper. Cover and grill over indirect heat for 30 minutes. Turn after 15 minutes. Brush with remaining apricot-mustard mixture and grill additional 15 to 20 minutes or until internal temperature registers 160° on an instant-read thermometer.

⑤ Serve turkey and potatoes with reserved glaze on the side.

PER SERVING 472 calories; 13 g fat (8 g sat.); 48 g protein; 41 g carbohydrate; 3 g fiber; 629 mg sodium; 154 mg cholesterol

**APRICOT-GLAZED
TURKEY BREAST**

This light and crisp grilled pizza is essentially pizza Margherita—just tomatoes, basil and mozzarella—embellished with delicious marinated grilled chicken. Serve it with a chilled white wine.

GRILLED CHICKEN PIZZA

MAKES 6 servings   **PREP** 15 minutes   **GRILL** chicken for 15 minutes, pizza for 6 minutes

CHICKEN

1   cup fresh basil leaves, torn
2   tablespoons olive oil
2   tablespoons vinegar
¼   teaspoon salt
¼   teaspoon pepper
1   pound boneless, skinless chicken breast halves

CRUST AND TOPPINGS

1   pound frozen pizza dough, thawed in the refrigerator
2   tablespoons olive oil
½   cup jarred pizza sauce
2   cups shredded mozzarella cheese
2   tablespoons grated Parmesan or Romano cheese
3   tablespoons shredded fresh basil leaves

① Prepare **Chicken.** Combine basil leaves, olive oil, vinegar, salt and pepper in a blender or mini chopper. While blender is running, add ⅓ cup water. Continue blending until fairly smooth. Place chicken in a glass dish and add contents of blender. Let stand while heating grill.

② **Crust and Toppings.** Divide thawed dough in half. Roll each half on a lightly floured surface to a 9-inch circle. Let rest.

③ Heat gas grill to medium-high or coals in charcoal grill to medium hot. Grill chicken for 15 minutes or until cooked through, turning once. Remove to a cutting board and slice into bite-size pieces.

④ Brush pizza doughs with some of the olive oil. Transfer doughs, oil-side down, onto grill. Brush dough tops with olive oil. Cover and grill 3 minutes. Using tongs and a spatula, flip over doughs. Working quickly, spread ¼ cup pizza sauce on each pie. Top with mozzarella. Cover and grill 2 minutes. Uncover and divide grilled chicken between pies. Grill 1 minute. Remove pizzas to cutting board and top with grated cheese and fresh basil and serve.

PER SERVING 401 calories; 16 g fat (6 g sat.); 32 g protein; 35 g carbohydrate; 1 g fiber; 680 mg sodium; 75 mg cholesterol

SALMON BURGERS

Juicy salmon patties are perfect for a speedy supper when prepped the night before.

SALMON BURGERS

MAKES 4 burgers **PREP** 15 minutes
GRILL 10 minutes

1¼ pounds salmon fillet
2 scallions, trimmed and roughly chopped
2 tablespoons chopped fresh dill
1 teaspoon lemon zest
⅓ cup panko bread crumbs
¼ teaspoon salt
¼ teaspoon pepper
¼ cup tartar sauce
1½ cups shredded lettuce
4 whole-wheat hamburger buns

① Remove skin from salmon fillet: With a sharp knife, cut a small corner of the skin away from the flesh. Then, gently pull and slice off remaining skin, trying to keep as much flesh intact to make the burgers. Discard skin; coarsely chop salmon.

② Heat gas grill to medium-high or coals in charcoal grill to medium hot. Transfer salmon to a food processor, along with scallions, 1 tablespoon of the dill, the lemon zest, panko, salt and pepper. Pulse until salmon is the consistency of ground beef but still has some shape. Do not overprocess.

③ Form mixture into 4 patties, each about 3½ inches in diameter. Coat patties with nonstick cooking spray. Grill patties 5 minutes. Flip over and continue to grill another 5 minutes. Meanwhile, stir remaining tablespoon of the dill into tartar sauce. Divide lettuce evenly among buns. Top each with a burger patty and 1 tablespoon tartar sauce.

PER BURGER 485 calories; 18 g fat (3 g sat.); 39 g protein; 42 g carbohydrate; 6 g fiber; 720 mg sodium; 95 mg cholesterol

MIXED GRILL KABOBS

MAKES 12 kabobs (6 servings) **PREP** 15 minutes **MARINATE** 30 minutes
MICROWAVE 2 minutes **GRILL** 8 minutes

BEEF KABOBS

1 pound sirloin, cut into 1½-inch pieces
⅓ cup light Vidalia onion salad dressing
1 green pepper, cored and cut into pieces
½ yellow pepper, cored and cut into pieces
1 red onion, peeled and cut into 1-inch half wedges
18 cherry tomatoes, rinsed

CHICKEN KABOBS

1 pound boneless, skinless chicken breasts, cut into 1½-inch pieces
⅓ cup light Vidalia onion salad dressing
1 medium zucchini, trimmed, halved lengthwise and cut into ½-inch rounds or pieces
1 each sweet orange and red pepper, cored and cut into pieces
½ yellow pepper, cored and cut into 1-inch pieces

① Soak twelve 12-inch bamboo skewers in warm water. **Beef Kabobs.** Combine steak and dressing in a resealable plastic bag. Refrigerate to marinate 30 minutes. Place peppers and onion in one side of a microwave-safe dish. Set aside.

② **Chicken Kabobs.** Combine chicken and dressing in a resealable plastic bag. Refrigerate to marinate 30 minutes. Add zucchini and peppers to dish with peppers and onion. Cover with plastic, venting one corner. Microwave 2 minutes to soften vegetables.

③ Heat gas grill to medium-high or coals in charcoal grill to medium hot. Begin threading kabobs. **Beef Kabobs.** Thread 1 beef cube, 1 piece onion, 1 tomato and 1 pepper piece onto a skewer. Continue threading until you have filled a total of 6 skewers. **Chicken Kabobs.** Thread chicken, pepper piece, zucchini and a different color pepper piece onto a skewer. Continue threading to fill 6 skewers.

④ Grill chicken kabobs 4 minutes per side, until cooked through, beef kabobs for 3 minutes per side until cooked through. Serve both kabobs with dipping sauce.

PER SERVING 327 calories; 11 g fat (2 g sat.); 39 g protein; 18 g carbohydrate; 3 g fiber; 188 mg sodium; 83 mg cholesterol

LONDON BROIL WITH RICE SALAD

LONDON BROIL WITH RICE SALAD

MAKES 6 servings   **PREP** 15 minutes
MICROWAVE 5 minutes   **GRILL** 12 minutes

STEAK & DRESSING

- ¼ cup raspberry vinegar
- 2 teaspoons honey mustard
- ½ teaspoon chili powder
- ¼ teaspoon salt
- ¼ teaspoon pepper
- ¼ teaspoon sugar
- ¼ cup olive oil
- 1 London broil steak (about 1¼ pounds)

RICE SALAD

- 1 bag (10 ounces) steam-in-bag rice and mixed veggies (such as Birds Eye Steamfresh)
- 1 sweet red pepper, cored and diced
- 3 scallions, trimmed and sliced
- ½ cup sliced seasoned almonds
- ½ cup goat cheese crumbles

① Heat gas grill to medium-high or coals in charcoal grill to medium hot. **Steak & Dressing.** In small bowl, whisk together the vinegar, honey mustard, chili powder, salt, pepper and sugar. While whisking, add olive oil in a thin stream. Place ¼ cup of the dressing in a glass dish with the steak. Marinate at room temperature while heating grill.

② **Rice Salad.** Microwave rice and veggies 3 to 5 minutes, as per package directions. Pour into bowl and add sweet red pepper and scallions. Whisk remaining dressing and stir into rice mixture. Gently stir in almonds and cheese.

③ Add steak to grill; cover and grill 7 minutes. Uncover and turn over steak. Grill an additional 5 minutes or to desired doneness. Let steak rest 5 minutes before slicing.

PER SERVING 357 calories; 21 g fat (5 g sat.); 25 g protein; 16 g carbohydrate; 2 g fiber; 208 mg sodium; 43 mg cholesterol

PULL-APART RIBS

MAKES 1 rack ribs (about 14)   **PREP** 15 minutes   **SLOW COOK** on LOW for 9 hours
COOK 5 minutes   **GRILL** 6 minutes

RUB AND RIBS

- 2 tablespoons dry mustard
- 2 tablespoons paprika
- 1 tablespoon dried oregano
- 1 teaspoon seasoned salt
- 1 tablespoon sugar
- 2 teaspoons black pepper
- 1 full rack pork spareribs (about 4 pounds)
- 1 bottle (12 ounces) beer or 1½ cups beef broth

SAUCE

- ⅓ cup packed light-brown sugar
- ⅓ cup cider vinegar
- 3 tablespoons ketchup

① **Rub.** In small bowl, stir together dry mustard, paprika, oregano, seasoned salt, sugar and pepper.

② **Ribs.** Remove ribs from packaging; rinse in cool water. Pat dry with paper towels. Cut rack in thirds.

③ Season ribs with ¼ cup of the dry rub, pressing on with your hands. Pour beer or broth and 1½ cups water into slow cooker. Stack ribs in cooker and cover. Slow cook on LOW for 9 hours.

④ Heat gas grill to medium-high or coals in charcoal grill to medium hot. **Sauce.** Place remaining rub, brown sugar, vinegar and ketchup in a small saucepan. Bring to a boil over high heat. Reduce heat to medium and simmer 5 minutes, stirring frequently.

⑤ Carefully remove ribs from slow cooker. Baste with sauce. Grill ribs 6 minutes, turning after 3 minutes.

PER RIB 278 calories; 19 g fat (7 g sat.); 18 g protein; 8 g carbohydrate; 1 g fiber; 203 mg sodium; 73 mg cholesterol

Old School Sweets

Tuck into these retro-style desserts that taste delightfully modern.

STICKY TOFFEE PUDDING, PAGE 143

BLACK & WHITE
COOKIES,
PAGE 143

CARAMEL APPLE CAKE

CARAMEL APPLE CAKE

MAKES 16 servings **PREP** 15 minutes
BAKE at 350° for 45 minutes

3   Granny Smith apples (8 ounces each), peeled, cored and cut into ¼-inch-thick slices
3   tablespoons lemon juice
¼   cup raisins
½   teaspoon cinnamon
⅛   teaspoon nutmeg
1   cup all-purpose flour
1   teaspoon baking powder
¼   teaspoon baking soda
¼   teaspoon salt
1   egg
⅔   cup dark-brown sugar
½   cup milk
¼   cup (½ stick) unsalted butter, melted, plus 2 tablespoons cold unsalted butter
1   teaspoon vanilla extract
⅔   cup caramel sauce
     Whipped cream (optional)

① Heat oven to 350°. Coat an 8 x 8 x 2-inch baking dish with nonstick cooking spray.

② Place apples in bottom of baking dish; drizzle with lemon juice. Top with raisins, cinnamon and nutmeg.

③ In large bowl, whisk flour, baking powder, baking soda and salt. In a small bowl, blend egg, sugar, ¼ cup of the milk, the melted butter and vanilla.

④ Make a well in the center of the flour mixture and stir in egg mixture. Pour batter over apples in baking dish.

⑤ In a small saucepan, combine remaining ¼ cup milk, 2 tablespoons butter and caramel sauce; bring to a boil, then remove from heat and pour over batter in baking dish.

⑥ Bake at 350° for 40 to 45 minutes or until toothpick tests clean. Spoon out servings and serve with whipped cream, if desired.

PER SERVING 325 calories; 9 g fat (6 g sat.); 3 g protein; 60 g carbohydrate; 2 g fiber; 275 mg sodium; 49 mg cholesterol

COCONUT CUSTARD PIE

MAKES 8 servings **PREP** 15 minutes **BAKE** at 400° for 18 minutes **COOK** 12 minutes
CHILL at least 4 hours

1   unbaked piecrust (from a 14.1-ounce package)
½   cup sugar
⅓   cup cornstarch
¼   teaspoon salt
1   cup milk
1   can (14.5 ounces) coconut milk
4   egg yolks
½   teaspoon coconut extract
⅔   cup toasted shredded coconut

① Heat oven to 400°. Fit pastry into a 9-inch pie plate. Prick with fork several times then bake crust at 400° for 18 minutes or until lightly browned; place on wire rack to cool completely.

② Whisk together sugar, cornstarch and salt in a medium-size saucepan.

③ Gradually whisk in milk and coconut milk. Whisk in egg yolks and coconut extract. Place over medium heat and cook for about 9 minutes, stirring occasionally, or until bubbles form. Reduce heat to low and cook 3 more minutes or until thickened.

④ Pour custard into cooled crust and smooth top. Cover and place in refrigerator for at least 4 hours or overnight. Sprinkle with toasted coconut and serve.

PER SERVING 273 calories; 13 g fat (7 g sat.); 4 g protein; 36 g carbohydrate; 0 g fiber; 209 mg sodium; 110 mg cholesterol

Slow Cooker Suppers

Make the living easy with summer favorites cooked conveniently in the slow cooker.

RATATOUILLE

Ratatouille—a Provençal vegetable dish that makes the best of the summer garden bounty—is delicious as a side to grilled meats.

RATATOUILLE

MAKES 6 servings **PREP** 15 minutes
LET STAND 20 minutes **SLOW COOK** for
3 hours on HIGH or 5 hours on LOW

- 1 small eggplant (about 1 pound), peeled and cut into ½-inch cubes
- ⅛ teaspoon plus ¼ teaspoon salt
- 1 medium-size red onion, chopped
- 2 medium-size sweet bell peppers, seeded and cut into ¾-inch pieces
- 1 package (10 ounces) mushrooms, cleaned and quartered
- 1 can (14.5 ounces) diced tomatoes
- 1 can (8 ounces) tomato sauce
- ¾ teaspoon black pepper
- ½ teaspoon Italian seasoning
- 1 medium-size yellow squash, quartered and cut into ¾-inch pieces
- 1 tablespoon fresh chopped basil
  Olive oil, for drizzling (optional)

① Place eggplant in a strainer and sprinkle with ⅛ teaspoon salt; let stand for 20 minutes and press out as much liquid as possible.

② In a 4- to 5-quart slow cooker, combine eggplant, onion, bell peppers and mushrooms. Drain diced tomatoes and stir in along with tomato sauce, black pepper and Italian seasoning. Cook on HIGH for 3 hours or LOW for 5 hours.

③ Add squash to slow cooker for last 45 minutes of cooking time. Before serving, stir in basil and remaining ¼ teaspoon salt. Drizzle with olive oil, if desired.

PER SERVING 82 calories; 0 g fat (0 g sat.); 5 g protein; 18 g carbohydrate; 6 g fiber; 446 mg sodium; 0 mg cholesterol

ALL-AMERICAN CHILI

MAKES 6 servings **PREP** 10 minutes **SLOW COOK** for 4 hours on HIGH or 6 hours on LOW

- 1½ pounds lean ground beef
- 2 onions, chopped
- 1 yellow bell pepper, seeded and chopped
- 2 garlic cloves, minced
- 2 cans (15.5 ounces each) kidney beans, drained and rinsed
- 1 can (14.5 ounces) diced tomatoes, drained
- 1 can (8 ounces) no-salt-added tomato sauce
- 1 cup low-sodium chicken broth
- 3 tablespoons chili powder
- 1 teaspoon ground cumin
- 1 teaspoon dried oregano
- ½ teaspoon salt
- 1 box (8.5 ounces) corn bread mix, prepared according to package directions (optional)

① Combine beef, onions, pepper, garlic, beans, tomatoes, tomato sauce, broth, 2 tablespoons of the chili powder, and ½ teaspoon each of the cumin and the oregano in slow cooker. Cover and cook on HIGH for 4 hours or LOW for 6 hours.

② Remove cover and stir in remaining 1 tablespoon chili powder, ½ teaspoon each cumin and oregano and the salt. Serve with corn bread, if desired.

PER SERVING 353 calories; 7 g fat (3 g sat.); 35 g protein; 37 g carbohydrate; 13 g fiber; 710 mg sodium; 71 mg cholesterol

BBQ PORK SANDWICHES

MAKES 8 servings **PREP** 5 minutes
SLOW COOK for 3 hours on HIGH or 5 hours on LOW

1   boneless pork loin roast (about 2½ pounds), trimmed and cut in half lengthwise
1¼ cups prepared low-sodium barbecue sauce
4   cups packaged coleslaw mix
½   cup reduced-fat coleslaw dressing
8   hamburger buns

① Place roast and 1 cup water in slow cooker. Cover and cook on HIGH for 3 hours or LOW for 5 hours.

② Remove pork from slow cooker and discard water. When cool enough to handle, shred pork into bite-size pieces; discard any excess fat. Stir pork together with barbecue sauce.

③ In another bowl, stir together coleslaw mix and dressing. Place ½ cup pork mixture on each bun and top each with ½ cup coleslaw. Serve immediately.

PER SERVING 456 calories; 16 g fat (5 g sat.); 31 g protein; 47 g carbohydrate; 2 g fiber; 1,050 mg sodium; 74 mg cholesterol

FRUIT COMPOTE

MAKES 6 servings **PREP** 15 minutes **SLOW COOK** for 3¾ hours on HIGH or 5¾ hours on LOW

3   cups fresh pineapple chunks
2   medium-size pears, peeled, cored and cut into ½-inch chunks (about 2 cups)
2   cups frozen sliced peaches
1   cup frozen pitted cherries
¾   cup dried apricots, quartered
⅔   cup frozen orange juice concentrate, thawed
1   tablespoon packed dark-brown sugar
1   teaspoon vanilla extract
2   tablespoons cornstarch
½   cup sliced almonds, toasted
    Vanilla ice cream (optional)

① Combine pineapple, pears, peaches, cherries, apricots, orange juice, brown sugar and vanilla extract in a slow cooker insert. Cover and cook on HIGH for 3½ hours or LOW for 5½ hours.

② Uncover and remove 2 tablespoons liquid. In a small bowl, stir together liquid and cornstarch. Stir cornstarch mixture back into slow cooker; cook 15 minutes more or until thickened. Sprinkle with almonds. Serve warm with ice cream, if desired.

PER SERVING 139 calories; 2 g fat (0 g sat.); 2 g protein; 29 g carbohydrate; 3 g fiber; 3 mg sodium; 0 mg cholesterol

MOLASSES BAKED BEANS

MAKES 10 servings **PREP** 10 minutes **COOK** 15 minutes **SLOW COOK** for 5 hours on HIGH or 6½ hours on LOW

- 1 **pound navy beans, picked over, rinsed and soaked overnight**
- ½ **tablespoon baking soda**
- 4 **slices bacon, finely chopped**
- 1 **medium-size onion, finely chopped**
- ¼ **cup molasses**
- ¼ **cup packed dark-brown sugar**
- 2 **cups boiling water**
- 2 **teaspoons dry mustard**
- 1 **teaspoon cider vinegar**
- ½ **teaspoon salt**
- ½ **teaspoon black pepper**

① Drain beans; place in a large saucepan. Cover with water by 2 inches; stir in baking soda. Bring to a boil over medium-high heat; boil for 15 minutes, skimming off any foam that accumulates.

② Meanwhile, heat a 10-inch nonstick skillet over medium-high heat. Add bacon to skillet; cook 4 minutes, stirring occasionally. Add onion to pan; cook 5 more minutes, stirring almost constantly.

③ Drain beans and transfer to slow cooker insert. Top with bacon mixture. Stir in molasses, sugar, boiling water and 1 teaspoon of the dry mustard. Cover; cook on HIGH for 5 hours or LOW for 6½ hours.

④ Remove cover; stir in remaining 1 teaspoon dry mustard, the cider vinegar, salt and pepper; serve immediately.

PER SERVING 261 calories; 6 g fat (2 g sat.); 11 g protein; 42 g carbohydrate; 7 g fiber; 238 mg sodium; 8 mg cholesterol

**CLASSIC CHEDDAR
SLIDERS, PAGE 160**

JULY

155

175

171

Bowled Over

Try a fresh spin on dinner with a hearty, main-dish salad.

**BEAN & CHERRY
TOMATO SPINACH
SALAD, PAGE 157**

**TUNA CAESAR SALAD,
PAGE 157**

No need to turn on the oven to make these satisfying, stay-cool, main-dish salads.

TEX-MEX SURIMI RICE SALAD

MAKES 4 servings **PREP** 15 minutes
MICROWAVE 2 minutes

3   tablespoons lime juice
2   tablespoons olive oil
2   tablespoons reduced-fat sour cream
¼   teaspoon chili powder
¼   teaspoon ground cumin
⅛   teaspoon black pepper
2   packages (8.8 ounces each) fully cooked microwavable rice
3   wedges Laughing Cow Light Queso Fresco & Chipotle cheese
½   pound surimi (imitation crab), cut into bite-size pieces
½   green bell pepper, core and seeds removed, finely diced
2   scallions, thinly sliced
1   head green leafy lettuce
    Lime wedges (optional)

① In a small bowl, whisk together lime juice, olive oil, sour cream, chili powder, cumin and pepper. Set aside.

② Heat rice in microwave following package directions, about 2 minutes; add to a large bowl. Add cheese and stir until melted. Stir in surimi, green pepper and scallions. Add lime juice mixture and stir to coat all ingredients.

③ Serve rice salad with lettuce leaves for wrapping. Squeeze with lime wedges, if desired.

PER SERVING 333 calories; 10 g fat (2 g sat.); 11 g protein; 50 g carbohydrate; 4 g fiber; 720 mg sodium; 23 mg cholesterol

CHICKEN WALDORF SALAD

MAKES 4 servings **PREP** 10 minutes

1   package (9 ounces) fully cooked grilled chicken
1   large apple, cored and diced
½   cup raisins
½   cup chopped walnuts
⅓   cup reduced-fat Miracle Whip
2   tablespoons nonfat milk
2   tablespoons lemon juice
4   heads endive, leaves separated

① Cut chicken into bite-size pieces and place in a large bowl. Add apple, raisins and nuts. In a smaller bowl, whisk together Miracle Whip, milk and lemon juice; add to chicken mixture and toss to coat all ingredients evenly.

② Line 4 salad plates with the endive leaves and spoon an equal amount of salad onto each.

PER SERVING 348 calories; 16 g fat (2 g sat.); 20 g protein; 36 g carbohydrate; 7 g fiber; 683 mg sodium; 42 mg cholesterol

**TEX-MEX SURIMI
RICE SALAD**

GREEK BULGUR SALAD WITH SHRIMP

MAKES 4 servings **PREP** 15 minutes **REFRIGERATE** 1 hour

3 tablespoons lemon juice
3 tablespoons olive oil
1 teaspoon prepared mustard
1 teaspoon fresh oregano, chopped
⅛ teaspoon salt
⅛ teaspoon black pepper
1 cup bulgur wheat
½ pound plum tomatoes, chopped
½ cucumber, peeled and chopped
¼ cup flat-leaf parsley, chopped
¼ cup fresh mint, chopped
1 pound cooked, peeled shrimp
½ head iceberg lettuce, shredded

½ large red onion, sliced
12 pitted black olives, chopped
2 ounces reduced-fat feta cheese (about ½ cup), crumbled

① In a small bowl, whisk together lemon juice, olive oil, mustard, oregano, salt and black pepper. Set aside.

② Place bulgur in a large bowl. Stir in 2 cups boiling water. Cover with plastic and allow to stand for 5 minutes. Stir in tomatoes, cucumber, parsley, mint and 2 tablespoons of lemon dressing. Cover and refrigerate 1 hour.

③ Toss the shrimp with 1 tablespoon of dressing and set aside.

④ In a large bowl, toss together lettuce, onion, olives and remaining dressing. Equally divide among 4 dinner plates. Top each serving with bulgur, shrimp and feta.

PER SERVING 410 calories; 17 g fat (3 g sat.); 28 g protein; 38 g carbohydrate; 8 g fiber; 692 mg sodium; 172 mg cholesterol

ROAST BEEF FAJITA SALAD

MAKES 4 servings **PREP** 15 minutes

1   head leafy lettuce, rinsed, dried and torn into bite-size pieces
2   beefsteak tomatoes, seeds removed, chopped
2   sweet red peppers, cored, seeds removed, cut into ½-inch slices
1   sweet onion, peeled and sliced
1   pound sliced deli roast beef
½   cup shredded reduced-fat taco-blend cheese
½   cup bottled fat-free Italian dressing

① Divide lettuce and tomato equally among 4 dinner plates. Arrange peppers, onion and roast beef over the lettuce. Sprinkle the cheese over the top. Drizzle 2 tablespoons dressing over each serving.

PER SERVING 413 calories; 18 g fat (5 g sat.); 41 g protein; 23 g carbohydrate; 7 g fiber; 683 mg sodium; 102 mg cholesterol

MANGO CHICKEN SALAD

Lean proteins, fruits, vegetables, and fresh homemade dressings make dinner light and delicious.

MANGO CHICKEN SALAD

MAKES 4 servings **PREP** 15 minutes
REFRIGERATE 1 hour

- ¼ cup 2% Greek yogurt
- ¼ cup reduced-fat mayonnaise
- 1 tablespoon lemon juice
- 2 teaspoons curry powder
- ¼ teaspoon salt
- 4 cups shredded rotisserie chicken
- 1 mango, diced (see "How to Dice a Mango," below)
- 1 cup red seedless grapes
- ½ cup sliced almonds
- 1 head Bibb lettuce

① In a large bowl, whisk together yogurt, mayonnaise, lemon juice, curry powder and salt. Fold in chicken, mango, grapes and half the almonds. Cover and refrigerate for at least 1 hour.

② Line 4 salad plates with lettuce leaves. Equally divide chicken mixture among plates and scatter with remaining nuts.

PER SERVING 386 calories; 16 g fat (3 g sat.); 40 g protein; 22 g carbohydrate; 3 g fiber; 358 mg sodium; 102 mg cholesterol

HOW TO DICE A MANGO

① Remove pit using slicer, or hold mango stem-end down and slice lengthwise as close to pit as possible with a sharp knife.

② Take one of the halves and, with a paring knife, make lengthwise and crosswise cuts without going through the peel.

③ Invert the peel and remove the square segments with your fingers or cut them away with the knife.

BEAN & CHERRY TOMATO SPINACH SALAD

MAKES 4 servings **PREP** 15 minutes
MICROWAVE 1 minute

- 2 tablespoons red wine vinegar
- 2 teaspoons prepared mustard
- 2 cloves garlic, finely chopped
- ⅛ teaspoon salt
- ⅛ teaspoon black pepper
- 3 tablespoons olive oil
- 2 cans (15 ounces) white beans, drained and rinsed
- 2 cups cherry tomatoes, halved
- ¼ cup flat-leaf parsley, chopped
- 8 cups spinach & spring mix salad
- 1 medium red onion, sliced
- 4 ounces white mushrooms, thinly sliced
- 8 slices fully cooked bacon

① In a small bowl, whisk together vinegar, mustard, garlic, salt and pepper. Gradually whisk in oil until mixture thickens. Set aside.

② In a medium-size bowl, mix together beans, tomatoes, parsley and 2 tablespoons of the dressing.

③ Place salad blend, onion and mushrooms in a large bowl and toss with the remaining dressing. Divide among 4 plates and top with bean mixture. Microwave bacon 1 minute; crumble 2 slices over each plate.

PER SERVING 306 calories; 16 g fat (3 g sat.); 12 g protein; 32 g carbohydrate; 10 g fiber; 730 mg sodium; 12 mg cholesterol

TUNA CAESAR SALAD

MAKES 4 servings **PREP** 15 minutes

- 2 cans (5 ounces each) tuna packed in water, drained
- ½ cup chopped celery
- 2 scallions, chopped
- ¼ cup reduced-fat mayonnaise
- 6 tablespoons Ken's Lite Caesar salad dressing
- 1 head romaine lettuce, rinsed and torn into bite-size pieces
- 1 cup whole-wheat croutons
- 2 tablespoons grated Parmesan cheese

① In a medium-size bowl, combine tuna, celery, scallions, mayonnaise and 2 tablespoons of salad dressing, breaking up tuna. Cover and refrigerate until serving.

② In a large bowl, toss lettuce, croutons, cheese and remaining 4 tablespoons of the dressing. Spoon salad onto 4 dinner plates and top with the tuna mixture.

PER SERVING 228 calories; 8 g fat (2 g sat.); 22 g protein; 15 g carbohydrate; 2 g fiber; 793 mg sodium; 53 mg cholesterol

Flipping Out

Try one (or more) of these six new takes on the classic American burger.

STACKED CHICKEN BURGER, PAGE 165

MOO SHU
PORK BURGER,
PAGE 162

CLASSIC CHEDDAR SLIDERS

MAKES 12 sliders **PREP** 15 minutes **GRILL** 4 minutes

- 1½ pounds ground round
- 12 thin slices sharp cheddar cheese (about 6 ounces)
- 12 dinner-size potato rolls
- ½ cup hamburger relish
- 2 large plum tomatoes, thinly sliced
- 12 small iceberg lettuce leaves

① Heat gas grill to medium-high or coals in a charcoal grill to medium-hot. Lightly coat grill rack with oil or cooking spray.

② Form the ground round into 12 equal-size patties. Grill for 2 minutes per side, covered, or until internal temperature registers 160° on an instant-read thermometer. Place cheese on top of each burger during last minute of cooking.

③ Spread cut side of each roll with 1 teaspoon relish. Top with slider, sliced tomato and lettuce. Serve immediately.

PER SLIDER 255 calories; 10 g fat (5 g sat.); 18 g protein; 22 g carbohydrate; 1 g fiber; 396 mg sodium; 45 mg cholesterol

PHILLY CHEESESTEAK BURGER

MAKES 6 servings **PREP** 15 minutes **COOK** 10 minutes **GRILL** 6 minutes

1½ pounds ground sirloin
1   tablespoon olive oil
1   large sweet onion
1   sweet red pepper, seeded and sliced
½   pound button mushrooms, sliced
12 thin slices provolone cheese
    (about 6 ounces)
¾   pound whole-wheat Italian bread,
    cut into 6 pieces and sliced in half
    horizontally

    Pepperoncini (optional)

① Form ground sirloin into 6 equal-size patties and refrigerate.

② Heat olive oil in a large nonstick skillet. Add onion and cook 5 minutes over medium heat, stirring occasionally. Add pepper and mushrooms and cook an additional 4 to 5 minutes or until tender.

③ Heat gas grill to medium-high or coals in a charcoal grill to medium-hot. Lightly coat grill rack with oil or cooking spray.

④ Grill burgers for 3 minutes per side, covered, or until internal temperature registers 160° on an instant-read thermometer. Turn off heat and place 2 slices of cheese on top of each burger. Cover and wait a few minutes until cheese melts.

⑤ Place burgers on Italian bread with onion and mushroom mixture spooned over top. Serve with pepperoncini, if desired.

PER SERVING 427 calories; 17 g fat (8 g sat.); 36 g protein; 34 g carbohydrate; 3 g fiber; 648 mg sodium; 80 mg cholesterol

At just 318 calories and 5 grams of fat, these peppery tuna steak sandwiches slathered with a mustard-shallot-sour cream sauce are super healthful and elegant.

TUNA "BURGER" AU POIVRE

MAKES 6 servings **PREP** 15 minutes
GRILL 6 minutes

½   cup reduced-fat sour cream
2   tablespoons chopped flat-leaf parsley
2   tablespoons chopped shallot
1   teaspoon honey Dijon mustard
6   tuna steaks, 4 ounces each, about 1 inch thick
2   teaspoons Montreal Steak seasoning
6   large slices sourdough bread, about 2 ounces each, cut in half crosswise
1   small head of frisée

① Heat gas grill to medium-high or coals in a charcoal grill to medium-hot. Lightly coat grill rack with oil or cooking spray.

② In a small bowl, stir together sour cream, parsley, shallot and mustard. Cover and refrigerate until ready to serve.

③ Rub both sides of tuna steaks with Montreal seasoning. Grill for 3 minutes per side. Remove to a plate and keep warm.

④ Spread top of each bread slice with 2 teaspoons of sour cream mixture. Sandwich a tuna steak and some frisée between bread slices and serve.

PER SERVING 318 calories; 5 g fat (2 g sat.); 33 g protein; 34 g carbohydrate; 1 g fiber; 656 mg sodium; 64 mg cholesterol

MOO SHU PORK BURGER

MAKES 6 servings **PREP** 15 minutes **GRILL** 6 minutes

6   tablespoons light mayonnaise
2   tablespoons hoisin sauce
1¼ pounds ground pork
4   ounces cremini mushrooms, finely chopped
2   scallions, trimmed and chopped
1   tablespoon light soy sauce
2   teaspoons ground ginger
6   fajita-size flour tortillas
1   cup arugula
½   cup thinly sliced radishes

① Heat gas grill to medium-high or coals in a charcoal grill to medium-hot. Lightly coat grill rack with oil or cooking spray.

② In a small bowl, stir together mayonnaise and 1 tablespoon of the hoisin sauce. Cover and refrigerate until ready to serve.

③ In a large bowl, mix together pork, mushrooms, scallions, soy sauce, remaining tablespoon hoisin sauce and ginger. Form into 6 equal-size patties. Grill for 3 minutes per side or until internal temperature registers 160° on an instant-read thermometer. Remove to a plate and keep warm.

④ To serve, spread 1 tablespoon of the mayonnaise mixture on one side of a tortilla. Place arugula and burger on top and fan radish slices over burger. Fold over.

PER SERVING 419 calories; 28 g fat (9 g sat.); 20 g protein; 22 g carbohydrate; 2 g fiber; 749 mg sodium; 73 mg cholesterol

TUNA "BURGER"
AU POIVRE

GYRO BURGER

Whether it's tucked in a pita or stacked on a bun, or between two pieces of hearty bread, a burger makes for fun eating.

GYRO BURGER

MAKES 6 servings **PREP** 15 minutes
GRILL 6 minutes

1   cup plain Greek yogurt
¼   cup crumbled reduced-fat feta cheese
½   cup chopped, peeled seedless cucumber
⅛   teaspoon salt
⅛   teaspoon black pepper
1¼   pounds ground lamb
2   teaspoons Greek seasoning (such as McCormick)
6   whole-grain pita breads
6   large Boston lettuce leaves
2   medium tomatoes, thinly sliced
½   red onion, peeled and thinly sliced

① Heat gas grill to medium-high or coals in a charcoal grill to medium-hot. Lightly coat grill rack with oil or cooking spray.

② In a medium-size bowl, stir together yogurt, feta cheese, cucumber, salt and pepper. Cover and refrigerate until ready to serve.

③ Mix together lamb and Greek seasoning. Form into 6 equal-size patties, about 4 inches in diameter. Grill for 2 to 3 minutes per side or until internal temperature registers 160° on an instant-read thermometer.

④ Cut off top quarter of pita bread to form a pocket. Fill each with lettuce, tomatoes, onion, some of the yogurt sauce and a lamb burger. Serve remaining yogurt mixture on the side.

PER SERVING 480 calories; 21 g fat (9 g sat.); 34 g protein; 40 g carbohydrate; 6 g fiber; 534 mg sodium; 95 mg cholesterol

STACKED CHICKEN BURGER

MAKES 6 servings   **PREP** 15 minutes   **GRILL** 6 minutes

¾   cup light mayonnaise
3   tablespoons ketchup
3   tablespoons pickle relish
2   tablespoons dried minced onion
1   tablespoon sugar
2¼   pounds ground chicken
1   tablespoon Worcestershire sauce
1   teaspoon garlic powder
½   teaspoon black pepper
9   sesame seed hamburger buns
1½   cups shredded lettuce

① Heat gas grill to medium-high or coals in a charcoal grill to medium-hot. Lightly coat grill rack with oil or cooking spray.

② In a medium-size bowl, blend mayonnaise, ketchup, relish, 1 tablespoon of the dried onion and sugar. Cover and refrigerate.

③ In a large bowl, mix together ground chicken, remaining tablespoon dried onion, Worcestershire sauce, garlic powder and pepper. Form into 12 equal-size patties.

④ Grill burgers for 2 to 3 minutes per side or until temperature registers 160° on an instant-read thermometer. Remove to a plate.

⑤ To serve, set aside 6 bun tops. Spread each bun bottom with 1 tablespoon sauce. Stack each with a burger and 2 tablespoons shredded lettuce. Top each with a bun half; repeat stacking with sauce, burger and lettuce. Top each with a reserved bun top. Serve with remaining sauce.

PER SERVING 598 calories; 31 g fat (9 g sat.); 35 g protein; 45 g carbohydrate; 2 g fiber; 858 mg sodium; 215 mg cholesterol

Have Treats, Will Travel

Seriously scrumptious, perfectly packable ways to end any picnic on a sweet note.

**BLUEBERRY CUPCAKES,
PAGE 171**

CHERRY RASPBERRY PIE,
PAGE 171

ALMOND POUND CAKE

MAKES 12 slices **PREP** 20 minutes
BAKE at 350° for 1 hour, 5 minutes

CAKE

2½ cups all-purpose flour
2½ teaspoons baking powder
½ teaspoon salt
¾ cup (1½ sticks) unsalted butter, softened
1¼ cups granulated sugar
3 large eggs
¾ cup milk
1 teaspoon almond extract

TOPPING

1 cup confectioners' sugar
½ teaspoon almond extract
2 tablespoons sliced almonds, lightly toasted

① Heat oven to 350°. Coat a 9 x 5 x 3-inch loaf pan with nonstick cooking spray.

② **Cake.** In medium-size bowl, combine flour, baking powder and salt. Set aside. In a large bowl, beat butter with an electric mixer until smooth. Add sugar and beat until light-colored, about 2 minutes. Add eggs, one at a time, beating well after each addition. On low speed, beat in half the flour mixture. Scrape down side of bowl and beat in milk. Add remaining flour mixture and the almond extract and beat until smooth. Spread into prepared pan.

③ Bake cake at 350° for 1 hour, 5 minutes or until crowned and set. Cool in pan on wire rack for 10 minutes, then invert to remove and cool upright on rack.

④ Make **Topping.** In medium-size bowl, combine confectioners' sugar, 4 teaspoons water and the almond extract. Whisk until smooth. Spread over cooled cake and top with toasted nuts. Let icing dry at least 15 minutes before slicing.

PER SLICE 349 calories; 14 g fat (8 g sat.); 5 g protein; 53 g carbohydrate; 1 g fiber; 206 mg sodium; 85 mg cholesterol

CHOCOLATE COCONUT BARS

MAKES 24 bars **PREP** 15 minutes **MICROWAVE** 2½ minutes **BAKE** at 350° for 40 minutes

BARS

1 cup (2 sticks) butter
4 squares (1 ounce each) unsweetened chocolate, broken up
1½ cups sugar
1½ cups all-purpose flour
4 eggs
½ teaspoon baking soda
¼ teaspoon salt
½ teaspoon coconut extract

TOPPING

1 cup sweetened flake coconut
½ cup (1 stick) unsalted butter, softened
2 cups confectioners' sugar
¼ teaspoon coconut extract

① Heat oven to 350°. Line a 13 x 9 x 2-inch baking pan with foil. Coat foil with nonstick cooking spray. Make **Bars.** Combine butter and chocolate in a microwave-safe bowl and microwave for 1 minute. Stir. Microwave another minute and stir. Microwave for 30 seconds more and stir until smooth.

② Stir in sugar, flour, eggs, baking soda, salt and coconut extract. Pour into prepared pan; smooth top. Bake at 350° for 30 minutes. Remove to rack.

③ While bar cools, prepare **Topping.** Spread coconut on a baking sheet and bake at 350° for 10 minutes or until golden. In a large bowl, combine butter and confectioners' sugar. Beat until smooth. Beat in coconut extract and 2 tablespoons water. Spread over cooled bar and top with toasted coconut. Cut into squares or refrigerate until serving.

PER BAR 255 calories; 19 g fat (9 g sat.); 3 g protein; 30 g carbohydrate; 1 g fiber; 67 mg sodium; 65 mg cholesterol

PEANUT BUTTER-CHOCOLATE CHUNK COOKIES

MAKES about 2½ dozen **PREP** 15 minutes **BAKE** at 375° for 15 minutes per batch

- 2   cups all-purpose flour
- 1   teaspoon baking soda
- ½   teaspoon salt
- ½   cup (1 stick) unsalted butter, softened
- ½   cup creamy peanut butter
- ¾   cup packed brown sugar
- ½   cup granulated sugar
- 2   large eggs
- 1   teaspoon vanilla extract
- 1   bag (11.5 ounces) chocolate chunks

① Heat oven to 375°. In a medium-size bowl, whisk together flour, baking soda and salt. Set aside.

② In large bowl, beat together butter and peanut butter with an electric mixer until smooth. Beat in both kinds of sugar until pale-colored. Add eggs and vanilla, beating until smooth. On low speed, beat in flour mixture just until combined, or, alternately, stir in by hand. Add chocolate chunks and stir until evenly distributed.

③ Using a small scoop, form mounds of cookie dough on a large cookie sheet (about 12). Press down with a fork in a crosshatch pattern. Bake at 375° for 15 minutes or until browned. Cool on wire rack; repeat with all dough.

PER COOKIE 231 calories; 11 g fat (5 g sat.); 4 g protein; 29 g carbohydrate; 2 g fiber; 135 mg sodium; 28 mg cholesterol

BLUEBERRY CUPCAKES

MAKES 12 cupcakes   **PREP** 15 minutes
BAKE at 375° for 25 minutes

CUPCAKES

1¾ cups all-purpose flour
2   teaspoons baking powder
¼   teaspoon salt
½   cup (1 stick) unsalted butter,
     softened
¾   cup sugar
2   eggs
¾   cup milk
1   teaspoon vanilla extract
¾   cup fresh blueberries

TOPPING

1⅓ cups heavy cream
3   tablespoons granulated sugar
⅔   cup fresh blueberries
1   tablespoon confectioners' sugar
     (optional)

① Heat oven to 375°. Line one 12-cup cupcake pan with foil or paper cupcake liners.

② **Cupcakes.** In medium-size bowl, combine flour, baking powder and salt. In large bowl, beat butter with an electric mixer until smooth. Add sugar and beat until pale and fluffy, about 2 minutes. Beat in eggs, one at a time. On low speed, add half the flour mixture. Beat in the milk and vanilla, followed by remaining flour mixture. Fold in fresh blueberries.

③ Spoon batter into pan, a scant ⅓ cup in each indent. Bake at 375° for 23 to 25 minutes, turning pan once. Cool in pan on wire rack, then remove cakes from pan to cool completely.

④ Prepare **Topping.** In large bowl, combine cream and granulated sugar. Beat until medium-stiff peaks are formed. Spoon onto cooled cupcakes, about ¼ cup on each. Scatter 6 or 7 blueberries over each cupcake, and dust with a little confectioners' sugar, if desired. Serve immediately or keep cool until serving.

PER CUPCAKE 317 calories; 19 g fat (11 g sat.); 4 g protein; 34 g carbohydrate; 1 g fiber; 144 mg sodium; 92 mg cholesterol

CHERRY RASPBERRY PIE

MAKES 12 servings   **PREP** 25 minutes
REFRIGERATE 2 hours or overnight
COOK 5 minutes   **BAKE** at 400° for 15 minutes, then at 375° for 45 minutes

PIECRUST (SEE NOTE)

2½ cups all-purpose flour
1   teaspoon salt
½   cup (1 stick) cold butter, cut into
     small pieces
½   cup solid vegetable shortening,
     chilled
6   to 8 tablespoons ice water

FILLING

¾   cup plus 2 teaspoons sugar
⅓   cup quick-cook tapioca
1   tablespoon cornstarch
¼   teaspoon salt
1½ cups cranberry juice blend
3   cups pitted fresh sweet cherries
     (or a 16-ounce package frozen pitted
     sweet cherries, thawed 1 hour)
1½ cups fresh raspberries
     (6-ounce container)
1   egg yolk, whisked with 2 tablespoons
     water

① Make **Piecrust.** Whisk flour and salt together in a large bowl. Cut in butter and shortening with a pastry blender until mixture resembles coarse meal. Sprinkle ice water, 1 tablespoon at a time, over mixture, incorporating with a fork until pastry is moist enough to hold together. Divide in half; shape each half into a disk and wrap in plastic. Refrigerate for at least 2 hours or overnight.

② Heat oven to 400°. Roll 1 crust out to a 12-inch circle. Gently transfer to a 9-inch pie plate. Prepare **Filling.** In medium-size saucepan, combine ¾ cup of the sugar, the tapioca, cornstarch and salt. Whisk to blend. Add juice and stir until smooth. Cook, stirring, for 5 minutes, until thickened and bubbly. Remove from heat and stir in cherries and raspberries.

③ Roll out remaining crust to a 12-inch circle. With a pastry cutter or pizza wheel, cut into 1-inch strips. Transfer pie filling to pastry-lined pie plate. Weave pastry into a lattice, alternating strips over and under each other. Fold edges under; crimp together. Brush pastry with egg yolk-water mixture, then sprinkle with remaining 2 teaspoons sugar.

④ Bake pie at 400° for 15 minutes. Reduce heat to 375° and bake an additional 45 minutes, covering pie edge with foil if browning too quickly. Cool at least an hour before slicing.

Note. You may substitute refrigerated rolled piecrusts, if desired.

PER SERVING 354 calories; 16 g fat (7 g sat.); 4 g protein; 49 g carbohydrate; 2 g fiber; 392 mg sodium; 0 mg cholesterol

CREAMY
STRAWBERRY PIE,
PAGE 191

AUGUST

183

187

199

5 Make-Ahead Suppers

Do the prep work beforehand, and it's no sweat to throw together a delicious meal.

**GRILLED BUFFALO
CHICKEN & VEGGIE SALAD,
PAGE 183**

**BEEF & BROCCOLINI
STIR-FRY, PAGE 183**

POACHED SALMON WITH SAUCE VERTE

Prepare the sauce and orzo ahead, and poach salmon and chill it if serving cold.

POACHED SALMON WITH SAUCE VERTE

MAKES 4 servings **PREP** 20 minutes
COOK 10 minutes **POACH** 12 minutes

- 1 container (7 ounces) 2% fat Greek yogurt
- ¼ cup watercress, chopped
- ¼ cup flat-leaf parsley, chopped
- 2 scallions, chopped
- 1 teaspoon salt
- ½ teaspoon black pepper
- 1½ cups orzo
- ½ pound green beans, trimmed and cut into 1-inch pieces
- 1 cup grape tomatoes, halved
- 3 tablespoons balsamic vinegar
- 2 tablespoons olive oil
- 4 pieces salmon fillet (about 4 ounces each)
- 1 lemon

① In a bowl, blend yogurt, watercress, parsley, scallions, ⅛ teaspoon of the salt and ⅛ teaspoon of the pepper. Cover and refrigerate until serving.

② Bring a large pot of lightly salted water to boiling. Add orzo and cook 3 minutes; add beans and cook an additional 6 to 7 minutes or until beans are tender. Drain and place into a serving bowl. Stir in tomatoes, vinegar, olive oil and remaining salt and pepper. Allow to cool; cover and refrigerate until serving.

③ Place salmon in a large skillet; add 1 cup water and top each with a lemon slice. Cover and bring to a simmer. Reduce heat to low and gently simmer for 10 to 12 minutes or until salmon is cooked through and flakes easily. Remove salmon from skillet and allow to cool. Cover and refrigerate until serving.

PER SERVING 424 calories; 17 g fat (3 g sat.); 35 g protein; 34 g carbohydrate; 4 g fiber; 734 mg sodium; 74 mg cholesterol

BURRITO CASSEROLE

MAKES 6 servings **PREP** 15 minutes **BAKE** at 350° for 35 minutes

- 2 packages (8.8 ounces each) fully cooked brown rice
- 1 jar (15½ ounces) salsa
- ½ teaspoon dried oregano
- 1 can (15 ounces) refried beans
- 1 package (10 ounces) frozen corn, thawed
- ½ teaspoon chipotle chile powder
- ½ teaspoon ground cumin
- 1½ cups shredded reduced-fat taco-cheese blend
- 2 packages (10 ounces each) frozen chopped spinach, thawed and squeezed dry
- 3 tablespoons chopped cilantro

① In a large bowl, combine rice, salsa and oregano. In a second bowl, combine refried beans, corn, chile powder and cumin.

② Coat a 12 x 8 x 2-inch baking dish with nonstick cooking spray. Spread half of the rice mixture evenly in dish. Layer refried bean mixture and half the cheese over the rice. Scatter spinach over cheese. Top with remaining rice mixture and cheese.

③ Cover with plastic wrap and refrigerate for up to 2 days.

④ Heat oven to 350°. Bake, uncovered, for 35 minutes or until internal temperature registers 140°. Sprinkle with cilantro before serving.

PER SERVING 382 calories; 9 g fat (4 g sat.); 19 g protein; 61 g carbohydrate; 10 g fiber; 788 mg sodium; 26 mg cholesterol

PORK RAGU & BOWTIE PASTA

MAKES 6 servings (plus 4 cups sauce for second meal) **PREP** 15 minutes **SLOW COOK** on HIGH for 6 hours or LOW for 8 hours

2   cans (14½ ounces each) Italian-seasoned diced tomatoes

1   medium-size onion, peeled and chopped

1   cup chopped carrots

4   cloves garlic, peeled and chopped

1   teaspoon salt

½   teaspoon black pepper

½   teaspoon dried oregano

¼   teaspoon red pepper flakes

2   pounds country-style pork ribs

½   pound zucchini, diced

1   pound whole-wheat bowtie (farfalle) pasta, cooked

1   cup shredded reduced-fat Italian 4-cheese blend

① Coat slow cooker bowl with nonstick cooking spray.

② Add tomatoes, onion, carrots, garlic, ½ teaspoon of the salt, ¼ teaspoon of the black pepper, oregano and pepper flakes. Stir to combine. Add ribs and cover with sauce. Scatter zucchini over top.

③ Cover and cook on HIGH for 6 hours or LOW for 8 hours.

④ Remove ribs and shred meat. Discard bones and stir shredded meat back into sauce; stir in the remaining ½ teaspoon salt and ¼ teaspoon black pepper.

⑤ Stir half the sauce (about 4 cups) into pasta, adding some of the cooking liquid, if desired. Stir in cheese and serve. Freeze extra sauce for future.

PER SERVING 474 calories; 10 g fat (4 g sat.); 32 g protein; 62 g carbohydrate; 4 g fiber; 559 mg sodium; 58 mg cholesterol

BEEF & BROCCOLINI STIR-FRY

MAKES 4 servings **PREP** 20 minutes
STIR-FRY 15 minutes

1 can (14½ ounces) reduced-sodium beef broth
3 tablespoons cornstarch
2 tablespoons reduced-sodium soy sauce
2 tablespoons ketchup
½ teaspoon Chinese five-spice
¾ pounds flank steak, cut against the grain into ¼-inch slices
1 pound Broccolini, cut into 2-inch pieces
2 sweet red peppers, seeds removed and cut into ½-inch slices
1 sweet onion, peeled, halved and cut into ½-inch slices
3 cloves garlic, peeled and finely chopped
2 tablespoons vegetable oil
½ pound shelled edamame
2 cups cooked brown rice

① In a medium-size bowl, whisk together broth and cornstarch. Add soy sauce, ketchup and five-spice.

② If prepping ahead, pour broth mixture into resealable bag and sliced steak into a second resealable bag. Place Broccolini, peppers, onion and garlic into another resealable bag. Refrigerate up to 2 days.

③ To prepare, heat 1 tablespoon oil in a large skillet over medium-high heat. Add sliced steak and stir-fry 3 minutes per side. Remove to a plate.

④ Add remaining tablespoon oil to skillet; add Broccolini, peppers, onion and garlic. Stir-fry 7 to 8 minutes or until vegetables are crisp-tender.

⑤ Add broth mixture and simmer 1 minute, until thickened. Stir in edamame, steak and any accumulated juices. Heat through.

⑥ Serve with cooked rice.

PER SERVING 497 calories; 15 g fat (2 g sat.); 34 g protein; 55 g carbohydrate; 6 g fiber; 714 mg sodium; 28 mg cholesterol

GRILLED BUFFALO CHICKEN & VEGGIE SALAD

MAKES 4 servings **PREP** 15 minutes
MARINATE 8 to 24 hours **GRILL** 12 minutes

CHICKEN
3 tablespoons Frank's hot sauce
3 tablespoons reduced-sodium chicken broth
1 tablespoon lemon juice
4 boneless, skinless chicken breasts (about 6 ounces each)

VEGETABLES
2 medium zucchini, cut in half lengthwise
2 ears of corn
½ pound cherry tomatoes, halved
⅛ teaspoon salt
⅛ teaspoon black pepper

SALAD & DRESSING
2 tablespoons white balsamic vinegar
1 teaspoon Dijon mustard
⅛ teaspoon garlic salt
⅛ teaspoon black pepper
5 tablespoons basil-infused olive oil
6 cups salad greens

① **Chicken.** Mix together hot sauce, broth and lemon juice. Place chicken in a large resealable bag and add hot sauce mixture. Seal and shake bag to coat chicken. Refrigerate 8 to 24 hours.

② Heat gas grill to medium-high or prepare charcoal grill with medium-hot coals. Lightly coat rack with oil or cooking spray. **Vegetables.** Place zucchini and corn on grill and cook for 10 to 12 minutes, turning a few times. Meanwhile, add

chicken and grill for 3 minutes per side or until internal temperature registers 160°.

③ Cut kernels from cobs and place in a medium-size bowl; cut zucchini into bite-size pieces and add to bowl. Add tomatoes; season with salt and pepper.

④ **Salad & Dressing.** Stir balsamic vinegar, mustard, garlic salt and pepper together in a small bowl. Gradually whisk in oil.

⑤ Dress greens with 3 tablespoons of the dressing. Drizzle remaining dressing over vegetables and serve with chicken.

PER SERVING 417 calories; 20 g fat (3 g sat.); 43 g protein; 19 g carbohydrate; 5 g fiber; 447 mg sodium; 99 mg cholesterol

The chicken can marinate in the spicy, vinegary Buffalo-style marinade for 8 to 24 hours—now that's getting ahead of the game!

Invite the Neighbors

New ideas to make your next backyard bash the talk of the town.

**CHOPPED SALAD WITH
ROASTED CORN RELISH,
PAGE 191**

**BEST BARBECUED
CHICKEN, PAGE 188**

SUMMER GAZPACHO WITH CRAB

MAKES 8 servings **PREP** 15 minutes **CHILL** 2 hours

½ slice white bread, torn into small pieces

2 tablespoons red wine vinegar

1 garlic clove, minced

1 jar (12.4 ounces) roasted red peppers, chopped

½ cucumber, peeled, seeded and roughly chopped

6 ripe tomatoes (about 2 pounds), seeded and roughly chopped

1 large yellow pepper, seeded and roughly chopped

½ small sweet onion (such as Vidalia), roughly chopped

3 tablespoons extra-virgin olive oil

½ teaspoon salt

¼ teaspoon black pepper

1 cup crabmeat, picked over for shells

① In a small bowl, stir together bread, vinegar, garlic and ¾ cup water.

② Combine bread mixture, red peppers and cucumber in a blender and puree until smooth, then transfer to a large bowl.

③ Stir together the tomatoes, yellow pepper and onion. Puree tomato mixture, slowly adding oil while blender is running.

Add to red pepper mixture and stir in salt and black pepper. Cover and refrigerate at least 2 hours.

④ To serve, divide soup evenly among 8 bowls and top each with 2 tablespoons of the crabmeat.

PER SERVING 142 calories; 6 g fat (1 g sat.); 9 g protein; 13 g carbohydrate; 2 g fiber; 470 mg sodium; 23 mg cholesterol

GRILLED ARUGULA BRUSCHETTA

MAKES 20 slices **PREP** 15 minutes **GRILL** 13 minutes

1   loaf (abut 12 ounces) Italian bread, cut diagonally into 1-inch slices
1   garlic clove, halved
1   tablespoon olive oil
1¼ cups shredded part-skim mozzarella
1¼ cups chopped arugula
7   tablespoons reduced-fat basil pesto

① Heat gas grill to medium-high or prepare charcoal grill with medium-hot coals. Grill bread about 2 to 3 minutes per side or until lightly toasted. Remove from grill. Rub one side of toasts with garlic; brush with olive oil.

② Reduce grill temperature to medium-low. Top each slice of toast with ½ tablespoon mozzarella, 1 tablespoon arugula and place another ½ tablespoon mozzarella over top.

③ Place toast slices back on grill, close cover and heat for 6 to 7 minutes or until cheese has melted. Top each slice with 1 teaspoon pesto; serve immediately.

PER SLICE 92 calories; 4 g fat (1 g sat.); 4 g protein; 10 g carbohydrate; 1 g fiber; 191 mg sodium; 6 mg cholesterol

This big bacon-and-asparagus-studded pasta dish dressed in a creamy, lemony ricotta sauce is perfect for sharing.

LEMONY HERB PASTA

MAKES 8 servings **PREP** 15 minutes
COOK 7 minutes

1   container (15 ounces) part-skim ricotta cheese
5   tablespoons lemon juice
¼   cup grated Parmesan cheese
⅓   cup chopped parsley
1   tablespoon olive oil
2   teaspoons lemon zest
½   teaspoon salt
¼   teaspoon black pepper
1   pound penne pasta
1   pound asparagus, trimmed and cut into 1-inch pieces
8   slices bacon, cooked and crumbled

① Bring a large pot of salted water to a boil. In a small bowl, whisk together ricotta, lemon juice, Parmesan, parsley, olive oil, lemon zest, salt and pepper. Set aside.

② Add penne to boiling water and cook for 7 minutes or until tender. Add asparagus to pot for final 3 minutes of cooking time. Set aside 1 cup pasta water, then drain pasta mixture and place in serving bowl.

③ Add ricotta mixture and bacon to serving bowl and stir well to combine, adding reserved pasta water by the ¼ cupful if necessary. Serve immediately.

PER SERVING 360 calories; 10 g fat (4 g sat.); 18 g protein; 47 g carbohydrate; 2 g fiber; 326 mg sodium; 26 mg cholesterol

BEST BARBECUED CHICKEN

MAKES 8 servings **PREP** 15 minutes **GRILL** 25 minutes **COOK** 15 minutes

1   package chicken pieces (about 3½ pounds), skin removed
1   tablespoon barbecue seasoning
¾   cup Homemade Barbecue Sauce
½   teaspoon each onion and garlic powder

① Heat gas grill to medium-high or prepare charcoal grill with medium-hot coals.

② Rub chicken with barbecue seasoning. Coat grill with nonstick spray. Grill chicken 20 to 25 minutes, covered, turning occasionally, or until chicken registers 165° internal temperature with thermometer.

③ Meanwhile, in a small saucepan, stir together barbecue sauce and onion and garlic powders over medium-low heat. Simmer for 15 minutes.

④ Brush chicken generously with sauce during the last 5 minutes of cooking; serve remaining sauce on the side.

PER SERVING 306 calories; 6 g fat (2 g sat.); 43 g protein; 17 g carbohydrate; 0 g fiber; 878 mg sodium; 139 mg cholesterol

HOMEMADE BARBECUE SAUCE

Whisk together 1¼ cups ketchup, ⅓ cup molasses, 2 tablespoons cider vinegar, ½ teaspoon hot sauce and ⅛ teaspoon liquid smoke in a small bowl until well blended.

LEMONY HERB PASTA

**CREAMY
STRAWBERRY PIE**

Strawberry pie is the essence of summer. This one features both lightly cooked and fresh strawberries in a vanilla-wafer crust, crowned with sweetened whipped cream.

CREAMY STRAWBERRY PIE

MAKES 10 servings **PREP** 15 minutes
BAKE at 350° for 14 minutes **COOK** 2 minutes
CHILL 4 hours

CRUST

6	ounces Nilla wafer cookies
2	tablespoons sugar
5	tablespoons unsalted butter, melted

FILLING

⅔	cup plus 2 tablespoons sugar
½	cup cran-raspberry juice
2	quarts strawberries (8 cups), hulled and thinly sliced
¼	cup cornstarch
½	cup heavy cream

① **Crust.** Heat oven to 350°. Combine Nilla wafers and sugar in a food processor. Pulse until fine crumbs are formed. Transfer to a bowl and add melted butter; stir together until all crumbs are moistened. Press crumbs into bottom and up side of a 9-inch pie plate. Bake crust at 350° for 14 minutes or until crust is lightly browned. Place on wire rack and cool completely.

② **Filling.** In medium-size saucepan, combine ⅔ cup of the sugar, juice, 2 cups strawberries and cornstarch. Gently mash berries with a potato masher. Bring to a boil over medium-high heat and cook 2 minutes or until clear and thickened. Remove from heat and let cool slightly. Stir in remaining strawberries, reserving several for garnish. Pour into cooled crust and refrigerate at least 4 hours.

③ In large bowl, beat together heavy cream and 2 tablespoons sugar until soft peaks form. Spread whipped cream over pie, leaving a 1-inch border around edges. Garnish with reserved berries and serve.

PER SERVING 296 calories; 13 g fat (7 g sat.); 2 g protein; 45 g carbohydrate; 3 g fiber; 81 mg sodium; 34 mg cholesterol

CHOPPED SALAD WITH ROASTED CORN RELISH

MAKES 8 servings **PREP** 15 minutes **GRILL** 34 minutes

4	tablespoons balsamic vinegar
1	minced garlic clove
¼	cup chopped basil
¼	teaspoon salt
¼	teaspoon black pepper
5	tablespoons olive oil
2	romaine hearts, washed and chopped into ½-inch slices
2	large sweet red peppers, seeded and cut into 4 quarters
4	ears corn, shucked and silks removed
1	large red onion

① Heat gas grill to medium-high or prepare charcoal grill with medium-hot coals.

② In small bowl, whisk together balsamic vinegar, garlic, basil, salt and pepper. Slowly whisk in olive oil; set aside. Place romaine in a large serving bowl.

③ Place peppers on grill and cover; grill for about 6 to 7 minutes per side or until skin is starting to turn black. Remove from grill and cut into ½-inch pieces; add to romaine in bowl.

④ Grill corn 10 minutes, turning, or until tender and beginning to brown. Remove corn from grill. Cut kernels from cob; add corn to romaine. Starting at root end, cut red onion into ½-inch-thick slices and secure with toothpicks to keep rings from separating. Grill slices 5 minutes per side, turning once. Remove and cut into ½-inch pieces; add to romaine mixture.

⑤ Toss salad with prepared dressing and serve immediately.

PER SERVING 172 calories; 10 g fat (1 g sat.); 4 g protein; 21 g carbohydrate; 4 g fiber; 100 mg sodium; 0 mg cholesterol

Pop Art

Simple, homemade frozen treats help everyone stay cool.

CHOCOLATE COOKIE PUDDING POPS

MAKES 10 ice pops (3 ounces each)
PREP 15 minutes **FREEZE** 6 hours or overnight

2¼ cups cold 2% milk
1   box (3.9 ounces) instant chocolate
    pudding and pie filling
1   cup Oreo cookies, crushed
1   ice pop mold (10 indentations)
10 wooden ice pop sticks

① Whisk together milk and pudding mix in medium-size bowl for 2 minutes. Fold in cookie chunks. Pour into ice pop mold and cover.

② Gently insert ice pop sticks into mold, keeping as upright as possible. Freeze 6 hours or overnight.

③ To unmold: Remove cover. Run outside of mold under warm water and gently pry pops from mold. Place in freezer-safe resealable plastic bag and store in freezer until serving.

PER POP 97 calories; 3 g fat (1 g sat.); 16 g carbs

Creamy and custardy, or light and fruity, these homemade freezer pops are the tops. Eat them before they melt!

MANGO YOGURT POPS

MAKES 10 ice pops (3 ounces each)
PREP 15 minutes **MICROWAVE** 1 minute
LET STAND 5 minutes **FREEZE** 6 hours
or overnight

1   envelope (.25 ounces) unflavored
    gelatin
1¼ pounds mangoes, peeled and pits
    removed (2 cups fruit)
1   container (7 ounces) 2% plain
    Greek yogurt
⅓   cup Quick Sugar Syrup (see below)
1   ice pop mold
10 wooden ice pop sticks

① Microwave ½ cup water for 1 minute.
Sprinkle gelatin over water and let stand
5 minutes.

② Combine mangoes, yogurt and sugar
syrup in blender. Puree until smooth. With
blender on, add gelatin mixture in thin
stream. Pour into ice pop mold and cover.

③ Insert ice pop sticks into mold,
keeping as upright as possible. Freeze
6 hours or overnight.

④ To unmold: Remove cover. Run outside
of mold under warm water and gently pry
pops from mold. Place in freezer-safe
resealable plastic bag and store in freezer
until serving.

PER POP 64 calories; 1 g fat (0 g sat.); 14 g carbs

QUICK SUGAR SYRUP

MAKES ⅔ cup **COOK** 2 minutes

Combine ½ cup sugar and ½ cup water
in a small saucepan. Heat over medium
heat just to a simmer, stirring once. Cook
2 minutes until sugar is completely
dissolved. Remove from heat and cool to
room temperature.

PER TABLESPOON 36 calories; 0 g fat; 9 g carbs

If you don't own ice pop molds, use paper cups. Cover each filled cup with a piece of aluminum foil. Poke the stick through it to keep it upright while freezing

MARGARITA POPS

MAKES 10 ice pops (3 ounces each)
PREP 5 minutes **FREEZE** 7 hours or overnight

1	**can (10 ounces) frozen Bacardi margarita mixer**
¼	**cup tequila**
2	**tablespoons orange liqueur**
1	**teaspoon lime zest**
⅛	**teaspoon salt**
1	**ice pop mold**
10	**wooden ice pop sticks**

① In a large pitcher, stir together frozen margarita mixer, 1 can (10 ounces) of water, tequila, orange liqueur, lime zest and salt. Stir until margarita mixer is dissolved.

② Pour into ice pop mold and cover. Freeze for 2 to 3 hours. Gently insert wooden sticks, keeping as upright as possible. Freeze at least another 4 hours or overnight.

③ To unmold: Remove cover. Run outside of mold under warm water and gently pry pops from mold. Place in freezer-safe resealable plastic bag and store in freezer until serving.

Note. For nonalcoholic pops replace tequila with ¼ cup water and orange liqueur with 2 tablespoons orange juice.

PER POP 66 calories; 0 g fat; 14 g carbs

POMEGRANATE-BLUEBERRY POPS

MAKES 10 ice pops (3 ounces each) **PREP** 5 minutes **FREEZE** 7 hours or overnight

2¼ cups blueberry-pomegranate juice blend (such as Minute Maid)
1 cup fresh blueberries
¼ cup Quick Sugar Syrup (page 193)
1 ice pop mold
10 wooden ice pop sticks

① Combine juice, blueberries and Quick Sugar Syrup in a blender. Puree until most of the berries are chopped. Pour into mold and cover. Freeze 2 to 3 hours.

② Gently insert ice pop sticks into pop mold, keeping as upright as possible. Freeze at least another 4 hours or overnight.

③ To unmold: Remove cover. Run outside of mold under warm water and gently pry pops from mold. Place in freezer-safe resealable plastic bag and store in freezer until serving.

PER POP 50 calories; 0 g fat; 13 g carbs

ICED COFFEE POPS

MAKES 10 ice pops (3 ounces each) **PREP** 15 minutes **FREEZE** 7 hours or overnight

2½ cups coffee, brewed with ¼ teaspoon cinnamon, chilled
⅔ cup half-and-half
¼ cup Quick Sugar Syrup (page 193)
1 ice pop mold
10 wooden ice pop sticks

① Combine brewed coffee, half-and-half and Quick Sugar Syrup until blended. Pour into ice pop mold and cover. Freeze 2 to 3 hours.

② Gently insert ice pop sticks into pop mold, keeping as upright as possible. Freeze at least another 4 hours or overnight.

③ To unmold: Remove cover. Run outside of mold under warm water and gently pry pops from mold. Place in freezer-safe resealable plastic bag and store in freezer until serving.

PER POP 36 calories; 2 g fat (1 g sat.); 4 g carbs

Slow Cooker Suppers

Celebrate the summer garden bounty with these veggie-packed dishes.

VEGGIE LASAGNA

MAKES 6 or 8 servings **PREP** 20 minutes **SLOW COOK** on HIGH for 4½ hours or LOW for 6½ hours **LET STAND** 10 minutes

- 2 small zucchini (12 ounces total), trimmed
- 1 package (8 ounces) sliced mushrooms
- 1 sweet red pepper, seeded and diced
- 1 container (15 ounces) part-skim ricotta cheese
- 1 package (8 ounces) reduced-fat shredded mozzarella or Italian-blend cheese
- ¼ cup packed parsley leaves, chopped
- 2 cloves garlic, chopped
- ¼ teaspoon black pepper
- 1 jar (26 ounces) roasted garlic pasta sauce
- 8 traditional lasagna noodles (uncooked), broken in half
- ¼ cup grated Parmesan cheese

① Coat slow cooker bowl with nonstick cooking spray.

② Insert slicing disk into food processor and thinly slice zucchini (or slice by hand). Transfer to a large bowl and add mushrooms and sweet pepper. In medium-size bowl, combine ricotta, 1 cup shredded cheese, parsley, garlic and black pepper.

③ Spread ½ cup pasta sauce over bottom of slow cooker. Top with 2 noodles (4 halves), overlapping as needed. Blend ¾ cup pasta sauce with ½ cup water and set aside. Stir remaining sauce and 2 tablespoons of the Parmesan into zucchini mixture. Layer half of the zucchini mixture over noodles. Top with 2 more noodles (4 halves). Spread with ricotta mixture and top with 2 more noodles. Finish layering with remaining zucchini mixture and remaining 2 noodles. Spread with reserved sauce-water mixture.

④ Cover and cook on HIGH for 4½ hours or on LOW for 6½ hours, adding remaining 1 cup shredded cheese and 2 tablespoons grated Parmesan for last 10 minutes of cook time. Let stand 10 minutes before serving.

PER SERVING 441 calories; 15 g fat (8 g sat.); 29 g protein; 49 g carbohydrate; 5 g fiber; 860 mg sodium; 45 mg cholesterol

TUSCAN SUMMER STEW

MAKES 6 servings **PREP** 15 minutes **COOK** 9 minutes **SLOW COOK** on HIGH for 6 hours or LOW for 8 hours

STEW

1   package (20 ounces) sweet Italian turkey sausage
½   pound green beans, trimmed and cut into 2-inch pieces
2   pounds tomatoes, cored, seeded and cut into 1-inch chunks
1   teaspoon chopped fresh rosemary
¼   cup white balsamic vinegar
2   ears corn, kernels cut from cobs (2 cups)
1   tablespoon instant polenta
     Fresh basil to garnish (optional)

POLENTA

¾   teaspoon salt
1   cup instant polenta
2   tablespoons grated Parmesan cheese

① **Stew.** Heat a large nonstick skillet over medium-high heat. Add sausages and brown on all sides, 4 minutes. Transfer to a slow cooker.

② Top sausages with green beans, tomatoes and chopped rosemary. Whisk balsamic vinegar together with ¾ cup water. Pour into slow cooker. Cover and cook on HIGH for 6 hours or LOW for 8 hours.

③ **Polenta.** Just before slow cooker is finished, bring 2 cups water and salt to a boil. While whisking, add 1 cup instant polenta in a steady stream. Continue to cook, whisking, for 5 minutes. Remove from heat and stir in Parmesan cheese.

④ Uncover slow cooker. Carefully remove sausage to cutting board. Stir corn kernels and 1 tablespoon instant polenta into slow cooker. Cover. Slice sausages and stir into stew. Serve stew over polenta; garnish with fresh basil, if desired.

PER SERVING 350 calories; 11 g fat (3 g sat.); 23 g protein; 41 g carbohydrate; 5 g fiber; 927 mg sodium; 57 mg cholesterol

CARROT SOUP

MAKES about 7 cups; 6 servings **PREP** 15 minutes
SLOW COOK on HIGH for 6 hours or LOW for 8 hours

1   medium onion, sliced
2   large cloves garlic, peeled and sliced
1½   pounds carrots, peeled, trimmed and cut into 3-inch pieces
1   box (32 ounces) vegetable broth
2   tablespoons packed brown sugar
1½   teaspoons ground ginger
2   tablespoons heavy cream
¼   teaspoon salt
3   tablespoons instant potato granules (for a thicker soup, if desired)
      Chopped cashews, to garnish (optional)
      Fresh cilantro, to garnish (optional)

① Scatter onion and garlic over bottom of slow cooker bowl. Top with carrots. Add vegetable broth and 2 cups water.

② Cover slow cooker and cook on HIGH for 6 hours or LOW for 8 hours.

③ Uncover and stir in brown sugar, ginger, heavy cream, salt and instant potato granules, if using. With a blender, an immersion blender or a food processor, carefully puree until desired consistency is reached.

④ Transfer soup to bowls and garnish with cashews and fresh cilantro, if desired.

PER SERVING 108 calories; 2 g fat (1 g sat.); 2 g protein; 21 g carbohydrate; 4 g fiber; 909 mg sodium; 7 mg cholesterol

Eating Well on a Budget

Great-tasting, affordable meals.

When zucchini and summer squash aren't readily available, sub in Swiss chard. You can try cannellini beans in place of the chickpeas for an Italian twist.

MINTED SQUASH ROTINI WITH CHICKPEAS

MAKES 6 servings **PREP** 15 minutes **COOK** 12 minutes

- 1 **pound rotini**
- 3 **tablespoons olive oil**
- ½ **cup chopped walnuts**
- ½ **pound zucchini, diced into 2 x ½-inch pieces**
- ½ **pound summer squash, cut into 2 x ½-inch pieces**
- ⅛ **teaspoon pepper**
- ½ **teaspoon salt**
- 1 **can (15.5 ounces) chickpeas, drained and rinsed**
- ¼ **cup fresh mint, chopped**
- ¾ **cup shredded Parmesan cheese**

① Bring a pot of lightly salted water to a boil. Add rotini and cook 8 to 10 minutes. Drain, toss in a large bowl with 1 tablespoon of the olive oil and set aside.

② Meanwhile, toast walnuts in a large sauté pan over medium heat, about 5 minutes. Shake pan about halfway through cooking time. Set aside.

③ Heat remaining 2 tablespoons olive oil in the same pan on medium-high. Add zucchini, summer squash, pepper and ¼ teaspoon of the salt; cook 5 minutes, until slightly tender but still crisp, stirring frequently. Add chickpeas and walnuts and heat through, about 2 minutes.

④ Add vegetable mixture to drained pasta along with remaining ¼ teaspoon salt, the mint and ½ cup of the Parmesan. Stir to combine, then top with remaining ¼ cup cheese.

PER SERVING 523 calories; 18 g fat (4 g sat.); 20 g protein; 71 g carbohydrate; 7 g fiber; 460 mg sodium; 7 mg cholesterol

CHEAP TRICKS

Instead of selecting prechopped walnuts, buy them in bulk, shelled but whole, and do the knife work yourself—for a savings of more than $2.50 per pound. (You'll pocket even more cash by stocking up on walnuts during the latter part of the year when they're on sale for the holidays.) Once opened, store them in a resealable plastic bag or airtight container in your freezer for up to a year.

WHEAT BERRY SALAD,
PAGE 213

SEPTEMBER

205

219

225

Join the Club

Ideas for the bundles of chicken, pork and fish the warehouse stores are famous for.

**PAN-SEARED PORK CHOPS,
PAGE 209**

CRUNCHY TILAPIA AND CARROT SLAW, PAGE 207

SAVORY ROAST CHICKEN & GRAVY

MAKES 6 servings **PREP** 15 minutes
ROAST at 450° for 30 minutes, 350° for
50 minutes **COOK** 4 minutes

- 2 whole chickens, giblets removed, about 4 pounds each
- 3 teaspoons McCormick Montreal Chicken Seasoning
- 1 lemon, thinly sliced
- 6 cloves garlic, sliced
- 1 pound parsnips, peeled and cut into 1-inch pieces
- 1 bag (1 pound) peeled baby carrots
- 1 small head cauliflower, cut into florets
- 2 tablespoons olive oil
- 2 tablespoons all-purpose flour
- 1 can (14½ ounces) reduced-sodium chicken broth

① Heat oven to 450°.

② Gently lift skin from breasts and legs and season each chicken with 1 teaspoon of the Montreal seasoning. Place some of the lemon and garlic slices under the skin.

③ Place chickens on a rack in a large roasting pan. Roast at 450° for 30 minutes. Reduce temperature to 350°. Roast for 50 minutes or until internal temperature registers 165°.

④ Meanwhile, place vegetables on a large rimmed baking sheet and toss with olive oil and remaining 1 teaspoon Montreal seasoning. Place in the 350° oven and roast for about 45 minutes or until tender. Stir after 25 minutes.

⑤ Reserve 1 chicken for future use. Pour out all but 3 tablespoons pan drippings from roasting pan and whisk in flour. Cook over medium-high heat for 1 minute; whisk in chicken broth and ½ cup water. Simmer 3 minutes until thickened, scraping browned bits from bottom of pan. Strain.

⑥ Serve chicken with gravy, vegetables and Olive Oil Smashed Potatoes (recipe, top left).

PER SERVING 474 calories; 15 g fat (2 g sat); 30 g protein; 57 g carbohydrate; 8 g fiber; 709 mg sodium; 77 mg cholesterol

OLIVE OIL SMASHED POTATOES

Cut 2½ pounds unpeeled potatoes into 1-inch pieces; cook in lightly salted water for 15 minutes, until tender. Drain. Smash with a potato masher and gradually beat in 3 tablespoons olive oil. Season with ½ teaspoon salt and ¼ teaspoon each pepper and nutmeg. Stir in 2 tablespoons chopped parsley.

CHICKEN FRIED RICE

MAKES 4 servings   **PREP** 15 minutes   **COOK** 22 minutes   **LET STAND** 5 minutes

3   eggs, lightly beaten
1   package (5.2 ounces) reduced-sodium chicken-flavor rice mix
3   cups shredded cooked chicken (dark meat from second roasted chicken, page 204)
1   bag (16 ounces) Asian stir-fry frozen vegetables, thawed
1   can (5 ounces) bamboo shoots, drained
2   tablespoons light soy sauce

2   teaspoons sesame oil
3   chopped scallions

①   Coat a large nonstick skillet with cooking spray. Add eggs and cook over medium heat until set, about 2 minutes; remove to a plate. Cut into strips.

②   Wipe out skillet. Prepare rice mix in skillet following package directions, about 20 minutes. During the last 7 minutes of cooking time, add chicken, vegetables, bamboo shoots and soy sauce. Stir in egg and cook, covered, for remaining 7 minutes.

③   Stir in sesame oil and scallions. Let stand, covered, 5 minutes.

PER SERVING 473 calories; 15 g fat (4 g sat); 41 g protein; 43 g carbohydrate; 5 g fiber; 800 mg sodium; 252 mg cholesterol

CREOLE TILAPIA & MASHED SWEET POTATOES

MAKES 4 servings **PREP** 15 minutes **BAKE** at 400° for 45 minutes **COOK** 8 minutes

- 2 **pounds sweet potatoes**
- 2 **tablespoons Brummel & Brown yogurt spread**
- 1½ **teaspoons paprika**
- ½ **teaspoon salt**
- ½ **teaspoon black pepper**
- ½ **teaspoon onion powder**
- ½ **teaspoon garlic powder**
- 4 **tilapia fillets, about 6 ounces each (preferably U.S. farm-raised)**
- 1 **tablespoon vegetable oil**

① Heat oven to 400°. Pierce sweet potatoes with a fork a few times and place directly on oven rack. Bake at 400° for 45 minutes or until tender. Slice potatoes in half and spoon flesh into a bowl, discarding skin. Mash with yogurt spread.

② In a small bowl, combine paprika, salt, pepper, onion powder and garlic powder. Stir ¾ teaspoon of mixture into sweet potatoes. Cover and keep warm.

③ Rub remaining spice mixture on both sides of fish. Heat oil in a large nonstick skillet over medium-high heat. Cook fish for 4 minutes per side or until cooked through.

④ Serve fish and sweet potatoes with Hearty Collard Greens.

PER SERVING 432 calories; 13 g fat (3 g sat); 40 g protein; 42 g carbohydrate; 9 g fiber; 750 mg sodium; 85 mg cholesterol

HEARTY COLLARD GREENS

In a large pot, heat 1 tablespoon vegetable oil over medium heat; add 1 cup sliced onion and 4 cloves smashed garlic. Cook 5 minutes or until browned; add 1 pound rinsed collards, cut into 2-inch pieces, 1 cup chicken broth and ¼ teaspoon salt. Cook, covered, 45 minutes, stirring occasionally, until tender. Season with red pepper flakes, if desired.

CRUNCHY TILAPIA

MAKES 4 servings **PREP** 15 minutes
COOK 35 minutes **BAKE** at 450° for 20 minutes

1 cup wild rice and lentil blend (such as Rice Select)
1 can (14½ ounces) reduced-sodium chicken broth
4 tilapia fillets, about 6 ounces each (preferably U.S. farm-raised)
2 egg whites, lightly beaten
1½ cups Progresso Lemon Pepper panko bread crumbs

① In a medium-size saucepan, combine rice blend and broth. Bring to a boil. Stir and cook, covered, on low for 35 minutes or until tender.

② Meanwhile, heat oven to 450°. Place a wire rack on a baking sheet and coat with nonstick cooking spray.

③ Dip fish in egg whites and then coat with panko. Place on prepared rack. Bake at 450° for 15 to 20 minutes, until fish is crispy and cooked through.

④ Serve fish with rice and Carrot Slaw (recipe, below).

PER SERVING 500 calories; 8 g fat (3 g sat); 46 g protein; 65 g carbohydrate; 5 g fiber; 671 mg sodium; 97 mg cholesterol

CARROT SLAW

In a large bowl, combine 1 pound shredded carrots, ½ cup jumbo raisins, ¼ cup reduced-fat Miracle Whip, ¼ cup reduced-fat sour cream, 3 tablespoons fat-free milk and ⅛ teaspoon salt. Cover and refrigerate for at least 1 hour.

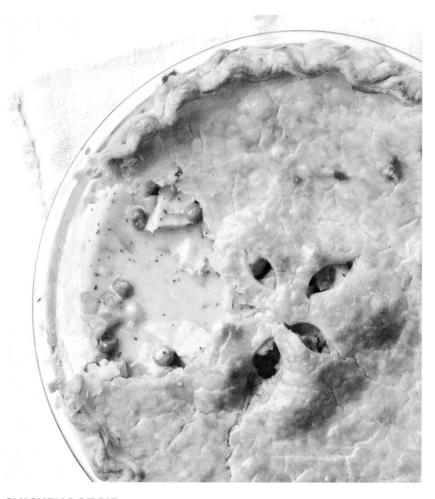

CHICKEN POT PIE

MAKES 2 pies, 4 servings each **PREP** 20 minutes **COOK** 3 minutes **BAKE** at 450° for 15 minutes and 350° for 30 minutes

1 package (14.1 ounces) ready-to-roll piecrust
⅓ cup all-purpose flour
1 can (14½ ounces) low-sodium chicken broth
1½ cups fat-free milk
1 cup diced celery
3 cups cubed cooked chicken (white meat from second roasted chicken, page 204)
1 package (10 ounces) frozen mixed vegetables, thawed
1 tablespoon dried onion flakes
1 tablespoon dried parsley flakes
1 teaspoon poultry seasoning
½ teaspoon garlic salt
½ teaspoon black pepper
1 egg, lightly beaten

① Heat oven to 450°. Coat bottoms of two 9-inch glass pie plates with nonstick cooking spray.

② Combine flour and broth; place in a large pot. Bring to a boil; add milk and celery. Simmer 3 minutes. Stir in chicken, vegetables, onion flakes, parsley, poultry seasoning, garlic salt and pepper.

③ Spoon chicken mixture into pie plates.

④ Unroll piecrusts, placing one on top of each pie plate and crimping edges.

⑤ Before baking, vent and lightly brush with beaten egg. Bake at 450° for 15 minutes; reduce heat to 350° and bake for an additional 25 to 30 minutes or until filling is bubbling and crust golden.

⑥ Allow to cool slightly before serving.

PER SERVING 404 calories; 18 g fat (7 g sat); 20 g protein; 38 g carbohydrate; 1 g fiber; 444 mg sodium; 58 mg cholesterol

ORANGE-DIJON PORK CHOPS

MAKES 4 servings **PREP** 10 minutes
COOK 7 minutes

½ cup orange marmalade
2 tablespoons reduced-sodium soy sauce
2 teaspoons Dijon mustard
1 tablespoon vegetable oil
4 bone-in center-cut pork chops, about 8 ounces each
⅛ teaspoon salt
⅛ teaspoon black pepper
¼ cup chopped toasted hazelnuts
2 cups cooked brown rice
   Tossed salad (optional)

① In a small bowl, stir together marmalade, soy sauce and mustard until combined. Set aside.

② Heat oil in a large nonstick skillet over medium-high heat. Season chops with salt and pepper; sauté 3 minutes, turn and sauté 2 more minutes. Spoon marmalade mixture over the top of the chops. Cook, covered, an additional 2 minutes or until internal temperature registers 145°.

③ Sprinkle hazelnuts over pork chops and serve with cooked brown rice and a tossed salad, if desired.

PER SERVING 491 calories; 18 g fat (4 g sat); 30 g protein; 52 g carbohydrate; 3 g fiber; 529 mg sodium; 73 mg cholesterol

GLAZED PORK CHOPS & GRAPES

MAKES 4 servings **PREP** 15 minutes
MARINATE 1 hour **COOK** 12 minutes

4 bone-in center-cut pork chops, about 8 ounces each
½ cup reduced-fat bottled balsamic vinaigrette dressing
1 tablespoon vegetable oil
⅛ teaspoon salt
⅛ teaspoon black pepper
½ cup reduced-sodium chicken broth
2 cups red seedless grapes, halved
1 package (5.6 ounces) couscous mix with pine nuts, prepared following package directions

① Marinate pork chops in ¼ cup of dressing in a resealable plastic bag in refrigerator for at least 1 hour.

② In a large nonstick skillet, heat oil over medium-high heat. Remove chops from marinade and season with salt and pepper. Cook chops 2 minutes per side and remove to a plate.

③ Add chicken broth, grapes and remaining ¼ cup dressing to skillet. Simmer gently for 3 minutes; add chops and simmer an additional 5 minutes, until internal temperature registers 145°.

④ Serve chops over cooked couscous; spoon grapes and sauce from skillet over chops.

PER SERVING 451 calories; 14 g fat (4 g sat); 32 g protein; 51 g carbohydrate; 3 g fiber; 708 mg sodium; 73 mg cholesterol

PAN-SEARED PORK CHOPS

MAKES 4 servings **PREP** 15 minutes **COOK** 10 minutes

1 tablespoon vegetable oil

4 bone-in center-cut pork chops, about 8 ounces each

⅛ teaspoon salt

⅛ teaspoon black pepper

2 tablespoons cornstarch

1 can (14½ ounces) reduced-sodium chicken broth

2 tablespoons capers

2 tablespoons lemon juice

¼ cup fresh parsley, chopped

½ pound whole wheat spaghetti, cooked following package directions

1 large head broccoli, cut into florets and steamed

① Heat oil in a large nonstick skillet over medium-high heat. Season chops with salt and pepper; sauté 3 minutes per side. Remove to a plate.

② Stir cornstarch into the broth; add to skillet and simmer 1 minute until thickened. Add in capers, lemon juice and pork chops. Cover and simmer 3 minutes or until internal temperature registers 145°. Stir in parsley.

③ Serve chops with cooked spaghetti and steamed broccoli. Spoon sauce over spaghetti.

PER SERVING 474 calories; 14 g fat (4 g sat); 36 g protein; 50 g carbohydrate; 7 g fiber; 499 mg sodium; 73 mg cholesterol

Grain Check

Whole grains make healthy versions of burritos, jambalaya—even rice pudding.

Millet

Wheat Berries

Brown Rice

Barley

Quinoa

BARLEY JAMBALAYA,
PAGE 214

WHEAT BERRY SALAD

Whole grains such as wheat berries and millet give a toothsome chewiness to salads and sandwich fillings.

WHEAT BERRY SALAD

MAKES 4 servings **SOAK** overnight
PREP 15 minutes **COOK** 45 minutes

- 1   cup wheat berries
- 1   Gala apple, cored and finely chopped
- ¾   cup dried cherries, cranberries or golden raisins
- 1   rib celery, finely chopped
- 2   scallions, trimmed and sliced
- ½   cup feta cheese, crumbled
- ⅓   cup cider vinegar
- 1   teaspoon honey mustard
- 1   teaspoon honey
- ⅛   teaspoon each salt and pepper
- 3   tablespoons olive oil

① Place wheat berries in a large bowl and add enough water to cover by 2 inches. Soak at room temperature overnight.

② Drain wheat berries and transfer to a medium-size saucepan. Add 3½ cups water. Bring to a boil, then reduce heat to medium and simmer for 45 minutes. Add a little more water, if needed, while cooking.

③ Drain and cool to room temperature. Meanwhile, in a large bowl, combine apple, dried fruit, celery, scallions and crumbled feta. In a small bowl, whisk together the vinegar, honey mustard, honey and salt and pepper. While whisking, add oil in a thin stream. Add wheat berries and dressing to apple mixture in bowl. Toss gently and serve.

PER SERVING 418 calories; 15 g fat (4 g sat.); 10 g protein; 60 g carbohydrate; 7 g fiber; 805 mg sodium; 17 mg cholesterol

CHICKEN & MILLET BURRITO

MAKES 6 servings **PREP** 15 minutes **COOK** 20 minutes **LET STAND** 5 minutes **BAKE** at 350° for 15 minutes

- ½   cup millet
- 1   cup baby spinach leaves, coarsely chopped
- ½   cup jarred salsa, plus more for serving
- 6   burrito-size tortillas (whole wheat, if desired)
- 1   can (15 ounces) refried beans, stirred to loosen
- 2   cups shredded cooked chicken (such as rotisserie)
- ¾   cup shredded cheddar cheese

① Bring 1¾ cups water to a boil. Add millet and simmer, covered, 20 minutes, stirring twice. Remove from heat and add spinach to pot. Cover and let stand 5 minutes.

② Heat oven to 350°. Stir ½ cup salsa into millet-spinach mixture. Spread centers of tortillas with refried beans, about ¼ cup for each. Top each with ⅓ cup shredded chicken, ⅓ cup millet mixture and 2 tablespoons cheese.

③ Fold sides of 1 tortilla in over filling and then fold bottom edge of tortilla over middle. Continue rolling to enclose filling. Repeat with all tortillas. Place all on a baking sheet and coat with nonstick cooking spray. Bake at 350° for 15 minutes or until heated through.

PER BURRITO 422 calories; 7 g fat (3 g sat.); 17 g protein; 76 g carbohydrate; 5 g fiber; 920 mg sodium; 29 mg cholesterol

BARLEY JAMBALAYA

MAKES 8 servings **PREP** 15 minutes
COOK 41 minutes

2   tablespoons olive oil
1   medium onion, chopped
1   green pepper, cored and chopped
2   ribs celery, trimmed and sliced
1   tablespoon creole seasoning
1   can (14.5 ounces) diced tomatoes
    with jalapeños
1½ cups pearl barley
1   can (14.5 ounces) low-sodium
    chicken broth
1   package (12 ounces) fully cooked
    smoked chicken sausage, sliced
1   pound cleaned shrimp

① Heat oil in a large lidded saucepan
over medium heat.

② Add onion, green pepper and celery
and cook 5 minutes. Stir in creole
seasoning and cook 1 minute.

③ Add tomatoes, barley, broth and
1½ cups water. Bring to a boil and then
reduce heat to medium-low. Simmer,
covered, 30 minutes.

④ Uncover saucepan and stir in sausage
and shrimp. Increase heat to medium-high.
Cover and cook 5 minutes, until shrimp is
opaque. Serve warm.

PER SERVING 315 calories; 11 g fat (3 g sat.);
22 g protein; 35 g carbohydrate; 7 g fiber;
963 mg sodium; 143 mg cholesterol

QUINOA PILAF

MAKES 6 servings **PREP** 5 minutes **COOK** 26 minutes

1   tablespoon unsalted butter
1   large shallot, peeled and chopped
8   baby carrots or 1 large carrot,
    peeled if needed, chopped
1   rib celery, trimmed and chopped
1   cup quinoa
1   can (14.5 ounces) vegetable broth
¼   teaspoon fresh thyme leaves
⅛   teaspoon salt

① Heat butter in a medium saucepan
over medium heat. Add shallot, carrot(s)
and celery and cook 5 minutes, stirring
occasionally.

② Add quinoa to saucepan and cook,
stirring, 1 minute. Pour in broth plus ¼ cup
water. Stir in thyme and salt.

③ Bring to a boil over medium-high heat.
Cover; reduce heat to medium-low and
cook until liquid is absorbed, about
20 minutes. Serve warm.

PER SERVING 140 calories; 4 g fat (1 g sat.);
4 g protein; 23 g carbohydrate; 2 g fiber;
396 mg sodium; 5 mg cholesterol

BROWN RICE PUDDING

MAKES eight ½-cup servings **PREP** 5 minutes **COOK** 55 minutes

¾ cup brown rice
½ cup sugar
2 tablespoons cornstarch
3 cups 2% milk
⅔ cup jumbo raisins
⅛ teaspoon ground cinnamon
⅛ teaspoon salt
   Pinch ground nutmeg

① In a medium saucepan, bring 2 cups water to a boil. Add rice and reduce heat to medium-low. Cover and cook for 45 minutes. Remove to a bowl.

② Whisk sugar and cornstarch into same saucepan. Add milk, stirring until smooth. Stir in cooked rice, raisins, cinnamon, salt and nutmeg.

③ Bring to a boil over medium-high heat. Reduce heat and simmer, stirring occasionally, 10 minutes. Let cool slightly before serving.

PER SERVING 207 calories; 2 g fat (1 g sat.); 5 g protein; 43 g carbohydrate; 2 g fiber; 78 mg sodium; 7 mg cholesterol

Healthy Snacks

Give your kids a pick-me-up with these five after-school specials.

BLACK BEAN
AND CORN
QUESADILLAS

Packed after-school schedules mean that sometimes supper has to wait. These hearty and healthy snacks will hold off hunger until then.

BLACK BEAN AND CORN QUESADILLAS

MAKES 8 servings **PREP** 5 minutes
COOK 3 minutes per batch **KEEP WARM** at 300°

- 1 package (8 ounces) shredded 4-cheese Mexican-blend cheese (2 cups)
- 8 8-inch whole wheat or flour tortillas
- 1½ cups bottled black bean and corn salsa
- 1 medium avocado, seeded, peeled and chopped
  Sour cream, for serving

① Heat oven to 300°. Divide cheese evenly among tortillas, sprinkling cheese over half of each tortilla. Top each tortilla with 1 tablespoon of the salsa. Divide avocado among tortillas. Fold tortillas in half, pressing gently.

② Heat a large skillet over medium-high heat for 2 minutes; reduce heat to medium. Cook 2 quesadillas for 2 to 3 minutes or until lightly browned and cheese is melted, turning once. Remove quesadillas from skillet; place on a baking sheet. Keep warm in 300° oven. Repeat with remaining quesadillas, cooking 2 at a time.

③ Cut quesadillas into wedges. Serve with sour cream and remaining salsa.

PER SERVING 312 calories; 16 g fat (8 g sat.); 12 g protein; 29 g carbohydrate; 6 g fiber; 584 mg sodium; 25 mg cholesterol

TURKEY PINWHEELS

MAKES 30 pieces **PREP** 15 minutes

- 1 package (8 ounces) cream cheese, softened
- ¼ cup jarred chutney
  Black pepper to taste
- 6 burrito-size flour tortillas or 6 pieces lavash bread
- 12 red-leaf lettuce leaves
- 1 pound thin-sliced smoked turkey
- 1 seedless cucumber, thinly sliced
- 3 to 4 plum tomatoes, thinly sliced

① Mix cream cheese and chutney in a food processor until smooth. Add pepper to taste.

② Spread a thin layer of cream cheese to the edge of each tortilla. Top each with 2 lettuce leaves. Divide sliced turkey among the tortillas; layer each tortilla equally with cucumber and tomatoes.

③ Tightly roll up; wrap in damp paper towels and refrigerate several hours. To serve, cut each roll-up into 5 pieces.

PER SERVING 94 calories; 4 g fat (2 g sat.); 5 g protein; 10 g carbohydrate; 1 g fiber; 247 mg sodium; 15 mg cholesterol

NUTTY CEREAL COOKIES

MAKES about 5 dozen cookies
PREP 30 minutes **BAKE** at 325° for 12 minutes
per batch **LET STAND** 2 minutes

1	cup all-purpose flour
½	cup flax seed meal
1	teaspoon baking powder
1	teaspoon baking soda
1	teaspoon ground cinnamon
1	cup butter, softened
1	cup granulated sugar
1	cup packed brown sugar
2	eggs
1	teaspoon vanilla
2	cups wheat cereal flakes
2	cups rolled oats
1½	cups chopped walnuts, toasted
1½	cups dried cranberries, raisins, dried cherries or dried blueberries

① Heat oven to 325°. In a medium bowl, combine flour, flax seed meal, baking powder, baking soda and cinnamon; set aside.

② In a very large bowl, beat butter with an electric mixer on medium to high speed for 30 seconds. Add granulated sugar and brown sugar. Beat until combined, scraping sides of bowl occasionally. Beat in eggs and vanilla until combined. Beat in as much of the flour mixture as you can with the mixer. Stir in any remaining flour mixture. Stir in wheat cereal, oats, walnuts and dried fruit.

③ Drop by well-rounded teaspoons 2 inches apart onto cookie sheets lined with parchment paper. Bake at 325° for 12 to 14 minutes or until golden and set. Let cool on cookie sheets 2 minutes. Transfer to a wire rack and cool.

PER COOKIE 110 calories; 6 g fat (2 g sat.); 2 g protein; 14 g carbohydrate; 1 g fiber; 58 mg sodium; 15 mg cholesterol

CREAMY PEANUT DIP

MAKES 4 servings (2 tablespoons sauce and 2 fruit wedges) **PREP** 10 minutes

2	tablespoons creamy peanut butter
1	tablespoon fat-free milk
⅓	cup frozen fat-free whipped dessert topping, thawed
1	medium red or green pear or apple, cored and cut into 16 slices

① In a small bowl, whisk together peanut butter and milk until combined. Gently fold in whipped dessert topping, leaving some streaks of whipped topping. Serve with fruit wedges.

PER SERVING 82 calories; 4 g fat (1 g sat.); 2 g protein; 10 g carbohydrate; 2 g fiber; 42 mg sodium; 0 mg cholesterol

MANGO-STRAWBERRY SMOOTHIE

MAKES three 8-ounce servings **PREP** 10 minutes

1½ cups orange juice, chilled

½ of a 12.3-ounce package light silken tofu, chilled and drained

1 medium mango, pitted, peeled and chopped (about 1 cup)

1 cup frozen unsweetened whole strawberries

Fresh mango chunks (optional)

Fresh whole strawberries (optional)

Orange sections (optional)

① In a blender, combine orange juice, tofu, cut up mango and strawberries. Cover and blend until smooth. If desired, for garnish, thread additional mango chunks, strawberries and orange sections on small skewers. Add a skewer to each serving. Serve immediately.

PER SERVING 142 calories; 1 g fat (0 g sat.); 5 g protein; 30 g carbohydrate; 2 g fiber; 52 mg sodium; 0 mg cholesterol

Slow Cooker Suppers

Beef brisket 5 ways.

Make the basic recipe and serve it in a vinegary-sweet tomato sauce or try one of the variations—Texas chili, Italian ragu, Chinese-style beef or an old-fashioned beef stew studded with peas and carrots.

SMOKY BEEF BRISKET

MAKES 8 servings **PREP** 10 minutes
SLOW COOK on HIGH for 6 hours or LOW for 9 hours

- 1   beef brisket, about 3 pounds
- 1   tablespoon smoked paprika
- 1   teaspoon salt
- ½   teaspoon black pepper
- 1   large onion, chopped
- 4   cloves garlic, chopped
- 1   can (14½ ounces) stewed tomatoes
- 1   can (14½ ounces) reduced-sodium beef broth
- ¼   cup cider vinegar
- ¼   cup brown sugar
- 8   hamburger rolls
      Pickles and coleslaw (optional)

① Coat slow cooker bowl with nonstick cooking spray.

② Season brisket with paprika, salt and pepper. Place in slow cooker. Scatter onion and garlic over brisket. Combine tomatoes, broth, vinegar and sugar. Pour over brisket.

③ Cover and cook on HIGH for 6 hours or LOW for 9 hours.

④ Remove meat from slow cooker and cool slightly. Slice or shred and stir into sauce.

⑤ Remove brisket with a slotted spoon and serve on rolls, with pickles and coleslaw, if desired.

PER SERVING 405 calories; 10 g fat (4 g sat.); 44 g protein; 36 g carbohydrate; 3 g fiber; 892 mg sodium; 73 mg cholesterol

TEXAS-STYLE CHILI

To make this classic, replace smoked paprika with regular paprika and stewed tomatoes with fire-roasted diced tomatoes. Eliminate sugar and add 3 tablespoons chili powder and 1 chopped green pepper. Serve with sour cream and shredded cheese, if desired.

HOME-STYLE STEW

Brisket is flavorful and inexpensive—but tough unless it's properly prepared. Long, moist cooking in the slow cooker turns it fall-apart tender.

BEEF RAGU

Try this Italian spin: Replace paprika with 1 teaspoon Italian seasoning, stewed tomatoes with 2 cans (14½ ounces) Italian-seasoned diced tomatoes and cider vinegar with balsamic. Eliminate broth and sugar and add 2 sliced Italian frying peppers. Shred meat into sauce and serve with cooked pappardelle pasta; top with grated Parmesan.

FIVE-SPICE BEEF

For an Asian twist, eliminate paprika, salt, pepper and sugar. Add 1 teaspoon Chinese five-spice and 1 tablespoons each light soy sauce and hoisin. Replace cider vinegar with rice vinegar. Add 1 can diced water chestnuts and 2 chopped scallions during last 30 minutes of cook time. Serve over rice with extra chopped scallions.

HOME-STYLE STEW

Replace smoked paprika with regular paprika. Eliminate vinegar and sugar. Add ½ teaspoon each dried oregano, thyme and sage. Stir in 1 package (10 ounces) thawed peas and carrots at end of cook time. Cool slightly; slice meat; stir back into slow cooker. Serve as a stew over mashed potatoes.

BEEF RAGU

FIVE-SPICE BEEF

Eating Well on a Budget
Great-tasting, affordable meals.

The creaminess of the polenta contrasting with the crunch of the kale and the buttery texture of roasted shrimp is a terrific combination—a simple-to-make restaurant-style meal at a very affordable price.

SHRIMP & KALE OVER ROASTED GARLIC POLENTA

MAKES 4 servings **PREP** 10 minutes **BAKE** at 400° for 1 hour, 5 minutes **COOK** 17 minutes

ROASTED GARLIC POLENTA
1   head garlic
1   teaspoon olive oil
1   cup yellow cornmeal
¾   teaspoon salt

KALE
2   teaspoons olive oil
1   bunch kale (about 1¼ pounds), tough stems removed, torn into bite-size pieces
¼   teaspoon salt
2   tablespoons balsamic vinegar

SHRIMP
1   pound cleaned and deveined shrimp
2   tablespoons olive oil
½   teaspoon red pepper flakes

① **Roasted Garlic Polenta.** Heat oven to 400°. Slice off top one-fourth of a head of garlic; drizzle with olive oil and wrap in foil, cut-side up. Bake until tender, 45 to 55 minutes. Cool slightly. Unwrap and squeeze out cloves; set aside. Discard skins.

② In saucepan, bring 4 cups of water to a boil. Slowly whisk in cornmeal. Stir until it begins to thicken, 1 minute. Reduce heat, cover and simmer 5 minutes. Add roasted garlic and salt.

③ **Kale.** Meanwhile, heat olive oil on medium-high in a large skillet. Stir in kale; cook about 2 minutes. Add ½ cup water, reduce heat to medium-low, cover and cook until tender, 15 minutes. Stir in salt and vinegar. Keep warm.

④ **Shrimp.** Toss shrimp with olive oil and red pepper flakes. Spread on a sheet pan; roast at 400° for 8 to 10 minutes, or until pink, turning halfway. Serve with kale and polenta.

PER SERVING 425 calories; 14 g fat (2 g sat.); 31 g protein; 46 g carbohydrate; 6 g fiber; 815 mg sodium; 172 mg cholesterol

CHEAP TRICKS

Shrimp that's been deveined can cost twice as much. Do it yourself by running a paring knife down the back of the shrimp; be careful not to slice too deeply. Remove and discard the dark vein. It isn't necessary to leave on the tail, but shrimp look nicer on the plate intact.

MINI WHOOPIE PIES, PAGE 267

NO-BAKE SPIDERWEB
CHEESECAKES, PAGE 267

OCTOBER

241

249

269

Weeknight Winners

Six simple, scrumptious suppers from our new cookbook, *Healthy Family Dinners*.

**ROASTED VEGETABLE & SHRIMP
SALAD, PAGE 233**

JERK-RUBBED LONDON
BROIL, PAGE 233

SMOKY BEEF & HOMINY STEW

MAKES 6 servings (12 cups) **PREP** 20 minutes **COOK** 1 hour, 35 minutes

6 tablespoons all-purpose flour
1 to 1½ teaspoons chipotle chile powder, depending on taste
¼ teaspoon salt
1 pound beef chuck, cut into 1-inch cubes
1 tablespoon canola oil
1 large onion, peeled, halved and thinly sliced
3 cloves garlic, peeled and coarsely chopped
3 cups reduced-sodium beef broth
1 can (14.5 ounces) no-salt-added stewed tomatoes
¾ teaspoon dried oregano
2 cans (15 ounces each) hominy, drained and rinsed
1 bag (1 pound) peeled baby carrots, sliced
1 large green pepper, cored, seeded and thinly sliced
3 tablespoons chopped cilantro
4½ cups cooked brown rice (1½ cups uncooked)

① In a shallow dish, whisk flour, 1 teaspoon of the chile powder and salt. Coat beef with flour mixture; reserve unused flour.

② Heat oil in a large pot or Dutch oven over medium-high heat. Add beef and cook, turning, until all sides are browned, about 5 minutes. Remove to a plate and reserve.

③ Add onion and garlic to pot and cook over medium heat, stirring to keep garlic from burning, about 4 to 5 minutes. Sprinkle with ¼ cup water, if needed. Scrape up any browned bits from bottom of pot.

④ Stir in beef and any accumulated juices, reserved flour mixture, broth, tomatoes, 1 cup water and dried oregano. Bring to a boil. Reduce heat to medium-low. Gently simmer 1 hour, stirring occasionally.

⑤ Add hominy, carrots, green pepper and remaining ½ teaspoon chile powder, if using. Simmer, covered, for 20 to 25 minutes or until carrots are tender.

⑥ Stir in cilantro and serve with cooked brown rice.

PER SERVING 469 calories; 7 g fat (2 g sat); 26 g protein; 72 g carbohydrate; 44 g fiber; 797 mg sodium; 33 mg cholesterol

GARAM MASALA LENTILS & POTATOES

MAKES 6 servings (12 cups) **PREP** 15 minutes
COOK 40 minutes

1 pound brown lentils, rinsed and picked over
1½ pounds all-purpose potatoes, peeled and cut into ¾-inch pieces
2 onions, peeled and chopped
1 can (14.5 ounces) no-salt-added diced tomatoes
2 teaspoons salt
1½ teaspoons garam masala seasoning
½ teaspoon ground cumin
½ teaspoon black pepper
2 yellow or red peppers, cored, seeded and cut into 1-inch pieces
½ cup cilantro leaves, chopped
¾ cup toasted slivered almonds

① In a large saucepan, combine 4 cups water, lentils, potatoes, onions, diced tomatoes, salt, garam masala, cumin and pepper. Cover and bring to a boil over high heat. Reduce heat to medium-low and simmer, covered, for 35 minutes. Stir occasionally. Add yellow peppers and simmer an additional 5 minutes.

② Stir in cilantro and sprinkle almonds over top.

PER SERVING 475 calories; 10 g fat (1 g sat); 27 g protein; 75 g carbohydrate; 22 g fiber; 786 mg sodium; 0 mg cholesterol

SCALLOP COUSCOUS PAELLA

MAKES 6 servings **PREP** 15 minutes **COOK** 11 minutes **LET STAND** 5 minutes

1   tablespoon olive oil
2   sweet red peppers, cored, seeded and cut into ½-inch pieces
1   large onion, chopped
4   cloves garlic, chopped
1   can (14.5 ounces) reduced-sodium chicken broth
½   teaspoon turmeric
½   teaspoon black pepper
¼   teaspoon salt
¼   teaspoon red pepper flakes
1¼   pounds sea scallops, rinsed
1   package (10 ounces) frozen peas, thawed

2   chipotle chorizo or jalapeño-flavor fully cooked chicken sausages from a 12-ounce package, cut into ½-inch coins
1   can (6½ ounces) chopped clams
3   cups whole wheat couscous
1   lemon, cut into wedges (optional)

① Heat oil in a large nonstick skillet over medium-high heat. Add red peppers, onion and garlic. Cook 6 minutes, stirring. Add broth, 1 cup water, turmeric, black pepper, salt and red pepper flakes. Bring to a simmer and add scallops. Simmer, covered, 3 minutes. Stir in peas, sausage and clams with their liquid. Simmer, covered, 2 minutes.

② Turn off heat; add couscous. Cover and let stand 5 minutes.

③ Fluff couscous with a fork. Serve with lemon wedges, if desired.

PER SERVING 460 calories; 8 g fat (2 g sat); 36 g protein; 64 g carbohydrate; 11 g fiber; 772 g sodium; 57 mg cholesterol

RAINBOW CHARD & WHITE BEAN CASSEROLE

MAKES 8 servings **PREP** 20 minutes **COOK** 15 minutes **BAKE** at 350° for 15 minutes

POLENTA AND ONIONS

- 4 cups fat-free milk
- 1 teaspoon garlic powder
- ¾ teaspoon salt
- ¼ teaspoon black pepper
- 1½ cups instant polenta
- ¾ cup shaved Asiago cheese
- ½ cup basil, shredded
- 1 tablespoon extra-virgin olive oil
- 2 onions, peeled, halved and thinly sliced

CHARD AND BEANS

- 2 tablespoons extra-virgin olive oil
- 2 bunches rainbow chard, trimmed and cut across leaves and 2 inches of stem into 1-inch pieces
- 4 cloves garlic, coarsely chopped
- ½ teaspoon dried Italian seasoning
- ¼ teaspoon salt
- ¼ teaspoon black pepper

- 2 cans (15 ounces each) cannellini beans, drained and rinsed
- ¾ cup shaved Asiago cheese

① **Polenta and Onions.** Lightly coat a 13 x 9 x 2-inch baking dish with nonstick cooking spray. In a large saucepan, combine milk, 1 cup water, garlic powder, salt and pepper. Bring to a simmer over medium-high heat. Gradually whisk in polenta. Cook, whisking continuously, for about 2 minutes, until thick. Add a little hot water if mixture becomes too thick. Stir in Asiago cheese and fresh basil. Spread polenta in prepared baking dish and allow to set at room temperature.

② Heat olive oil in a large nonstick skillet over medium to medium-high heat. Add onions and cook 8 minutes, stirring occasionally, until golden. Remove to a plate and wipe out skillet.

③ **Chard and Beans.** Heat olive oil in same skillet over medium heat. Add chard (in batches) and garlic and cook 5 minutes, stirring occasionally. Season with Italian seasoning, salt and pepper. Stir in beans and heat through.

④ Assemble casserole. Heat oven to 350°. Spoon chard and beans evenly over polenta. Sprinkle ½ cup of the Asiago cheese over chard and beans. Scatter onions and remaining cheese over top. Bake, uncovered, at 350° for 15 minutes.

⑤ Allow to cool slightly before slicing. May also be served at room temperature.

PER SERVING 383 calories; 12 g fat (5 g sat); 16 g protein; 51 g carbohydrate; 6 g fiber; 681 mg sodium; 21 mg cholesterol

ROASTED VEGETABLE & SHRIMP SALAD

MAKES 6 servings **PREP** 20 minutes
REFRIGERATE 15 minutes **ROAST** at 450° for
30 minutes **GRILL/BROIL** 4 minutes

2 large zucchini, cut into ½-inch
   slices on the diagonal
2 summer squash, cut into ½-inch
   slices on the diagonal
6 carrots, peeled and cut into ½-inch
   slices on the diagonal
2 sweet red peppers, cored, seeds
   removed and cut into ½-inch slices
10 tablespoons reduced-fat Italian
   dressing
½ teaspoon black pepper
¼ teaspoon salt
1½ pounds medium-size shrimp, peeled
   and deveined
6 cups watercress
3 ounces reduced-fat feta cheese,
   crumbled

① Heat oven to 450°. Spray two
15 x 11-inch baking pans with nonstick
cooking spray.

② Place zucchini, squash, carrots and
red peppers in a large bowl. Toss with
2 tablespoons of the dressing. Spoon
vegetables evenly into prepared baking
pans and season with pepper and salt.
Roast at 450° for 30 minutes, turning once
after 15 minutes.

③ While vegetables are roasting, place
shrimp in a resealable plastic food-storage
bag with 2 tablespoons of the dressing.
Shake to coat. Marinate in refrigerator
15 minutes.

④ Grill or broil shrimp for 2 minutes per
side. Set aside.

⑤ Evenly distribute watercress among
6 large salad plates and top with roasted
vegetables. Drizzle each with 1 tablespoon
of remaining dressing. Scatter cooked
shrimp and feta over each salad. Serve
immediately.

PER SERVING 214 calories; 5 g fat (2 g sat);
22 g protein; 21 g carbohydrate; 6 g fiber;
762 mg sodium; 144 mg cholesterol

JERK-RUBBED LONDON BROIL

MAKES 6 servings **PREP** 15 minutes
REFRIGERATE 4 hours or overnight
COOK 25 minutes **BROIL** 12 minutes

JERK RUB
1 teaspoon garlic powder
1 teaspoon onion powder
1 teaspoon sugar
1 teaspoon dried thyme
1 teaspoon ground allspice
1 teaspoon black pepper
½ teaspoon cayenne pepper
½ teaspoon salt
¼ teaspoon ground cloves
1½ pounds top round for London broil

POTATO SALAD
1½ pounds fingerling potatoes
1 green pepper, seeded and thinly
   sliced
1 yellow pepper, seeded and thinly
   sliced
½ red onion, thinly sliced
½ cup light mayonnaise
¼ cup reduced-fat sour cream
¼ cup fat-free milk
½ teaspoon salt

① **Jerk Rub.** In a small bowl, mix together
garlic powder, onion powder, sugar, thyme,
allspice, black pepper, cayenne, salt and
cloves. Reserve 1 teaspoon of mixture for
potato salad. Press rub evenly into both
sides of London broil and place in a
resealable plastic food storage bag.
Refrigerate 4 hours or overnight.

② **Potato Salad.** Place potatoes in a
medium-size saucepan and cover with
lightly salted water. Simmer for 20 to
25 minutes until fork-tender. Drain and
cut into bite-size pieces.

③ Place peppers and onion in a large
bowl. Add potatoes. Cover with plastic
wrap and let cool on counter 15 to
30 minutes.

④ Meanwhile, in a small bowl, whisk
together mayonnaise, sour cream, milk,
salt and reserved teaspoon of rub. Fold
into potatoes and peppers. Cover and
refrigerate for at least 4 hours.

⑤ **Steak.** Heat broiler and coat a broiler
pan with nonstick cooking spray. Broil
steak 6 minutes. Turn and broil 5 to
6 minutes more or until internal
temperature registers 135° on an instant-
read thermometer for medium-rare. Let
rest 5 minutes before slicing.

PER SERVING 388 calories; 17 g fat (6 g sat);
29 g protein; 29 g carbohydrate; 3 g fiber;
639 mg sodium; 57 mg cholesterol

Amp up the flavor of lean
meat with a spice rub—this
one does double duty to
perk up potato salad.

Lighten Up!
Scaling back is a cinch with delicious dinner options under 350 calories.

**ZUCCHINI PARMESAN,
PAGE 241**

DILLED CUCUMBER SALAD,
PAGE 241

CHICKEN & FETA ROLL-UPS,
PAGE 241

BEEF & MIXED MUSHROOM SKEWERS

MAKES 4 servings (2 skewers per serving) **PREP** 30 minutes **COOK** 20 minutes **BROIL** 10 minutes

1 pound small red-skinned potatoes, about 1 inch in diameter

2 tablespoons balsamic vinegar

5 tablespoons olive oil

2 tablespoons chopped oregano

2 teaspoons chopped thyme

2 teaspoons McCormick Montreal Steak Seasoning

1½ pounds mixed mushrooms, such as button, shiitake and cremini

1 large rib eye steak, 8 to 10 ounces, cut into 24 cubes

① Place potatoes in a medium-size saucepan and cover with lightly salted water. Bring to a boil; simmer for 15 to 20 minutes, until fork-tender. Drain and set aside.

② In a small bowl, whisk together vinegar, olive oil, oregano, thyme and 1 teaspoon of the steak seasoning. Set aside.

③ Heat broiler. Spray a large broiler pan with nonstick cooking spray.

④ Thread potatoes, mushrooms and beef on 8 metal skewers. Place on prepared broiler pan and brush generously with the oil and vinegar mixture. Season with ½ teaspoon of the steak seasoning. Broil on middle rack for 5 minutes; turn, brush with remaining vinegar and oil mixture and season with remaining ½ teaspoon steak seasoning. Broil for additional 5 minutes or until vegetables are tender.

⑤ Serve with salad, if desired.

PER SERVING 350 calories; 15 g fat (4 g sat); 18 g protein; 38 g carbohydrate; 5 g fiber; 385 mg sodium; 31 mg cholesterol

GRILLED SCALLOPS WITH ALMOND-ARUGULA PESTO

MAKES 4 servings **PREP** 15 minutes
COOK 2 minutes **GRILL** 6 minutes

PESTO

- ⅓ cup sliced almonds
- 2 cups arugula
- 1 cup basil leaves
- 2 cloves garlic
- ½ cup olive oil
- ⅓ cup grated Parmesan cheese
- ½ teaspoon black pepper
- ½ teaspoon salt

SQUASH AND SCALLOPS

- 1 pound zucchini, coarsely shredded
- 1 pound summer squash, coarsely shredded
- 1½ pounds sea scallops
- ¼ teaspoon salt
- ⅛ teaspoon black pepper

① **Pesto.** In bowl of food processor, add almonds, arugula, basil and garlic. Process 1 minute. Gradually add oil and process until fully incorporated. Add cheese, pepper and salt; process until blended. Reserve ½ cup. Cover and refrigerate remainder for another use for up to a week.

② **Squash and Scallops.** Heat a large nonstick skillet over medium-high heat.

Spray lightly with nonstick cooking spray and add zucchini and squash. Stir-fry for 2 minutes. Place in a medium-size bowl.

③ Meanwhile, heat a grill pan over medium-high heat; lightly brush with oil. Season scallops with salt and pepper. Grill scallops for 2 to 3 minutes per side or until cooked through. Remove from grill pan and keep warm.

④ Toss squash with ¼ cup of the reserved pesto. Serve immediately with scallops and remaining ¼ cup of pesto.

PER SERVING 350 calories; 18 g fat (3 g sat); 35 g protein; 13 g carbohydrate; 3 g fiber; 692 mg sodium; 62 mg cholesterol

**FLATBREAD PIZZA WITH
ROASTED CHERRY TOMATOES
& PORTOBELLO MUSHROOMS**

A veggie-packed pizza and breaded and baked pork cutlets make healthy eating taste indulgent.

FLATBREAD PIZZA WITH ROASTED CHERRY TOMATOES & PORTOBELLO MUSHROOMS

MAKES 4 servings **PREP** 15 minutes
BAKE at 400° for 50 minutes

- 1   pound cherry tomatoes
- 6   ounces sliced portobello mushrooms
- 4   large scallions, cut into 1-inch pieces
- 1   tablespoon olive oil
- ¼   teaspoon salt
- ⅛   teaspoon black pepper
- ¼   cup torn basil leaves
- 1   tablespoon chopped oregano
- 1   prepared flatbread or prepared pizza crust
- 3   ounces sliced reduced-fat provolone

① Heat oven to 400°. Coat a large rimmed baking pan with nonstick cooking spray.

② Place tomatoes, mushrooms and scallions in prepared baking pan and toss with olive oil. Season with salt and pepper and bake at 400° for 30 minutes. Remove from oven and toss with basil and oregano.

③ Place flatbread on a baking sheet. Spoon vegetable mixture over top; tear cheese into bite-size pieces and scatter over vegetables. Bake at 400° for 15 to 20 minutes or until flatbread is crispy.

④ Allow to cool slightly before slicing.

PER SERVING 339 calories; 12 g fat (3 g sat); 14 g protein; 44 g carbohydrate; 4 g fiber; 788 mg sodium; 11 mg cholesterol

PORK CUTLETS WITH MUSTARD & DILL

MAKES 4 servings **PREP** 25 minutes **BAKE** at 400° for 15 minutes **COOK** 10 minutes

- 1   tablespoon Dijon mustard
- 1   tablespoon chopped fresh dill
- 2   cloves garlic, chopped
- 1   tablespoon olive oil
- 4   thin boneless pork chops, 4 ounces each
- 3   tablespoons unseasoned bread crumbs
- 1   can (14½ ounces) reduced-sodium chicken broth
- 3   cloves garlic, peeled and smashed
- 1   pound small potatoes about 1 inch in diameter
- 1   pound Japanese eggplant, cut into 2 x 1-inch pieces
- ½   pound baby carrots
- ¼   teaspoon salt
- ¼   teaspoon black pepper

① Heat oven to 400°. Coat a baking dish with nonstick cooking spray.

② In a small bowl, combine mustard, dill, garlic and olive oil. Place pork chops in prepared dish and spread tops with an equal amount of mustard and dill mixture. Sprinkle bread crumbs over each chop. Bake at 400° for 15 minutes or until internal temperature registers 145°. Place under broiler for 1 minute, if desired, until browned.

③ Meanwhile, place broth, garlic and potatoes in a large pot, cover and bring to a boil. Reduce heat to medium and simmer, covered, 10 minutes. Add eggplant, carrots, salt and pepper. Simmer for 8 to 10 minutes, stirring occasionally, or until vegetables are tender. Serve pork with vegetables.

PER SERVING 333 calories; 7 g fat (1 g sat); 30 g protein; 38 g carbohydrate; 8 g fiber; 740 mg sodium; 62 mg cholesterol

ROASTED COD & STONE FRUIT SALSA

MAKES 4 servings **PREP** 20 minutes **BAKE** at 450° for 15 minutes **COOK** 15 minutes

2   nectarines
2   peaches
2   plums
½   cup chopped red onion
1   large jalapeño pepper, seeds removed and finely chopped
2   tablespoons lime juice
¼   cup cilantro, chopped
1   tablespoon olive oil
¾   teaspoon salt
1¼ pounds cod
1   teaspoon McCormick Lemon & Herb seasoning

6   ounces Lundberg roasted brown rice couscous, from a 10-ounce package, about 1 cup

① Heat oven to 450°. Coat glass baking dish with nonstick cooking spray.

② Pit nectarines, peaches and plums; dice and place in medium-size bowl. Add onion, jalapeño, lime juice, cilantro, oil and ¼ teaspoon of the salt. Gently stir; cover and refrigerate until ready to serve.

③ Place cod in prepared baking dish and season with ¾ teaspoon of the lemon and

herb seasoning and ¼ teaspoon of the salt. Bake at 450° for 15 minutes or until cooked through.

④ Meanwhile, cook roasted brown rice couscous following package directions, adding remaining ¼ teaspoon each of the salt and lemon and herb seasoning.

⑤ Serve cod with couscous and fruit salsa.

PER SERVING 350 calories; 6 g fat (1 g sat); 27 g protein; 52 g carbohydrate; 6 g fiber; 590 mg sodium; 54 mg cholesterol

④ Cut chicken into 1-inch slices and serve with cooked orzo and Dilled Cucumber Salad. Garnish with parsley and remaining lemon.

PER SERVING 348 calories; 6 g fat (2 g sat); 34 g protein; 36 g carbohydrate; 2 g fiber; 606 mg sodium; 69 mg cholesterol

DILLED CUCUMBER SALAD

In a medium-size bowl, combine 2 thinly sliced peeled cucumbers, ¼ cup fresh dill sprigs, ¼ cup red wine vinegar, ¼ cup water and 1 teaspoon sugar. Cover and refrigerate for at least one hour or until serving.

CHICKEN & FETA ROLL-UPS

MAKES 4 servings **PREP** 20 minutes
BAKE at 400° for 30 minutes

- 4 thinly sliced boneless, skinless chicken breasts, about 4 ounces each
- 3 ounces fat-free feta cheese
- 2 tablespoons chopped fresh oregano
- 2 tablespoons chopped fresh basil
  1 cup reduced-sodium chicken broth
- ¼ cup white wine
- ¼ teaspoon salt
- ¼ teaspoon black pepper
- 1 lemon, halved and thinly sliced
- 1¼ cups whole wheat orzo, cooked following package directions
- 2 tablespoons chopped parsley

① Heat oven to 400°.

② Spread chicken out on a flat work surface and pound lightly. Place one-fourth of the cheese on short end of each chicken breast. Sprinkle an equal amount of oregano and basil over each breast and roll up tightly.

③ Place chicken, seam sides down, in an 11 x 7 x 2-inch glass baking dish. Pour broth and wine over chicken. Season with salt and pepper; place a slice of lemon on each. Loosely cover with foil and bake at 400° for 30 minutes.

ZUCCHINI PARMESAN

MAKES 8 servings **PREP** 30 minutes
COOK 12 minutes **BAKE** at 375° for 40 minutes

- ½ cup flour
- 3 eggs, lightly beaten
- 1½ cups seasoned bread crumbs
- 3 large zucchini, about 2 pounds, cut lengthwise into ¼-inch-thick slices
- ¼ cup canola oil
- 1 jar (25 ounces) prepared marinara sauce (such as Muir Glen)
- 2 cups shredded reduced-fat mozzarella cheese
- 1 cup basil leaves
- ¼ cup grated Parmesan cheese

① Heat oven to 375°. Coat a 13 x 9 x 2-inch baking dish with nonstick cooking spray.

② Place flour, eggs and bread crumbs in separate shallow bowls. Lightly coat zucchini slices with flour. Dip in egg and coat with bread crumbs. Set aside.

③ Heat 2 tablespoons of the oil in a large nonstick skillet over medium-high heat. Cook zucchini 1½ to 2 minutes per side until golden brown. Cook in three batches, adding more oil as needed.

④ Spoon ½ cup of sauce in bottom of prepared baking dish. Evenly place one-third of the zucchini in dish; top with ¾ cup of sauce and ⅔ cup mozzarella cheese. Repeat layering twice, adding basil between second and third layers.

⑤ Sprinkle Parmesan cheese over top and loosely cover with nonstick foil. Bake at 375° for 30 minutes; remove foil and bake for an additional 10 minutes.

⑥ Cool slightly before slicing. Serve with a green salad, if desired.

PER SERVING 304 calories; 15 g fat (5 g sat); 17 g protein; 27 g carbohydrate; 5 g fiber; 762 mg sodium; 100 mg cholesterol

Even the pickiest eaters in the family will gobble up this cheesy dish that's a healthy cross between lasagna and eggplant Parmesan.

Higher Ground

Ten new and delicious recipes for ground beef that go way beyond burgers.

**KOREAN RICE BOWL,
PAGE 249**

STUFFED ACORN SQUASH,
PAGE 246

JAMAICAN BEEF PATTIES

JAMAICAN BEEF PATTIES

MAKES 6 servings **PREP** 5 minutes
COOK 13 minutes **BAKE** at 400° for 15 minutes

- 2   teaspoons vegetable oil
- 1   medium onion, finely chopped
- 2   teaspoons curry powder
- 1   pound lean ground beef
- ½   teaspoon dried thyme
- ¼   teaspoon ground allspice
- ½   teaspoon salt
- ¼   teaspoon pepper
- ½   cup low-sodium beef broth
- ½   cup dry bread crumbs
- 2   packages (8 ounces each) crescent dough sheets
- 1   large egg, lightly beaten

① Heat oven to 400°. Heat oil in a large nonstick skillet over medium heat. Add onion and cook, stirring occasionally, for 5 minutes. Add curry powder; cook 1 minute. Stir in ground beef, thyme, allspice, salt and pepper. Cook 5 minutes, breaking meat apart with a wooden spoon. Stir in broth and bread crumbs; cook 2 minutes. Remove from heat.

② Unroll crescent dough. Cut each piece crosswise into 3 (8 x 4-inch) pieces, for a total of 6. Roll each piece out slightly. Place ½ cup of filling on one half of one piece. Fold dough over to enclose filling. Press edges to seal, using a fork. Transfer to a large baking sheet and brush with a little of the egg. Repeat with all the pieces of dough.

③ Bake at 400° for 15 minutes or until golden. Serve warm.

PER PATTY 488 calories; 25 g fat (7 g sat); 23 g protein; 38 g carbohydrate; 1 g fiber; 949 mg sodium; 81 mg cholesterol

BEEF TAGINE

MAKES 4 servings **PREP** 10 minutes **COOK** 16 minutes

- 2   teaspoons vegetable oil
- 1   medium onion, peeled, trimmed, halved and sliced
- 2   medium carrots, peeled and cut into coins
- 1   pound ground beef (see note, page 250)
- 2   teaspoons ground cinnamon
- 1   teaspoon each ground ginger and cumin
- ¼   teaspoon each salt and pepper
- 1   cup low-sodium beef broth
- 1   tablespoon all-purpose flour
- 1   can chickpeas (15.5 ounces), drained and rinsed
- ½   cup dried apricots, chopped
- ½   cup golden raisins
- 1   cup couscous
- ¼   cup cilantro, chopped

① Heat oil in a large, lidded nonstick skillet over medium heat. Add onion and carrots and cook, stirring, 5 minutes.

② Crumble in ground beef. Increase heat to medium-high and cook 5 minutes. Stir in cinnamon, ginger, cumin, salt and pepper. Cook 1 minute.

③ In measuring cup, whisk broth and flour until smooth. Add to skillet, along with chickpeas, apricots and raisins. Cover and simmer over medium-low heat for 5 minutes.

④ Meanwhile, prepare couscous according to package directions. Spoon onto platter and add beef mixture. Top with cilantro and serve.

PER SERVING 576 calories; 14 g fat (4 g sat); 35 g protein; 78 g carbohydrate; 10 g fiber; 697 mg sodium; 69 mg cholesterol

STUFFED ACORN SQUASH

MAKES 4 servings **PREP** 15 minutes **COOK** 14 minutes **BAKE** at 350° for 1 hour

2　medium acorn squash, halved and seeds removed
4　slices bacon, diced
1　medium onion, trimmed and diced
1　Granny Smith apple, peeled, cored and diced
1　pound ground beef (see note, page 250)
¼　cup packed dark brown sugar
1　teaspoon pumpkin pie spice
½　teaspoon dried sage
¼　teaspoon salt
¼　teaspoon pepper
2　tablespoons dry bread crumbs

① Heat oven to 350°. Place squash halves cut sides down on a rimmed dish. Add 2 cups water to dish and bake at 350° for 40 minutes.

② Meanwhile, cook bacon in a large nonstick skillet over medium heat for 4 minutes. Add onion and apple. Cook an additional 4 minutes, stirring occasionally.

③ Stir in ground beef. Cook, breaking meat apart with a wooden spoon, 5 minutes. Add brown sugar, pumpkin pie spice, sage, salt and pepper. Cook 1 minute. Remove from heat and stir in bread crumbs.

④ Drain water from baking dish and flip over squash. Spoon meat mixture into squash halves. Return to oven and bake at 350° for 20 minutes. Serve warm.

PER SERVING 398 calories; 12 g fat (5 g sat); 27 g protein; 48 g carbohydrate; 5 g fiber; 399 mg sodium; 76 mg cholesterol

SOUTHWEST SALAD

MAKES 4 servings **PREP** 25 minutes
COOK 8 minutes

BEEF TOPPING
1　pound ground beef (see note, page 250)
2　teaspoons chili powder
1　teaspoon garlic powder
1　can red kidney beans, drained and rinsed

DRESSING AND SALAD
¼　cup chipotle mayo
¼　cup milk
2　tablespoons lime juice
1　teaspoon sugar
1　head green leaf lettuce, trimmed, rinsed and torn into bite-size pieces
½　each sweet red and green pepper, cored and cut into thin strips
1　cup cherry tomatoes, halved
⅓　cup shredded cheddar
1　cup tortilla strips (such as Ortega)

① **Beef Topping.** Cook beef in a large nonstick skillet over medium heat for 5 minutes, breaking apart with a wooden spoon. Drain off excess fat. Add chili and garlic powders and cook 1 minute. Stir in beans; heat through, about 2 minutes.

② **Dressing and Salad.** In a small bowl, whisk mayo, milk, lime juice and sugar. Set aside.

③ In a large bowl, toss lettuce, pepper strips and cherry tomatoes with dressing. Top with beef mixture, shredded cheddar and tortilla strips.

PER SERVING 440 calories; 21 g fat (7 g sat); 32 g protein; 31 g carbohydrate; 9 g fiber; 524 mg sodium; 85 mg cholesterol

SOUTHWEST SALAD

BEEF SOUVLAKI

BEEF SOUVLAKI

MAKES 4 servings **PREP** 20 minutes
BROIL 7 minutes

SANDWICHES

1	pound ground beef (see note, page 250)
1½	teaspoons Greek seasoning or ½ teaspoon each dried oregano, minced onion and marjoram
2	cloves garlic, chopped
2	tablespoons lemon juice
⅛	teaspoon each salt and pepper
4	whole wheat pitas
2	cups leaf lettuce, shredded
½	cup crumbled feta cheese

SAUCE

½	of a cucumber, grated
1	container (7 ounces) Greek 2% yogurt
3	tablespoons chopped mint
2	tablespoons lemon juice
⅛	teaspoon each salt and pepper

① **Sandwiches.** Heat broiler. In a large bowl, combine ground beef, Greek seasoning, garlic, lemon juice, salt and pepper. Divide into 16 pieces, shaping into balls, and thread onto 2 or 3 metal skewers. Coat broiler pan with nonstick cooking spray; place skewers on pan. Set aside.

② **Sauce.** Squeeze excess water from cucumber in paper towels. In a small bowl, stir cucumber, yogurt, mint, lemon juice, salt and pepper. Set aside.

③ Wrap pitas in foil and place in bottom of oven. Broil skewers for 4 minutes. Carefully flip over and broil an additional 3 minutes. Remove warmed pitas from oven. Top each with some sauce, shredded lettuce, 4 pieces meat and 2 tablespoons feta.

PER SANDWICH 446 calories; 16 g fat (8 g sat); 36 g protein; 42 g carbohydrate; 6 g fiber; 783 mg sodium; 88 mg cholesterol

KOREAN RICE BOWL

MAKES 4 servings **PREP** 15 minutes **COOK** 20 minutes **LET STAND** 10 minutes

1½	cups sushi rice
¼	cup rice vinegar
3	tablespoons low-sodium soy sauce
1	tablespoon peeled, minced fresh ginger
2	cloves garlic, minced
1	tablespoon cornstarch
2	teaspoons sesame oil
2	teaspoons chili-garlic paste (such as Sriracha)
1	zucchini, cut into matchsticks
2	cups shiitake mushroom caps (¼ pound), thinly sliced
1	cup shredded carrots
1	pound ground beef (see note, page 250)
4	large eggs (optional)

① Prepare rice: Combine 2 cups water and rice in a medium, lidded saucepan. Bring to a soft boil. Cover and simmer over medium-low heat, 20 minutes. Remove from heat and let stand 10 minutes.

② Meanwhile, in a small bowl, blend rice vinegar, soy sauce, ginger, garlic, cornstarch, sesame oil and chili-garlic sauce. Set aside.

③ Coat a large nonstick skillet with nonstick cooking spray. Add vegetables and 3 tablespoons water. Cook over medium-high heat for 4 minutes or until just softened. Remove to a bowl and keep warm.

④ Crumble beef into same skillet. Cook 5 minutes, breaking apart with a spoon. Add sauce mixture and cook 2 minutes.

⑤ Meanwhile, in a second skillet, fry eggs, if using: Coat skillet with nonstick spray; heat over medium to medium-high heat. Crack 2 eggs into skillet. Cook 1 minute, then flip. Cook 1 more minute. Transfer to a plate. Repeat with remaining 2 eggs. Place a mound of rice into 4 bowls. Top each with ½ cup meat mixture and ⅓ cup vegetables. Finish each with a fried egg, if using.

PER SERVING (with eggs) 532 calories; 17 g fat (5 g sat); 34 g protein; 59 g carbohydrate; 4 g fiber; 461 mg sodium; 282 mg cholesterol

PAD THAI WITH BEEF

MAKES 4 servings **PREP** 15 minutes
SOAK 10 minutes **COOK** 10 minutes

½   of a 14-ounce package rice noodles
1   pound lean ground beef (see note, left)
4   scallions, trimmed and cut into 1-inch pieces
2   cloves garlic, minced
3   tablespoons fresh lime juice, plus lime wedges, for serving
2   tablespoons fish sauce
2   tablespoons rice vinegar
2   teaspoons sugar
2   large eggs
⅔   cup mung bean sprouts
¼   cup chopped peanuts

① Soak rice noodles in a bowl of lukewarm water for 10 minutes.

② Meanwhile, brown beef in a large nonstick skillet over medium-high heat, breaking apart with a spoon, 5 minutes. Pour into colander to drain.

③ Return skillet to medium heat and add scallions and garlic. Sauté 1 minute. Add soaked noodles, lime juice, fish sauce, vinegar and sugar. Cook, stirring, 1 minute.

④ Push noodle mixture to one side of skillet and crack eggs into skillet. Scramble eggs, cooking 1 minute. Fold eggs and reserved ground beef into noodle mixture. Add ⅓ cup of the bean sprouts and cook 1 to 2 minutes, until noodles are tender and beef is heated through. Add ¼ to ½ cup water if mixture is too dry. Transfer to a serving platter and top with remaining ⅓ cup sprouts and peanuts. Serve with lime wedges.

PER SERVING 450 calories; 17 g fat (5 g sat); 31 g protein; 43 g carbohydrate; 2 g fiber; 800 mg sodium; 174 mg cholesterol

PATTY MELT PANINI

MAKES 4 servings **PREP** 15 minutes **COOK** 30 minutes

2   tablespoons unsalted butter
1   large Vidalia or other sweet onion, sliced
1   pound lean ground beef (see note, below)
1   tablespoon Worcestershire sauce
½   teaspoon garlic powder
½   teaspoon dried oregano
¼   teaspoon black pepper
8   slices seedless rye
¼   pound thinly sliced reduced-fat American cheese, about 8 slices
¼   cup light Thousand Island salad dressing

① Heat butter in large nonstick skillet over medium heat. Add onion and cook, stirring occasionally, 20 minutes.

② Meanwhile, combine ground beef, Worcestershire sauce, garlic powder, oregano and pepper in a medium bowl.

Shape into 4 patties, trying to mimic the shape of the rye bread.

③ Heat a panini press or an indoor grill to medium hot. Grill beef patties for 3 to 4 minutes. Remove to a plate.

④ Place 4 slices of rye on a cutting board. Top each with 1 slice of cheese, 1 beef patty, ½ cup onions, 1 cheese slice and another slice of bread. Grill 2 sandwiches for 3 minutes, then repeat with remaining 2 sandwiches. Serve with salad dressing on the side.

PER SERVING 523 calories; 26 g fat (13 g sat); 36 g protein; 39 g carbohydrate; 3 g fiber; 931 mg sodium; 104 mg cholesterol

Note: You can substitute ground turkey, chicken or even meatloaf mix for the ground beef in these recipes.

PAD THAI
WITH BEEF

CHEESEBURGER QUICHE

CHEESEBURGER QUICHE

MAKES 6 servings **PREP** 15 minutes
COOK 13 minutes **BAKE** at 400° for 47 minutes
LET STAND 5 minutes

1   refrigerated piecrust (from a
    15-ounce package)
1   pound lean ground beef (see note,
    page 250)
¼   cup ketchup
1   tablespoon Worcestershire sauce
1   medium red onion, diced
2   packed cups baby spinach
1   cup grape tomatoes, halved
¼   teaspoon each salt and pepper
5   large eggs
¾   cup 2% milk
2   tablespoons Dijon mustard
1   cup shredded sharp cheddar cheese

① Heat oven to 400°. Unroll crust and roll out slightly. Fit into the bottom and up the sides of a 9-inch deep pie dish. Flute edge. Line crust with nonstick foil. Bake at 400° for 12 minutes. Remove foil.

② Meanwhile, cook beef in a large nonstick skillet over medium-high heat, 5 minutes, breaking apart with a spoon. Spoon into a bowl and stir in ketchup and Worcestershire sauce.

③ In same skillet, cook onion for 5 minutes over medium heat. Add spinach and tomatoes; cook 3 minutes. Season with ⅛ teaspoon each of the salt and pepper. Stir in beef.

④ Transfer beef mixture to crust. In medium bowl, whisk together eggs, milk, mustard and remaining ⅛ teaspoon each salt and pepper. Sprinkle cheese over filling. Carefully add egg mixture. Bake at 400° for 35 to 40 minutes. Let stand 5 minutes before slicing.

PER SERVING 458 calories; 26 g fat (12 g sat); 27 g protein; 27 g carbohydrate; 1 g fiber; 740 mg sodium; 248 mg cholesterol

ASIAN LETTUCE WRAPS

MAKES 4 servings **PREP** 20 minutes **COOK** 14 minutes

NOODLES
1   cup frozen shelled edamame
2   packages (3 ounces each) ramen
    noodles, seasoning packets reserved
⅓   cup bottled peanut sauce

LETTUCE WRAPS
1   pound lean ground beef (see note,
    page 250)
1   sweet red pepper, cored and cut
    into matchsticks
4   scallions, trimmed and thinly sliced
3   cloves garlic, sliced
3   tablespoons low-sodium teriyaki
    sauce
2   tablespoons lime juice
2   tablespoons rice vinegar
2   teaspoons sugar
¼   teaspoon red pepper flakes
½   of a cucumber, shaved into strips
    with a vegetable peeler
½   cup fresh mint leaves
2   heads Boston lettuce, trimmed and
    leaves separated

① **Noodles.** Bring a medium saucepan of water to a boil. Add edamame; cook 1 minute. Add ramen and cook 3 minutes. Drain, rinse with cold water and toss with sauce.

② **Lettuce Wraps.** Heat a large nonstick skillet over medium-high heat. Crumble in ground beef and cook, breaking apart with a spoon, 4 minutes. Add sweet pepper, scallions and garlic. Cook 4 minutes.

③ Meanwhile, whisk together teriyaki sauce, lime juice, vinegar, sugar and red pepper flakes. Add to skillet and cook 2 minutes. Let everyone assemble their own wraps: Layer cucumber, meat mixture and mint into lettuce leaves. Roll up and eat with noodles on the side.

PER SERVING 415 calories; 12 g fat (4 g sat); 33 g protein; 44 g carbohydrate; 8 g fiber; 537 mg sodium; 69 mg cholesterol

Slow Cooker Suppers

Chicken 5 ways.

**ITALIAN-STYLE
CHICKEN STEW**

With a few simple twists and tweaks, a basic chicken stew goes Italian, Indian, Mexican, French and Hawaiian.

ITALIAN-STYLE CHICKEN STEW

MAKES 6 servings **PREP** 15 minutes
SLOW COOK on HIGH for 6 hours or LOW for 8 hours

2	pounds skinless chicken thighs
1½	teaspoons dried Italian seasoning
¾	teaspoon garlic salt
¼	teaspoon black pepper
1	large onion, thinly sliced
1	can (14½ ounces) diced tomatoes
1	cup reduced-sodium chicken broth
2	tablespoons quick-cooking tapioca
1	can (15 ounces) cannellini beans, drained and rinsed
½	cup sliced black pitted olives
½	cup fresh basil, torn into small pieces
6	biscuits (such as Pillsbury Grands) baked following package directions

① Coat slow cooker with nonstick cooking spray.

② Place chicken thighs in slow cooker and season with Italian seasoning, garlic salt and black pepper. Scatter onion over chicken. Stir together tomatoes, broth and tapioca; pour over onion.

③ Cover and cook on HIGH for 5½ hours or LOW for 7½ hours. Stir in beans and olives and cook an additional 30 minutes. Remove bones.

④ To serve, stir in basil and spoon over biscuits.

PER SERVING 485 cal; 19 g fat (5 g sat); 44 g protein; 33 g carbohydrate; 5 g fiber; 941 mg sodium; 136 mg cholesterol

SPICY CURRY

Replace Italian seasoning and black pepper with 3 teaspoons curry powder and ¼ teaspoon cayenne pepper. Add 1 pound peeled potatoes, cut into ½-inch pieces, when adding onion. Substitute 1 can (15 ounces) chickpeas for cannellini beans. Eliminate olives and basil. Serve with cooked basmati rice and naan, if desired. Make it kid-friendly by reducing cayenne to a pinch.

CHICKEN MOLE
SOFT TACOS

Chicken thighs can hold up to slow cooking without getting dry, as chicken breast often does—and because they're skinless, they're healthful too.

CHICKEN MOLE SOFT TACOS

Replace Italian seasoning and black pepper with 2 tablespoons unsweetened cocoa powder, 1 teaspoon chipotle chile powder and ½ teaspoon each ground cumin and cinnamon. Substitute 1 can (15 ounces) pinto beans for cannellini beans. Eliminate olives and basil. Serve with 6 flour tortillas and Spanish rice, if desired.

EASIEST-EVER COQ AU VIN

Replace Italian seasoning with herbes de Provence and sliced onion with 2 cups thawed frozen pearl onions. Eliminate diced tomatoes, tapioca, beans, olives and basil. Substitute with 1 cup dry red wine and 2 tablespoons tomato paste. Add 2 cups quartered white mushrooms and 2 large chopped carrots when adding onions. Serve over cooked egg noodles.

SWEET & TANGY CHICKEN

Substitute Italian seasoning, garlic salt and black pepper with ½ teaspoon ground ginger and ¼ teaspoon allspice. Add 1 large chopped green pepper, 1 can (8 ounces) drained pineapple chunks, ¼ cup rice vinegar, 2 tablespoons reduced-sodium soy sauce and 1 tablespoon sugar when adding onion. Eliminate olives and basil. Serve over cooked angel hair pasta.

EASIEST-EVER COQ AU VIN

SWEET & TANGY CHICKEN

Ripe for the Picking

Apple desserts that are tasty to the core.

**MAPLE, APPLE & CHEDDAR PIE,
PAGE 261**

APPLE-RAISIN BARS

MAKES 12 bars **PREP** 15 minutes **BAKE** at 350° for 35 minutes

2   cups all-purpose flour
2   teaspoons baking powder
1½   teaspoons cinnamon
½   teaspoon salt
2   cups packed light brown sugar
2   eggs
½   cup (1 stick) butter or margarine, softened
1   teaspoon vanilla extract
1½   cups diced Golden Delicious apple
¾   cup raisins

① Heat oven to 350°. Liberally coat a 13 x 9 x 2-inch baking pan with nonstick cooking spray; set aside.

② In a medium-size bowl, whisk together flour, baking powder, cinnamon and salt; set aside.

③ In a large bowl, with an electric mixer on medium speed, blend together sugar, eggs, butter and vanilla for 3 minutes or until smooth.

④ Reduce speed to low and gradually add flour mixture; mix for 2 minutes or until just incorporated. Stir in diced apples and raisins and spread into prepared pan.

⑤ Bake at 350° for 35 minutes or until toothpick inserted in center comes out clean. Cool completely before cutting into bars and serving.

PER BAR 338 calories; 9 g fat (5 g sat); 4 g protein; 63 g carbohydrate; 2 g fiber; 194 mg sodium; 55 mg cholesterol

UPSIDE-DOWN APPLE CAKE

MAKES 9 servings **PREP** 25 minutes **BAKE** at 350° for 50 minutes **COOL** 25 minutes

⅓ cup cold unsalted butter, cut up

6 very small red cooking apples
(1¼ to 1½ pounds total)

⅓ cup packed brown sugar

1⅓ cups all-purpose flour

⅔ cup granulated sugar

2 teaspoons baking powder

1 teaspoon ground ginger

1 teaspoon ground cinnamon

⅔ cup milk

¼ cup butter, softened

1 egg

1 teaspoon vanilla extract
Ice cream (optional)

① Heat oven to 350°. Place cold butter in a 9 x 9 x 2-inch baking pan. Place in 350° oven for about 5 minutes or until butter is melted. Meanwhile, halve apples; remove stems. With a melon baller or small spoon, scoop out apple cores. Sprinkle brown sugar over melted butter; stir. Arrange 9 apple halves in butter mixture, cut sides down. Return to oven and bake 10 to 15 minutes or until bubbly.

② Meanwhile, peel and coarsely shred remaining 3 apple halves; set aside. In a medium bowl, combine flour, granulated sugar, baking powder and spices. Add shredded apple, milk, ¼ cup softened butter, egg and vanilla. Beat with an electric mixer on low speed until combined. Beat on medium speed for 1 minute. Spoon batter gently over apples in pan, spreading evenly (some apple may still be exposed and some butter mixture may come to the surface).

③ Bake at 350° for about 35 minutes or until a wooden toothpick inserted near center comes out clean. Cool cake in pan on a wire rack for 5 minutes. Loosen edges and invert onto serving platter. Spoon any topping left in pan over the top of cake. Cool about 20 minutes; serve warm with ice cream.

PER SERVING 313 calories; 13 g fat (8 g sat); 3 g protein; 47 g carbohydrate; 2 g fiber; 157 mg sodium; 56 mg cholesterol

APPLE BISTRO TART

MAKES 8 servings **PREP** 30 minutes
BAKE at 425° for 20 minutes

½ of a recipe Pastry for a Double-Crust Pie (right) or ½ of a 15-ounce package refrigerated piecrust (1 crust)

3 tablespoons granulated sugar

1 teaspoon ground cinnamon

1 teaspoon finely shredded lemon peel

2 medium tart green apples, peeled, cored and cut into ½-inch-thick slices

½ cup chopped pecans

½ cup prepared caramel apple dip
Confectioners' sugar

① Heat oven to 425°. Prepare and roll out pastry into a 12-inch circle or let the piecrust stand according to package directions. In a bowl, combine granulated sugar, cinnamon and lemon peel. Add apple slices and pecans; toss to coat.

② Place piecrust on a large baking sheet. Spread caramel apple dip over crust to within 2 inches of edges. Place apple mixture over caramel. Fold edges of crust 2 inches up and over apple mixture, folding edges as necessary.

③ Bake at 425° for 20 minutes or until crust is golden brown and apples are just tender. Remove tart from oven. Sprinkle with confectioners' sugar before serving. Serve warm.

PER SERVING 273 calories; 12 g fat (3 g sat); 2 g protein; 41 g carbohydrate; 2 g fiber; 174 mg sodium; 5 mg cholesterol

MAPLE, APPLE & CHEDDAR PIE

MAKES 8 servings **PREP** 30 minutes
BAKE at 375° for 1 hour **COOL** 1 hour

Pastry for a Double-Crust Pie (recipe follows)

½ cup sugar

2 tablespoons all-purpose flour

½ teaspoon ground cinnamon

¼ teaspoon salt

5 cups thinly sliced peeled apples, such as Jonathan or McIntosh (5 medium)

1½ cups shredded white cheddar cheese (6 ounces)

6 tablespoons maple syrup

1 tablespoon whipping cream

¼ cup toasted chopped pecans (optional)

① Heat oven to 375°. Prepare Pastry for a Double-Crust Pie. On a lightly floured surface, slightly flatten one portion of dough. Roll dough from center to edge into a 12-inch circle. Wrap pastry circle around rolling pin; unroll into a 9-inch pie pan or plate. Ease pastry into pie pan without stretching it; set aside.

② For the filling, in a bowl, stir together sugar, flour, cinnamon and salt. Add apples; toss to coat. Add cheese and 4 tablespoons of the maple syrup; stir to combine. Transfer to pastry-lined pie pan. Drizzle with cream.

③ Trim pastry even with edge of pie pan. Roll the remaining dough into a 12-inch circle. Cut slits in pastry. Place pastry circle on filling; trim pastry to ½ inch beyond edge of pie pan. Fold top pastry edge under bottom pastry. Crimp edge as desired. Cover edge of pie with foil to prevent overbrowning.

④ Bake at 375° for 40 minutes. Remove foil. Bake about 20 minutes more or until apples are tender and pastry is golden brown. Transfer to a wire rack. Brush with the 2 tablespoons maple syrup. If desired, sprinkle with pecans. Cool for 1 hour. Serve slightly warm.

Pastry for a Double-Crust Pie In a large bowl, stir 2½ cups all-purpose flour and 1 teaspoon salt. Using a pastry blender, cut in ½ cup shortening and ¼ cup butter, cut up, until pieces are pea size. Sprinkle 1 tablespoon ice water over flour mixture; toss gently with a fork. Push moistened dough to side of bowl. Repeat with additional ice water, 1 tablespoon at a time (½ to ⅔ cup total), until all the flour mixture is moistened. Gather mixture into a ball. Divide in half; shape into balls.

PER SERVING 504 calories; 23 g fat (8 g sat); 10 g protein; 65 g carbohydrate; 3 g fiber; 498 mg sodium; 25 mg cholesterol

The sweetness of maple syrup and the tangy taste of cheddar cheese infuse this apple pie with fabulous flavor. An aged white cheddar will have the most piquancy.

Eating Well on a Budget

Great-tasting, affordable meals.

Make this meal vegetarian by substituting vegetable broth for the chicken. Just don't use water—broth or stock adds another layer of flavor and is worth the extra 2 bucks.

THAI BUTTERNUT SQUASH SOUP

MAKES 6 servings **PREP** 20 minutes **COOK** 27 minutes

- 1   tablespoon olive oil
- 1   medium sweet onion, chopped
- 1   piece of ginger (1 to 2 inches), peeled and grated
- 2   cloves garlic, minced
- 1   tablespoon red curry paste
- 1   can (14.5 ounces) coconut milk
- 4   cups low-sodium chicken broth
- 3   pounds butternut squash, peeled, seeded and cut into 1-inch cubes
- 1   lime, juiced (about 3 tablespoons)
- 1   teaspoon salt
- ⅓   cup unsalted peanuts, chopped
- ⅓   cup sliced scallions
- 3   whole wheat pitas or flatbreads, halved

① Heat oil in a large, lidded pot over medium heat. Add onion and sauté until softened, about 5 minutes. Add ginger and garlic and cook 1 minute. Stir in curry paste and cook another minute.

② Pour in coconut milk and chicken broth; stir well to break up the curry paste. Add squash, bring to a boil and then lower to a simmer. Cover partially and cook 15 to 20 minutes or until squash is tender.

③ Puree soup with an immersion blender until smooth. Stir in lime juice and salt. Serve with peanuts, scallions and bread.

PER SERVING 420 calories; 22 g fat (14 g sat); 10 g protein; 54 g carbohydrate; 9 g fiber; 947 mg sodium; 0 mg cholesterol

CHEAP TRICKS

Homemade soup is generally inexpensive—even more so if you make your own stock. It's also a good way to use leftovers, such as roasted chicken, salad extras or precooked pasta and rice. Dive into your pantry: Chances are there's a can of beans, tomatoes or something else that you could incorporate with terrific results. Don't be afraid to experiment—flavors often meld as ingredients simmer.

All Hallow's Eats

Sweet treats for a spirited celebration.

CEMETERY CAKE, PAGE 267

NO-BAKE SPIDERWEB
CHEESECAKES, PAGE 267

MINI WHOOPIE PIES

MINI WHOOPIE PIES

MAKES 24 sandwich cookies **PREP** 15 minutes
BAKE at 375° for 13 minutes per batch

COOKIES

2   cups all-purpose flour
½   cup unsweetened cocoa powder
1   teaspoon baking powder
¼   teaspoon salt
½   cup (1 stick) unsalted butter, softened
¾   cup granulated sugar
2   large eggs
¾   cup milk
½   teaspoon vanilla extract

FILLING

2   cups confectioners' sugar
¼   cup (½ stick) unsalted butter, softened
½   teaspoon vanilla extract
    Orange food coloring

① Heat oven to 375°. Line 2 or 3 large baking sheets with nonstick foil.

② **Cookies.** In medium-size bowl, whisk flour, cocoa, baking powder and salt. In a large bowl, beat together the butter and sugar until smooth. Beat in eggs, one at a time, beating well after each, until mixture is a pale yellow color. On low speed, beat in half of the flour mixture. Beat in milk and vanilla and then remaining flour mixture.

③ Drop dough by level tablespoonfuls onto prepared sheets, spacing at least 1½ inches apart, spreading slightly to a 2-inch round (about 48 rounds total). Bake at 375° for 12 to 13 minutes or until tops are dry. Cool completely.

④ Meanwhile, prepare **Filling.** In a medium-size bowl, beat together confectioners' sugar, butter, 2 tablespoons water, vanilla and food coloring until smooth and desired color. Once cookies are cool, sandwich together (flat side to flat side) with a scant tablespoon of filling. Store in airtight container.

PER COOKIE 166 calories; 7 g fat (4 g sat); 2 g protein; 26 g carbohydrate; 1 g fiber; 51 mg sodium; 33 mg cholesterol

NO-BAKE SPIDERWEB CHEESECAKES

MAKES 16 servings **PREP** 10 minutes
MICROWAVE 30 seconds plus 1 minute
REFRIGERATE at least 4 hours

CRUST AND CHEESECAKES

16 Nilla Wafers
1   envelope (0.25 ounce) unflavored gelatin
2   packages (8 ounces each) cream cheese, softened
⅔   cup sugar
1   teaspoon vanilla extract
2   cups whipped topping or whipped cream
½   cup mini semisweet chocolate chips

SPIDERWEBS

½   cup mini semisweet chocolate chips
1   teaspoon vegetable oil

① **Crust and cheesecakes.** Line 16 indents of 2 cupcake pans with foil liners. Coat liners with nonstick spray. Place 1 Nilla wafer in bottom of each prepared cup.

② Sprinkle gelatin over ¼ cup water in a glass measuring cup and let soak for 1 minute. Microwave 30 seconds to dissolve.

③ Beat cream cheese and sugar in a large bowl until smooth. Beat in vanilla, then fold in whipped topping or whipped cream. While beating over medium speed, add dissolved gelatin in thin stream. Fold in mini chips. Spoon ¼ cup batter into each prepared cup, smoothing tops.

④ **Spiderwebs.** Combine chips and oil in a microwave-safe bowl. Microwave 1 minute and stir until smooth. Transfer to a resealable plastic bag or piping bag. Snip off a small corner and pipe in a spiral pattern on each cake. Starting at the center, run a thin knife through each spiral to resemble a spider-web. Refrigerate at least 4 hours.

PER SERVING 247 calories; 16 g fat (10 g sat); 4 g protein; 23 g carbohydrate; 1 g fiber; 97 mg sodium; 32 mg cholesterol

CEMETERY CAKE

MAKES 12 servings **PREP** 15 minutes
BAKE at 350° for 33 minutes
MICROWAVE 1 minute **DECORATE** 30 minutes

CAKE

1   box (18.25 ounces) chocolate cake mix
3   large eggs
½   cup vegetable oil

FROSTING AND DECORATIONS

6   ounces semisweet chocolate, chopped
¾   cup heavy cream
4   rectangular cookies (such as Social Tea Biscuits)
4   Pepperidge Farm Milano cookies (trim ¼ inch from one end of each cookie)
5   pumpkin candies (such as Jelly Belly)

① Heat oven to 350°. Coat a 13 x 9 x 2-inch baking pan with nonstick cooking or baking spray.

② **Cake.** Prepare cake mix with 1¼ cups water, the eggs and oil as per package directions. Transfer batter to prepared pan. Bake at 350° for 31 to 33 minutes, or as per package directions. Cool completely.

③ Trim crowned area from top of cake; reserve scraps for later use. Invert cake onto serving platter.

④ **Frosting and decorations.** Place chopped chocolate in a medium bowl. Heat cream in a glass measuring cup in microwave for 1 minute. Pour over chocolate and let stand 5 minutes. Whisk until smooth. Let cool an additional 5 minutes.

⑤ Transfer ½ cup of the chocolate mixture to a pastry bag or resealable plastic bag. Pour and spread remaining frosting over cake, allowing some to drip down cake sides. Snip a small corner from plastic bag. Pipe decorations onto cookies. Let dry. With a knife, cut slits into cake and insert decorated cookies into slits. Crumble reserved cake scraps and place on cake in front of cookies. Scatter pumpkin candies over cake.

PER SERVING 434 calories; 26 g fat (8 g sat); 4 g protein; 49 g carbohydrate; 3 g fiber; 429 mg sodium; 75 mg cholesterol

Cake Pops

This is no trick: These treats are simple to make—and so impressive!

Use this master recipe to create Jack-O'-Lanterns, Black Cats, Yummy Mummies and Pirate Pops. A mini ice cream scoop is the secret to uniform-size balls.

BASIC CAKE BALLS

MAKES 48 cake balls **PREP** 1 hour

1 box (18.25 ounces) cake mix
   13 x 9 x 2-inch cake pan
   Large mixing bowl
1 container (16 ounces) prepared frosting
   Large metal spoon
   Wax paper
2 baking sheets
   Plastic wrap

① Bake cake as directed on the box, using a 13 x 9 x 2-inch cake pan. Let cool completely.

② Once cake is cooled, get organized and set aside at least 1 hour to crumble, roll and dip 4 dozen cake balls.

③ Crumble cooled cake into a large mixing bowl: Cut a baked 13 x 9-inch cake into 4 equal sections. Remove a section from the pan, break it in half and rub the 2 pieces together over a large bowl, making sure to crumble any large pieces that fall off. You can also use a fork to break apart any larger pieces. Repeat with each section until entire cake is crumbled into a fine texture. (If large pieces are mixed in, the cake balls may turn out lumpy and bumpy.) You should not see any large pieces of cake.

④ Add three-fourths of the container of frosting. Mix it into the crumbled cake, using the back of a large metal spoon, until thoroughly combined. (You will not need the remaining frosting; if you use the entire container, the cake balls will be too moist.)

⑤ The mixture should be moist enough to roll into 1½-inch balls and still hold a round shape. After rolling the cake balls by hand, place them on a wax paper–covered baking sheet.

⑥ Cover with plastic wrap and chill for several hours in the refrigerator, or place in the freezer for about 15 minutes. You want the balls to be firm but not frozen.

⑦ If you're making a project that calls for uncoated cake balls, stop here and proceed to decorate the cake balls, following the project instructions.

JACK-O'-LANTERNS

48 uncoated Basic Cake Balls (see recipe, page 269)
48 ounces (3 pounds) orange candy coating (see below for info on where to buy supplies)
Deep, microwave-safe bowl
48 paper lollipop sticks
48 green Tic Tac mints or similarly shaped candy
Styrofoam block
Black edible-ink pen

① Have the cake balls chilled and in the refrigerator.

② Melt the orange candy coating in a microwave-safe plastic bowl, following instructions on the package. The coating should be about 3 inches deep for easier dipping. (It's best to work with about 16 ounces of coating at a time.)

③ When you are ready to dip, remove a few cake balls from the refrigerator at a time.

④ One at a time, dip about ½ inch of the tip of a lollipop stick into the melted candy coating, and insert the stick straight into a cake ball, pushing it no more than halfway through. Dip the cake pop into the melted coating, and tap off any excess coating: Hold the pop over the bowl in one hand, and tap your wrist gently with your other hand. (If you use the hand holding the cake pop to shake off excess coating, the force of the movement will be too strong and could cause the cake ball to loosen or fly off the lollipop stick.) The excess coating will fall off, but you will need to rotate the lollipop stick so the coating doesn't build up on one side, making it too heavy on that side. If too much coating starts to build up at the base of the stick, simply use your finger to wipe it off, spinning the lollipop stick at the same time. This can happen if the coating is too thin or too hot. It's not as hard as it sounds; it just takes a little practice.

⑤ Immediately insert a Tic Tac into the very top of the pumpkin pop. Hold in place until set, and let dry completely in the Styrofoam block. Repeat with the remaining pumpkins until they all have stems.

⑥ Add jack-o'-lantern faces with a black edible-ink pen, and let dry completely in the Styrofoam block.

BLACK CATS

48 uncoated Basic Cake Balls (see recipe, page 269)
48 ounces (3 pounds) white candy coating
Deep, microwave-safe plastic bowl
Black candy coloring (not food coloring)
48 paper lollipop sticks
Styrofoam block
96 chocolate chips
48 red rainbow chip sprinkles
96 yellow or white oval sprinkles
Black edible-ink pen
Kitchen knife
Toothpicks

① Have the cake balls chilled and in the refrigerator.

② Melt the white candy coating in a microwave-safe plastic bowl, following instructions on the package. The coating should be about 3 inches deep for easier dipping. (It's best to work with about 16 ounces of coating at a time.)

③ Tint the coating with black candy coloring. Keep adding color, stirring, until the coating is dark enough.

④ When you are ready to dip, remove a few cake balls at a time from the refrigerator, keeping the rest chilled.

⑤ One at a time, dip about ½ inch of the tip of a lollipop stick into the melted candy coating, and insert the stick straight into a cake ball, pushing it no more than halfway through. Dip the cake pop into the melted coating, and tap off any excess coating: Hold the pop over the bowl in one hand, and tap your wrist gently with your other hand. (If you use the hand holding the cake pop to shake off excess coating, the force of

the movement will be too strong and could cause the cake ball to loosen or fly off the lollipop stick.) The excess coating will fall off, but you will need to rotate the lollipop stick so the coating doesn't build up on one side, making it too heavy on that side. If too much coating starts to build up at the base of the stick, simply use your finger to wipe it off, spinning the lollipop stick at the same time. This can happen if the coating is too thin or too hot. It's not as hard as it sounds; it just takes a little practice.

⑥ Let dry in a Styrofoam block.

⑦ Now work on the ears. Submerge the chocolate chips in the black candy coating, one at a time. Remove (you can use the end of a kitchen knife to lift them out) and attach two to the top of each pop for the ears. Hold them in place until the candy coating sets like glue, and place in the Styrofoam block to dry. Repeat until all the cake pops have black ears.

⑧ When the pops are dry, use a toothpick to dot a small amount of melted candy coating in position for the nose, and attach a red rainbow chip sprinkle. Use the same technique to attach two oval sprinkles for the eyes.

⑨ Using a black edible-ink pen, draw a straight line down the center of each oval sprinkle to finish the eyes. Let dry completely.

Tip You can also use round confetti sprinkles for the eyes.

Supplies: Look for candy coating disks, candy coloring, candy writers, paper pop sticks, edible-ink pens and Styrofoam blocks in the baking section of your local crafts supply store or at michaels.com

YUMMY MUMMIES

48 uncoated Basic Cake Balls (see recipe, page 269), formed into oval shapes
64 ounces (4 pounds) white candy coating
    Deep, microwave-safe plastic bowl
48 paper lollipop sticks
    Styrofoam block
    Large squeeze bottle
    Green candy writer

① Have the oval cake balls chilled and in the refrigerator.

② Melt the white candy coating in a microwave-safe plastic bowl, following the instructions on the package. The coating should be about 3 inches deep for easier dipping. (It's best to work with about 16 ounces of coating at a time.)

③ When you are ready to dip, remove a few cake balls from the refrigerator at a time, keeping the rest chilled.

④ One at a time, dip about ½ inch of the tip of a lollipop stick into the melted candy coating, and insert the stick straight into the bottom of an oval-shape cake ball, pushing it no more than halfway through. Dip the cake pop into the melted coating, and tap off any excess coating: Hold the pop over the bowl in one hand, and tap your wrist gently with your other hand. (If you use the hand holding the cake pop to shake off excess coating, the force of the movement will be too strong and could cause the cake ball to loosen or fly off the lollipop stick. Tapping the wrist holding the cake pop absorbs some of the impact.) The excess coating will fall off, but you will need to rotate the lollipop stick so the coating doesn't build up on one side, making it too heavy on that side. If too much coating starts to build up at the base of the stick,

simply use your finger to wipe it off, spinning the lollipop stick at the same time. This can happen if the coating is too thin or too hot. It's not as hard as it sounds; it just takes a little practice.

⑤ Let dry completely in a Styrofoam block.

⑥ Pour the remaining melted white coating into a plastic squeeze bottle and pipe lines across the front of each mummy face. Let dry completely in the Styrofoam block.

⑦ Use a green candy writer to pipe two dots of dark green candy coating on the front of each cake pop for the eyes.

⑧ Let dry completely.

Tip If you don't need or want to make 48 cake balls, simply divide the cake in half for 24 cake balls or in quarters for 12 and freeze the remaining cake for later use. Remember to reduce the amount of frosting proportionally.

PIRATE POPS

48 uncoated Basic Cake Balls (see recipe, page 269)
48 ounces (3 pounds) white candy coating
2   deep, microwave-safe plastic bowls
48 paper lollipop sticks
    Styrofoam block
24 ounces red candy coating
    About 15 white confetti sprinkles per cake pop
    Toothpicks
48 red M&M's Minis
48 red jumbo heart sprinkles
    Black edible-ink pen

① Have the cake balls chilled and in the refrigerator.

② Melt the white candy coating in a microwave-safe plastic bowl, following the instructions on the package. The coating should be about 3 inches deep for easier dipping. (It's best to work with about 16 ounces of coating at a time.)

③ When you are ready to dip, remove a few cake balls at a time from the refrigerator, keeping the rest chilled.

④ One at a time, dip about ½ inch of the tip of a lollipop stick into the melted candy coating, and insert the stick straight into a

cake ball, pushing it no more than halfway through. Dip the cake pop into the melted coating, and tap off any excess coating: Hold the pop over the bowl in one hand, and tap your wrist gently with your other hand. (If you use the hand holding the cake pop to shake off excess coating, the force of the movement will be too strong and could cause the cake ball to loosen or fly off the lollipop stick. Tapping the wrist holding the cake pop absorbs some of the impact.) The excess coating will fall off, but you will need to rotate the lollipop stick so the coating doesn't build up on one side, making it too heavy on that side. If too much coating starts to build up at the base of the stick, simply use your finger to wipe it off, spinning the lollipop stick at the same time. This can happen if the coating is too thin or too hot. It's not as hard as it sounds; it just takes a little practice.

⑤ Let dry completely in a Styrofoam block.

⑥ For the bandannas, melt the red candy coating in the second microwave-safe bowl and dip the top half of each cake pop into it, holding the pop at a diagonal. Before the red candy coating sets, place miniature white confetti sprinkles randomly on top. (You can also attach the sprinkles after the coating dries by using a toothpick to dot on coating and then attaching the sprinkles.)

⑦ Let dry completely in the Styrofoam block.

⑧ To finish the bandannas, use a toothpick to dab a little red candy coating onto one side of the pop, and attach a red M&M's Mini. Hold it in place until the candy coating sets like glue. Use the same technique to attach a jumbo heart sprinkle, with the pointed end toward the cake pop, for the final touch, and let dry.

⑨ For the faces, use a black edible-ink pen to draw on eyes, patches and mouths. Let dry completely.

GOLDEN ROASTED
TURKEY WITH PAN GRAVY,
PAGE 279

NOVEMBER

278

300

305

Fall Harvest

Freshly picked fall veggies make dinner flavorful and oh-so-satisfying.

**ROTINI & CAULIFLOWER,
PAGE 279**

ROOT VEGETABLE GRATIN,
PAGE 279

NOT-STUFFED CABBAGE

NOT-STUFFED CABBAGE

MAKES 4 servings **PREP** 15 minutes
BAKE at 350° for 15 minutes **COOK** 23 minutes

MEATBALLS

- 1   pound lean ground beef
- 2   tablespoons dried onion flakes
- 1   tablespoon dried parsley
- ½   teaspoon ground allspice
- ¼   teaspoon salt
- ⅛   teaspoon black pepper

SAUCE

- 1   pound cabbage, thinly sliced
- ½   teaspoon salt
- ¼   teaspoon black pepper
- 1   can (28 ounces) crushed tomatoes
- ⅓   cup raisins
- 2   tablespoons sugar
- 1   tablespoon onion flakes
- 3   cups cooked brown rice

① Heat oven to 350°. Coat a rimmed baking pan with nonstick cooking spray.

② **Meatballs.** In a bowl, combine ground beef, onion flakes, parsley, allspice, salt and pepper. Form into 28 meatballs, using about 1 tablespoon of mixture each. Place on prepared baking pan and bake at 350° for 15 minutes.

③ **Sauce.** Coat a large nonstick skillet with cooking spray. Add cabbage, salt and pepper; simmer over medium-high heat 8 minutes, stirring often. Stir in tomatoes, raisins, sugar and onion flakes. Bring to boil; reduce heat and simmer, covered, 10 minutes. Add meatballs and simmer 5 minutes.

④ Serve meatballs and sauce over rice.

PER SERVING 497 calories; 7 g fat (3 g sat); 33 g protein; 72 g carbohydrate; 8 g fiber; 793 mg sodium; 70 mg cholesterol

CHICKEN TERIYAKI & FALL VEGETABLES

MAKES 4 servings **PREP** 20 minutes **BAKE** at 450° for 15 minutes **COOK** 16 minutes

- 1   pound sweet potatoes, peeled and cut into 1-inch cubes
- ½   cup reduced-sodium chicken broth
- ¼   cup reduced-sodium teriyaki sauce
- 3   tablespoons rice vinegar
- 1   teaspoon sugar
- 1   teaspoon Asian chili paste
- 2   tablespoons vegetable oil
- 1   pound boneless, skinless chicken thighs, cut into 1-inch pieces
- 1   medium head broccoli, cut into florets
- 2   sweet red peppers, seeds removed, cut into ¼-inch slices
- 4   ounces soba noodles, cooked following package directions

① Heat oven to 450°. Coat rimmed baking pan with nonstick cooking spray.

② Spread out sweet potatoes on pan and bake at 450° for 15 minutes or until tender.

③ Combine broth, teriyaki sauce, vinegar, sugar and chili paste. Set aside.

④ In a large nonstick skillet, heat 1 tablespoon of the oil over medium-high heat. Add chicken; cook 4 minutes per side. Remove chicken to a plate. Add remaining tablespoon oil to skillet and add broccoli and red peppers. Stir-fry 6 to 8 minutes, until broccoli is tender.

⑤ Add sweet potatoes, reserved chicken, teriyaki mixture and soba noodles. Stir to coat all ingredients. Heat through.

PER SERVING 476 calories; 18 g fat (3 g sat); 33 g protein; 51 g carbohydrate; 6 g fiber; 762 mg sodium; 110 mg cholesterol

DEEP-DISH VEGGIE & PEPPERONI PIZZA

MAKES 6 servings **PREP** 15 minutes **BAKE** at 450° for 1 hour

½ pound eggplant cut into quarters lengthwise and then into ¼-inch slices

½ pound brown mushrooms, such as cremini, stems removed, quartered

1 small red onion, peeled and quartered

1 pound frozen pizza dough, thawed

1½ cups shredded reduced-fat Italian-blend cheese

¼ teaspoon salt

¼ teaspoon dried oregano

⅛ teaspoon black pepper

1 can (8 ounces) no-salt-added tomato sauce

2 ounces turkey pepperoni, coarsely chopped

3 plum tomatoes, sliced

① Heat oven to 450°. Coat a rimmed baking sheet and a 10-inch deep-dish pizza pan with nonstick cooking spray.

② Place eggplant, mushrooms and onion on prepared baking sheet. Bake at 450° for 30 minutes, turning once.

③ On a lightly floured surface, roll out dough to form a circle slightly larger than the pizza pan. Place dough in prepared pan, pressing excess dough to the sides.

④ Layer half the cheese and all the vegetables onto dough. Season with salt, oregano and pepper. Spoon sauce over vegetables and scatter pepperoni over sauce.

⑤ Bake at 450° for 15 minutes. Scatter remaining cheese and fan tomato slices over top. Bake for an additional 15 minutes. Remove from oven and cool slightly.

⑥ Use a sharp knife to cut into 6 slices; remove with pie server or spatula.

PER SERVING 335 calories; 12 g fat (5 g sat); 17 g protein; 43 g carbohydrate; 4 g fiber; 753 mg sodium; 27 mg cholesterol

ROTINI & CAULIFLOWER

MAKES 6 servings **PREP** 10 minutes
COOK 14 minutes

1   head cauliflower, cut into florets
1   package (14½ ounces) Barilla Plus rotini pasta
¼   cup olive oil
4   cloves garlic, peeled and sliced
1   teaspoon salt
¼   teaspoon red pepper flakes
1   can (15 ounces) cannellini beans, drained and rinsed
½   cup packed basil leaves
½   cup grated Parmesan cheese
¼   cup plain bread crumbs

① Bring a large pot of lightly salted water to boil. Add cauliflower and cook 4 minutes. Remove with a slotted spoon to a bowl. Add pasta to pot and cook 10 minutes. Drain, reserving 1 cup cooking liquid. Place pasta back into pot.

② Meanwhile, heat oil in a large nonstick skillet over medium-high heat. Add garlic and cook 1 minute. Stir in cooked cauliflower, ½ teaspoon of the salt, red pepper flakes and beans. Heat through.

③ Spoon cauliflower and bean mixture into pasta. Add some of the reserved cooking liquid and season with remaining salt.

④ To serve, tear in basil and stir in cheese. Top with bread crumbs.

PER SERVING 479 calories; 14 g fat (2 g sat); 21 g protein; 69 g carbohydrate; 12 g fiber; 662 mg sodium; 6 mg cholesterol

ROOT VEGETABLE GRATIN

MAKES 6 servings **PREP** 25 minutes **BAKE** at 375° for 1 hour, 30 minutes **BROIL** 45 seconds
LET STAND 10 minutes

1   teaspoon salt
½   teaspoon black pepper
½   teaspoon dried thyme
¼   teaspoon nutmeg
⅛   teaspoon cayenne pepper
1½ cups shredded Swiss cheese
3   cloves garlic, finely chopped
1   medium-size butternut squash, peeled, seeds removed and sliced into ⅛-inch-thick half moons
½   pound parsnips, peeled and sliced into ⅛-inch-thick half moons
½   pound carrots, peeled and thinly sliced
1   can (15 ounces) chickpeas, drained and rinsed
1   large onion, thinly sliced
1   pound white turnip, peeled and sliced into ⅛-inch-thick half-moons
¼   cup reduced-fat chicken broth
1   cup panko bread crumbs
2   tablespoons olive oil

① Heat oven to 375°. Coat a 13 x 9 x 2-inch baking dish with nonstick cooking spray.

② In a small bowl, combine salt, pepper, thyme, nutmeg and cayenne. In another bowl, combine cheese and garlic.

③ Layer half the butternut squash in dish; sprinkle with ½ teaspoon seasoning and ½ cup cheese mixture. Layer parsnips and carrots over squash and season with ½ teaspoon seasoning and ½ cup cheese, followed by chickpeas, onion and ½ teaspoon seasoning and ½ cup cheese. Top with turnip, remaining butternut squash and seasoning. Pour chicken broth over top. Cover with foil and bake at 375° for 60 minutes. Remove foil and bake for an additional 30 minutes.

④ Combine panko and olive oil. Sprinkle evenly over vegetables. Broil 45 seconds or until lightly browned. Let stand 10 minutes.

PER SERVING 328 calories; 13 g fat (5 g sat); 15 g protein; 41 g carbohydrate; 8 g fiber; 687 mg sodium; 25 mg cholesterol

Dinner Tonight = Lunch Tomorrow

Two-for-one recipes that yield deliciously different meals.

**TURKEY SCALOPPINE WITH
TARRAGON-MUSHROOM SAUCE**

TURKEY SCALOPPINE WITH TARRAGON-MUSHROOM SAUCE

MAKES 6 servings   **PREP** 15 minutes
COOK 30 minutes

BARLEY

2   cups reduced-sodium chicken broth
2   cups barley
¼   teaspoon salt
¼   teaspoon black pepper
1   cup frozen peas, thawed

TURKEY

2   pounds turkey breast for scaloppine
¾   teaspoon salt
¾   teaspoon black pepper
¼   cup all-purpose flour
2   tablespoons olive oil
½   pound cremini mushrooms, quartered
1   large shallot, finely chopped
2   cloves garlic, finely chopped
2   cups reduced-sodium chicken broth
⅛   teaspoon ground nutmeg
1   tablespoon chopped tarragon

① **Barley.** In a medium-size saucepan, bring broth and 2 cups water to a boil. Stir in barley, salt and pepper. Simmer, covered, on low for 20 minutes. Stir in peas during last 2 minutes.

② **Turkey.** Season turkey with ½ teaspoon each of the salt and black pepper. Coat with flour. Reserve unused flour.

③ Heat 1 tablespoon olive oil over medium-high heat. Cook turkey 2 minutes per side. Reserve.

④ Add the remaining tablespoon of oil, the mushrooms, shallot and garlic. Cook 4 minutes, stirring occasionally. Sprinkle 2 tablespoons of the remaining flour over mushrooms and cook, stirring, 1 minute. Gradually stir in broth and the remaining ¼ teaspoon each salt and pepper. Add nutmeg and cook 1 minute until thickened; add reserved turkey and tarragon and heat through. For each lunch, reserve one serving of turkey before adding to sauce.

PER SERVING 493 calories; 6 g fat (1 g sat); 48 g protein; 62 g carbohydrate; 12 g fiber; 584 mg sodium; 60 mg cholesterol

LUNCH SPIN-OFF:
GREEK SALAD WITH TURKEY

In a salad container, combine 2 cups shredded lettuce and 1 tablespoon each sliced black olives and crumbled feta. Add 5 ounces sliced turkey scaloppine. Just before eating, toss with 2 tablespoons reduced-fat red wine dressing.

LEMON PEPPER CHICKEN AND BALSAMIC SUCCOTASH

MAKES 6 servings   **PREP** 15 minutes   **BAKE** at 425° for 75 minutes   **COOK** 10 minutes

CHICKEN AND CARROTS

1   chicken, 2½ to 3 pounds, cut into 8 pieces, skin removed
2   tablespoons lemon pepper seasoning
1   lemon, sliced
1   pound peeled baby carrots
1   tablespoon olive oil
¼   teaspoon salt
¼   teaspoon black pepper

SUCCOTASH

1   tablespoon olive oil
1   onion, chopped
2   cloves garlic, chopped
1   sweet red pepper, cored, seeded and cut into ½-inch pieces
2   cups frozen corn, thawed
2   cups frozen lima beans, thawed
3   tablespoons balsamic vinegar
1   teaspoon lemon pepper seasoning
1   tablespoon chopped parsley

① **Chicken and Carrots.** Heat oven to 425°. Place chicken in a roasting pan; season with lemon pepper and place a lemon slice on top of each piece. Bake at 425° for 40 to 45 minutes or until internal temperature reaches 170°. Place carrots on a rimmed baking dish and toss with olive oil, salt and pepper. Bake for 30 minutes, turning once, or until tender.

② **Succotash.** Heat oil in a large nonstick skillet over medium heat. Add onion, garlic and red pepper. Cook 5 minutes, stirring occasionally. Stir in corn, lima beans, balsamic vinegar and lemon pepper. Cook for an additional 5 minutes. Stir in parsley.

③ Serve chicken with carrots and succotash. For each lunch, reserve one serving of chicken.

PER SERVING 480 calories; 16 g fat (4 g sat); 49 g protein; 34 g carbohydrate; 7 g fiber; 596 mg sodium; 135 mg cholesterol

LUNCH SPIN-OFF:
CHEF'S SALAD WRAP

Combine 1½ cups shredded leafy lettuce, 4 ounces shredded lemon pepper chicken, ¼ cup reduced-fat cheese, and sliced onion, if desired. Spread one side of a burrito-size flour tortilla with 2 tablespoons reduced-fat Thousand Island dressing; spoon salad down center and roll up tightly. Wrap in plastic.

ITALIAN STEAK & "FRIES"

MAKES 6 servings   **PREP** 10 minutes   **MARINATE** 4 hours or overnight   **BAKE** at 450° for 35 minutes   **BROIL OR GRILL** 6 minutes   **LET STAND** 5 minutes

STEAK

2	tablespoons canola oil
2	tablespoons red wine vinegar
2	tablespoons honey Dijon mustard
2	tablespoons ketchup
2	cloves garlic, chopped
1	teaspoon Italian seasoning
1¾	pounds lean flank steak
½	teaspoon salt
¼	teaspoon black pepper

FRIES

2	pounds potatoes cut into 1-inch wedges
2	tablespoons canola oil
1	teaspoon Italian seasoning
½	teaspoon salt
¼	teaspoon black pepper
1	tablespoon basil-infused olive oil

① **Steak.** Whisk canola oil, vinegar, mustard, ketchup, garlic and Italian seasoning in a medium bowl. Combine with steak in a large resealable plastic bag; shake to coat steak. Refrigerate for 4 hours or overnight.

② **Fries.** Heat oven to 450°. Toss potato wedges with the canola oil, Italian seasoning, salt and pepper. Place on a baking sheet; bake at 450° for 30 to 35 minutes, turning once.

③ Heat broiler or stovetop grill pan; lightly grease. Season steak with salt and pepper. Broil or grill steak 3 minutes per side or until internal temperature reaches 125° for medium-rare. Let stand 5 minutes; thinly slice against grain. For each lunch, set aside one serving of steak.

④ Toss fries with basil oil and serve with steak.

PER SERVING 405 calories; 18 g fat (4 g sat); 32 g protein; 30 g carbohydrate; 2 g fiber; 577 mg sodium; 56 mg cholesterol

LUNCH SPIN-OFF:
PHILLY CHEESESTEAK

Spread 1 teaspoon yellow mustard on each side of a small sub roll and fill with 4 ounces sliced steak. Top with 3 tablespoons reduced-fat cheddar and pickled jalapeños, if desired. Wrap tightly in microwave-safe plastic wrap. Microwave for 1 minute.

PORK TENDERLOIN WITH CREAMY APPLE CIDER SAUCE

MAKES 6 servings **PREP** 15 minutes
COOK 13 minutes **BAKE** at 425° for 12 minutes
LET STAND 5 minutes

- 2 small pork tenderloins, about ¾ pound each
- 1 teaspoon salt
- ½ teaspoon black pepper
- 1 tablespoon olive oil
- 2 tablespoons all-purpose flour
- 2 cups reduced-sodium chicken broth
- 1 cup apple cider
- ½ cup heavy cream
- 2 tablespoons Dijon mustard
- 2 tablespoons chopped parsley
- 1½ cups couscous

① Heat oven to 425°.

② Season pork with ½ teaspoon of the salt and ¼ teaspoon of the pepper. Heat oil in a large ovenproof nonstick skillet over medium-high heat. Brown pork on all sides, about 7 minutes total. Place skillet in oven and bake for 12 minutes or until internal temperature registers 145°. Carefully remove from oven (handle will be hot), place meat on a serving platter and cover.

③ Stir flour into 1 cup of the broth until flour is dissolved; add to skillet. Add apple cider and simmer 5 minutes, stirring occasionally. Stir in cream and ¼ teaspoon each of the salt and pepper; add mustard and simmer 1 minute. Add parsley.

④ Meanwhile, place the remaining 1 cup broth, ½ cup water and the remaining ¼ teaspoon salt in a medium-size saucepan and bring to a simmer. Turn off heat and stir in couscous. Cover; let stand 5 minutes. Fluff with a fork.

⑤ Thinly slice pork and serve with sauce and couscous. For each lunch, reserve one serving of pork.

PER SERVING 464 calories; 14 g fat (6 g sat); 32 g protein; 51 g carbohydrate; 3 g fiber; 577 mg sodium; 101 mg cholesterol

LUNCH SPIN-OFF:
VIETNAMESE SANDWICH

Combine ¼ cup shredded carrot, 2 tablespoons each sliced onion and rice vinegar and 1 teaspoon each sugar and soy sauce. Spread 2 teaspoons reduced-fat mayonnaise on a split crusty roll. Arrange 4 ounces thinly sliced pork tenderloin over bottom half and spoon carrot mixture over top. Sprinkle with fresh cilantro leaves; wrap tightly in plastic.

CHIPOTLE SALMON & SOUTHWESTERN RICE

MAKES 6 servings **PREP** 15 minutes
BAKE at 450° for 20 minutes **COOK** 18 minutes

SALMON AND PEPPERS

- 1½ pounds salmon fillet
- ½ teaspoon salt
- 1 canned chipotle in adobo sauce, seeds removed, chopped and mixed with 1 tablespoon each adobo sauce and water
- 3 red sweet peppers, cored, seeded and sliced into ½-inch-thick slices
- 1 tablespoon olive oil
- ¼ teaspoon black pepper

RICE PILAF

- 1 tablespoon olive oil
- ½ medium onion, chopped
- 1 cup rice
- 2 cups vegetable broth
- ¼ teaspoon salt
- 1 package (10 ounces) frozen corn, thawed
- 2 tablespoons chopped cilantro

① **Salmon and Peppers.** Heat oven to 450°. Coat baking dish with nonstick cooking spray.

② Place salmon in prepared dish, skin-side down. Season with ¼ teaspoon of the salt and the chipotle mixture. Bake at 450° until fish is cooked through, about 20 minutes.

③ Meanwhile, place peppers on a baking sheet and toss with olive oil, the remaining ¼ teaspoon salt and the pepper. Roast for 20 minutes.

④ **Rice Pilaf.** Heat oil in a medium-size saucepan; add onion and cook over medium-high heat for 3 minutes, stirring occasionally. Stir in rice, broth and salt. Bring to boil; simmer, covered, for 10 minutes. Add corn and simmer for 5 additional minutes. Stir in cilantro.

⑤ Serve salmon with rice and roasted peppers. For each lunch, reserve one serving salmon and rice.

PER SERVING 440 calories; 18 g fat (3 g sat); 27 g protein; 43 g carbohydrate; 3 g fiber; 689 mg sodium; 67 mg cholesterol

LUNCH SPIN-OFF:
TACOS

In each of two hard taco shells, place 2 ounces flaked chipotle salmon and ¼ cup rice pilaf. Spoon on 1 tablespoon salsa and wrap each in microwave-safe plastic wrap. Microwave, wrapped, 1 minute before serving.

Season's Eatings

Ten delicious new takes on Thanksgiving classics.

GOLDEN ROASTED TURKEY WITH PAN GRAVY, PAGE 293

GREEN BEANS & BRUSSELS
SPROUTS, PAGE 293

MEDITERRANEAN PUFFS

Two classic appetizers get a modern makeover. Pastry palmiers are filled with a savory stuffing, and the much-beloved cheese ball is made with goat cheese.

MEDITERRANEAN PUFFS

MAKES 40 puffs **PREP** 10 minutes
REFRIGERATE 30 minutes **BAKE** at 400° for 15 minutes

- 1   bag (3 ounces) sun-dried tomatoes
- 1   box (10 ounces) frozen artichokes, thawed
- 1   cup pitted kalamata olives
- 1   cup shredded Parmesan
- ¼   teaspoon black pepper
- 2   sheets (17.3-ounce box) frozen puff pastry, thawed

① Heat oven to 400°. In a small bowl, cover tomatoes with warm water and rehydrate for 10 minutes; remove and pat dry with paper towels. Add to food processor with artichokes, olives, Parmesan and pepper. Pulse to combine until finely chopped.

② Gently roll out one pastry sheet on parchment paper. Spread half the mixture evenly on top. Fold the short ends of the dough over about 2 inches; fold each side again until the edges almost touch. Fold one more time, bringing one side on top of the other, and press lightly with the rolling pin. Repeat with second sheet. Cover both with plastic wrap and refrigerate 30 minutes.

③ Beat 1 egg with 1 tablespoon water in a small bowl. Remove pastries from refrigerator and brush with the egg mixture. Slice each roll into 20 pieces and divide among four parchment paper-lined baking sheets, leaving a 2-inch space between each puff. Bake at 400° for 12 to 15 minutes or until golden.

PER PUFF 68 calories; 4 g fat (1 g sat); 2 g protein; 5 g carbohydrate; 1 g fiber; 168 mg sodium; 2 mg cholesterol

GOAT CHEESE–PISTACHIO BALL

MAKES 2 cups **PREP** 10 minutes **REFRIGERATE** 1 hour

- 4   ounces plain goat cheese, room temperature
- 8   ounces cream cheese, room temperature
- 2   tablespoons honey
- 2   teaspoons chopped fresh thyme
- ½   cup pistachios, chopped

① Blend cheeses, honey and thyme in a stand mixer. Mix on medium speed until combined.

② Transfer mixture to work surface with a spatula. Form into a ball and roll in the pistachios. Refrigerate 1 hour. When firm, reshape, if needed. Plate and serve with crackers or a baguette, sliced and toasted.

PER TABLESPOON 50 calories; 4 g fat (2 g sat); 2 g protein; 2 g carbohydrate; 0 g fiber; 34 mg sodium; 9 mg cholesterol

Sure, everybody loves the turkey, but some say the best part of the meal is the stuffing. This version is studded with sweet sausage and tart Granny Smith apple.

APPLE-SAUSAGE STUFFING

MAKES 8 servings **PREP** 15 minutes
BAKE at 350° for 35 minutes **COOK** 13 minutes

10	slices whole wheat bread, cut into ½-inch cubes
½	pound sweet sausage, casing removed
1	Granny Smith apple, peeled, cored and diced
1	medium onion, chopped
2	medium carrots, peeled and diced
2	ribs celery, trimmed and diced
2	cloves garlic, minced
1	cup low-sodium chicken broth
1	teaspoon each chopped sage, thyme and rosemary
¼	teaspoon each salt and pepper

① Heat oven to 350°. Spread bread cubes onto two large baking sheets. Toast at 350° for 15 minutes and transfer to a large bowl.

② Heat a large nonstick skillet over medium-high heat. Crumble sausage into pan, breaking apart with a spoon. Cook until no longer pink, 5 minutes.

③ Stir in apple, onion, carrots, celery and garlic. Reduce heat to medium and cook 5 minutes, stirring occasionally. Add broth, sage, thyme, rosemary, salt and pepper. Heat through, about 3 minutes. Pour over bread cubes and stir gently to moisten.

④ Loosely pack stuffing into turkey before roasting, placing excess in a small covered dish. Or spoon all stuffing into a 13 x 9 x 2-inch baking dish. Cover with foil and bake 20 minutes, uncovering for last 5 minutes to crisp top, if desired.

PER SERVING 160 calories; 4 g fat (1 g sat); 10 g protein; 22 g carbohydrate; 4 g fiber; 432 mg sodium; 9 mg cholesterol

WILD MUSHROOM SOUP

MAKES 8 servings plus 2 cups for Green Beans & Brussels Sprouts, page 293
PREP 15 minutes **COOK** 28 minutes

3	tablespoons butter
2	large shallots, diced
1½	pounds mixed wild mushrooms (such as cremini, shiitake and oyster), sliced
1	tablespoon chopped fresh thyme
3	tablespoons all-purpose flour
7	cups low-sodium chicken broth
¾	cup heavy cream
¼	cup dry sherry
2	teaspoons salt
⅛	teaspoon black pepper
¼	cup parsley, chopped

① Melt butter in a large lidded pot over medium heat. Add shallots and sauté for 2 to 3 minutes, or until softened. Add mushrooms and thyme and cook 8 minutes. Sprinkle in flour and cook 2 minutes, stirring constantly. Add stock and bring to a boil. Turn down to a simmer, cover and cook 15 minutes.

② Stir in heavy cream, sherry, salt and pepper, and bring to a simmer (do not boil). Mix in parsley and serve, reserving 2 cups for the Green Beans & Brussels Sprouts (page 293).

PER SERVING 145 calories; 10 g fat (6 g sat); 4 g protein; 11 g carbohydrate; 1 g fiber; 494 mg sodium; 32 mg cholesterol

CRANBERRY-APPLE MOLD,
PAGE 293

CLASSIC MASHED POTATOES WITH GREEN ONION & CHIVES

MAKES 12 servings **PREP** 10 minutes
COOK 12 minutes

4   pounds russet potatoes, peeled and cut into 2-inch chunks
1   teaspoon salt plus more for boiling the potatoes
1¼   cups 2% milk
¼   cup (½ stick) unsalted butter, cut up
3   green onions, trimmed and sliced
1   tablespoon snipped fresh chives

① Place potato chunks in a large pot. Add enough cool water to cover by an inch. Bring to a boil over high heat. Add a little salt to the water. Cook 12 minutes, until potatoes are tender, and drain.

② Transfer potatoes to a serving dish and mash with a potato masher. Add milk, butter and 1 teaspoon salt; mash until smooth. Stir in green onions and chives and serve.

PER SERVING 166 calories; 4 g fat (3 g sat); 4 g protein; 29 g carbohydrate; 2 g fiber; 212 mg sodium; 12 mg cholesterol

ROASTED CAULIFLOWER WITH CHEESE SAUCE

MAKES 8 servings **PREP** 10 minutes **BAKE** at 450° for 30 minutes **COOK** 6 minutes

CAULIFLOWER
1   medium head cauliflower (about 2¼ pounds), trimmed and cut into florets
6   cloves garlic, halved lengthwise
3   tablespoons olive oil
½   teaspoon salt
¼   teaspoon black pepper

CHEESE SAUCE
2   tablespoons unsalted butter
2   tablespoons all-purpose flour
1½   cups 2% milk
¼   teaspoon salt
     Pinch ground nutmeg
6   ounces cheddar cheese, shredded (1½ cups)

① **Cauliflower.** Heat oven to 450°. Combine cauliflower and garlic in a large bowl. Drizzle with olive oil. While stirring, season with salt and pepper. Transfer to a large rimmed baking sheet. Roast at 450° for 30 minutes, stirring once.

② Meanwhile, prepare **Cheese Sauce.** Melt butter over medium heat in a medium-size saucepan (not nonstick). Whisk in flour and cook 2 minutes. Gradually add milk, whisking constantly until smooth. Bring to a simmer, whisking occasionally. Season with salt and nutmeg. Simmer 4 minutes and remove from heat. Stir in shredded cheese, whisking until smooth.

③ Transfer roasted cauliflower and garlic to a platter. Top with cheese sauce and serve immediately.

PER SERVING 207 calories; 16 g fat (8 g sat); 9 g protein; 9 g carbohydrate; 2 g fiber; 391 mg sodium; 33 mg cholesterol

CHECKERBOARD SWEET POTATOES

MAKES 8 servings **PREP** 10 minutes **COOK** 15 minutes **BAKE** at 350° for 30 minutes

3   pounds sweet potatoes, peeled and cut into 2-inch chunks

½   cup whole milk

4   tablespoons butter

1   can (8 ounces) crushed pineapple, drained

¼   cup brown sugar, packed

1   teaspoon pumpkin pie spice

¼   teaspoon salt

20 marshmallows

40 pecan halves

① Cover sweet potatoes with cold water and bring to a boil. Reduce to a simmer and cook 12 to 15 minutes or until knife-tender. Drain and return to pot. Mash potatoes with a potato masher, then stir in milk, butter, pineapple, brown sugar, pumpkin pie spice and salt.

② Transfer mixture to a 2½-quart oval casserole dish; smooth out top. Starting at the top left, alternate one marshmallow with two pecan halves until the entire casserole is covered. Bake at 350° for 25 to 30 minutes, or until marshmallows are browned and puffed.

PER SERVING 343 calories; 11 g fat (4 g sat); 5 g protein; 59 g carbohydrate; 6 g fiber; 191 mg sodium; 17 mg cholesterol

GOLDEN ROASTED TURKEY WITH PAN GRAVY

MAKES 12 servings (plus leftovers)
PREP 15 minutes **BAKE** at 350° for 30 minutes,
at 325° for 2½ hours **LET STAND** 20 minutes

TURKEY

1 frozen turkey (about 14 pounds), thawed as per package directions
Apple-Sausage Stuffing (recipe, page 288)

3 tablespoons butter

2 tablespoons honey

2 teaspoons each chopped fresh thyme leaves, rosemary and sage

¼ teaspoon salt

¼ teaspoon black pepper

PAN GRAVY

1½ cups low-sodium chicken broth

2 tablespoons all-purpose flour

① **Turkey.** Heat oven to 350°. Remove giblets from turkey and rinse turkey inside and out. Pat dry with paper towels. Place turkey on a rack in a roasting pan. Tuck wings under breast.

② Loosely pack Apple-Sausage Stuffing into cavity. Tie legs together.

③ Combine butter, honey, herbs, salt and pepper in a small saucepan over medium heat. Cook 2 to 3 minutes, until butter is melted. Brush over turkey, and also under skin on breast, if desired.

④ Roast turkey at 350° for 30 minutes. Baste with any remaining glaze. Lower oven temperature to 325°. Cover with foil and continue to roast until thigh meat registers 165° on an instant-read thermometer, about 2½ more hours, or about 15 minutes per pound. Transfer turkey to platter and let stand 20 minutes.

⑤ **Pan Gravy.** Strain pan drippings into a fat separator. Pour ½ cup defatted juices into a small saucepan along with 2 tablespoons of the turkey fat. Whisk in chicken broth and flour. Bring to a boil over medium-high heat. Cook 3 minutes. Garnish turkey with extra herbs and orange sections. Serve with gravy alongside.

PER SERVING 482 calories; 15 g fat (6 g sat); 78 g protein; 3 g carbohydrate; 0 g fiber; 306 mg sodium; 240 mg cholesterol

Have foil at the ready as the buttery honey glaze may burn. Tent foil over top of breast and over wings to avoid overbrowning.

CRANBERRY-APPLE MOLD

MAKES 8 servings **COOK** 15 minutes
REFRIGERATE 8 hours or overnight

1 bag (12 ounces) fresh cranberries

1 Fuji or Gala apple, peeled, cored and diced into ½-inch pieces

1 2-inch piece of ginger, peeled and grated

1 cup sugar

1 envelope unflavored gelatin
Pinch of salt

① Combine cranberries, apple, ginger, sugar and 1 cup water in a medium pot. Bring to a boil, then reduce to a simmer and cook 15 minutes.

② Meanwhile, in a small bowl, combine gelatin with 2 tablespoons hot water. Stir to dissolve. Add pinch of salt. Set aside for 5 minutes or until gelatin swells.

③ Pour ½ cup of the cooked cranberry mixture into the dissolved gelatin; mix to combine. Pour back into the pot and stir. Transfer to a 4-cup mold and cool slightly. Cover with plastic wrap and refrigerate at least 8 hours or overnight.

PER SERVING 91 calories; 1 g fat (0 g sat); 1 g protein; 25 g carbohydrate; 2 g fiber; 3 mg sodium; 0 mg cholesterol

GREEN BEANS & BRUSSELS SPROUTS

MAKES 8 servings **PREP** 18 minutes
COOK 11 minutes **BAKE** at 350° for 20 minutes

10 ounces Brussels sprouts, trimmed and halved

1 pound green beans, halved

4 slices thick-cut bacon, diced

3 tablespoons all-purpose flour

2 cups reserved Wild Mushroom Soup (recipe, page 288)

1 cup French's Fried Onions

¼ teaspoon salt

¼ teaspoon pepper

① Bring a large pot of lightly salted water to a boil. Add Brussels sprouts; after 3 minutes, add the beans to the same pot. Boil for another 4 minutes. Drain and set aside.

② Meanwhile, cook bacon in a large nonstick skillet on medium heat for 8 minutes or until slightly crisp. Stir in flour and cook for 1 minute. Add soup and bring to a simmer; cook 2 more minutes or until thickened. Stir in reserved vegetables, salt and pepper. Pour into a 2½-quart casserole dish and top with fried onions. Bake at 350° for 20 minutes or until fried onions are browned.

PER SERVING 171 calories; 11 g fat (4 g sat); 5 g protein; 15 g carbohydrate; 4 g fiber; 329 mg sodium; 14 mg cholesterol

Baked to Perfection

Last served, first remembered—seven irresistible desserts.

PEAR & CRANBERRY
CROSTATA, PAGE 301

PUMPKIN MOUSSE–FILLED
CUPCAKES, PAGE 301

**STRAWBERRY LINZER
COOKIE TART**

STRAWBERRY LINZER COOKIE TART

MAKES 16 servings **PREP** 15 minutes
FREEZE 25 minutes **BAKE** at 400° for 12 minutes
and at 350° for 40 minutes

2¼ cups all-purpose flour
1 teaspoon ground cinnamon
½ teaspoon salt
⅛ teaspoon ground nutmeg
14 tablespoons butter (1¾ sticks), cut into small pieces and chilled
1 cup sugar
2½ cups walnuts, ground (about ⅔ pound)
1 egg, lightly beaten
1 egg yolk, lightly beaten
1 jar (12 ounces) seedless strawberry jam
1 egg, beaten with 1 teaspoon water
¼ cup slivered almonds
1 tablespoon confectioners' sugar

① Heat oven to 400°. In a large bowl, whisk flour, cinnamon, salt and nutmeg. Cut in butter until mixture resembles coarse crumbs. Add sugar and walnuts.

② Stir in whole egg and yolk. Work into ball; divide dough in half. Press half of dough into the bottom and up sides of a 9-inch nonstick tart pan with removable bottom.

③ Bake at 400° in bottom rack of oven for 10 to 12 minutes until barely colored.

④ Meanwhile, roll remaining dough between sheets of wax paper to ¼-inch thickness. Put on baking sheet; freeze 25 minutes.

⑤ Reduce oven temperature to 350°. Spread jam over baked tart bottom. Remove top piece of wax paper from chilled dough; cut into 1-inch-wide strips. Arrange over jam in lattice pattern, without weaving, about ½ inch apart, piecing strips if necessary. Press ends of strips to edge.

⑥ Brush egg over pastry; scatter almonds around edge.

⑦ Bake at 350° for 40 minutes or until browned. Cool on wire rack. Gently remove ring; dust tart with confectioners' sugar.

PER SERVING 383 calories; 24 g fat (8 g sat); 6 g protein; 40 g carbohydrate; 2 g fiber; 84 mg sodium; 66 mg cholesterol

PUMPKIN SWIRL CHEESECAKE

MAKES 16 servings **PREP** 25 minutes **MICROWAVE** 1 minute
BAKE at 350° for 1 hour, 20 minutes **REFRIGERATE** overnight

CRUST
1 box (9 ounces) Nabisco Famous Chocolate Wafers, finely crushed
2 tablespoons sugar
6 tablespoons butter, melted

FILLING
1½ pounds cream cheese, softened
½ cup granulated sugar
½ cup packed brown sugar
2 tablespoons cornstarch
1 teaspoon pumpkin pie spice
1 cup pumpkin pie mix
4 eggs
1 teaspoon vanilla
½ cup milk chocolate baking chips

① Heat oven to 350°. Wrap bottom and sides of a 9-inch springform pan with foil.

② **Crust.** Mix together cookie crumbs, sugar and butter. Press over bottom and partially up sides of prepared pan. Refrigerate while making filling.

③ **Filling.** In a large bowl, beat cream cheese until smooth. Beat in sugars, cornstarch and pumpkin pie spice until combined. Beat in pie mix, and eggs one at a time; add vanilla and beat until smooth. Reserve ½ cup batter.

④ Microwave chocolate for 30 seconds, stir and microwave another 15 seconds. Stir again and mix into reserved batter; microwave an additional 15 seconds.

⑤ Pour batter into prepared pan. Dollop heaping tablespoons of the chocolate mixture over top of cake and swirl with a small knife or spatula. Place in roasting pan, adding enough hot water to come halfway up side of foil.

⑥ Bake at 350° for 70 to 80 minutes, until just set. Run a knife around edge of pan. Cool in pan on rack. Cover; refrigerate overnight. Remove side of pan to serve.

PER SERVING 370 calories; 24 g fat (14 g sat); 7 g protein; 33 g carbohydrate; 2 g fiber; 267 mg sodium; 115 mg cholesterol

CARROT CAKE

MAKES 18 servings **PREP** 25 minutes **BAKE** at 350° for 40 minutes **REFRIGERATE** 1 hour

2½ **cups all-purpose flour**
2 **teaspoons baking soda**
1 **teaspoon pumpkin pie spice**
1 **teaspoon ground cinnamon**
½ **teaspoon salt**
1½ **cups sugar**
1¼ **cups vegetable oil**
4 **eggs**
2½ **teaspoons vanilla extract**
3 **large carrots, finely shredded (about 1½ cups)**
1 **can (8 ounces) crushed pineapple in juice**
1 **cup chopped walnuts**
½ **cup golden raisins**
1 **pound reduced-fat cream cheese (Neufchâtel)**
4 **tablespoons unsalted butter, softened**
3 **cups confectioners' sugar**
   Chopped walnuts, for garnish (optional)

① Heat oven to 350°. Coat bottoms of three 8 x 2-inch round cake pans with nonstick cooking spray. Line bottom of pans with wax paper; coat with spray.

② In a medium-size bowl, whisk together flour, baking soda, pumpkin pie spice, cinnamon and salt. In a large bowl, beat sugar, oil, eggs and 1½ teaspoons of the vanilla until blended. On low speed, gradually beat in flour mixture until smooth. Stir in carrots, pineapple with its juice, nuts and raisins. Divide batter among prepared pans, about 2 generous cups in each. Spread evenly.

③ Place two of the pans on the middle rack of the oven and the third pan in the middle of the top rack. Bake at 350° for 40 minutes or until toothpick inserted in centers of cake layers comes out clean. Cool in pans on wire rack for 10 minutes.

Turn out onto wire racks, removing pans and wax paper. Cool completely.

④ In a large bowl, beat cream cheese, butter and remaining teaspoon vanilla until light and creamy, about 2 minutes. On low speed, gradually beat in confectioners' sugar. Beat until fluffy, about 2 minutes.

⑤ With a serrated knife, trim tops of layers to make level. Place one layer on serving plate. Spread ¾ cup frosting over top. Repeat with second layer. Place third layer on top and spread with 1 cup frosting; spread remaining frosting around side of cake. Garnish with chopped nuts around top edge of cake, if desired. Refrigerate cake for at least 1 hour, or until frosting is set.

PER SERVING 515 calories; 29 g fat (7 g sat); 7 g protein; 58 g carbohydrate; 2 g fiber; 276 mg sodium; 72 mg cholesterol

PEAR & CRANBERRY CROSTATA

MAKES 8 servings **PREP** 20 minutes
REFRIGERATE 30 minutes
MICROWAVE 30 seconds **BAKE** at 400° for
45 minutes

PASTRY

1   cup all-purpose flour
3   tablespoons sugar
⅛   teaspoon salt
¼   cup reduced-fat cream cheese
     (Neufchâtel), chilled
2   tablespoons solid vegetable
     shortening, chilled

FILLING

⅓   cup sweetened dried cranberries
3   tablespoons apple or orange juice
3   Bartlett pears (about 1½ pounds)
3   tablespoons sugar
1   tablespoon cornstarch
½   teaspoon ground cinnamon
1   egg yolk, lightly beaten

① **Pastry.** In a bowl, whisk flour, sugar
and salt. With pastry blender, cut in cream
cheese and shortening until coarse crumbs
form. Sprinkle with 3 tablespoons cold
water, 1 tablespoon at a time, until dough
just holds together. Shape into 6-inch disk.
Wrap well; refrigerate 30 minutes.

② **Filling.** In a small microwave-safe
bowl, combine cranberries and juice.
Microwave 30 seconds and set aside.

③ Heat oven to 400°.

④ Peel and core pears; halve and cut into
thin slices. In a large bowl, combine pears,
2 tablespoons of the sugar, the cornstarch
and cinnamon. Stir in cranberries and
any liquid.

⑤ On a lightly floured surface, with
floured rolling pin, roll pastry to a 13-inch
circle. Roll up pastry onto pin; unroll onto
large ungreased baking sheet. Mound pear
filling into center, leaving a 2½-inch
border. Fold border up and partway over
filling (crostata should measure 8 inches
across). Brush edge with egg; sprinkle with
remaining tablespoon of sugar.

⑥ Bake at 400° for 40 to 45 minutes or
until pears are tender.

PER SERVING 204 calories; 5 g fat (2 g sat);
3 g protein; 37 g carbohydrate; 3 g fiber;
69 mg sodium; 31 mg cholesterol

If dough gets too soft to work
with, refrigerate on baking
sheet before adding filling.

PUMPKIN MOUSSE-FILLED CUPCAKES

MAKES 16 cupcakes **PREP** 20 minutes
BAKE at 375° for 20 minutes
MICROWAVE 45 seconds

CUPCAKES

2   cups all-purpose flour
2½   teaspoons baking powder
¼   teaspoon salt
½   cup (1 stick) unsalted butter,
     softened
1¼   cups sugar
2   eggs
1   teaspoon vanilla extract
¾   cup milk
1   cup whipped topping, thawed
½   cup canned pumpkin pie filling

FROSTING

5   ounces semisweet chocolate,
     chopped
5   tablespoons brewed coffee
⅓   cup unsalted butter, cut up

① **Cupcakes.** Heat oven to 375°.
Line 16 muffin cups with paper liners.

② In a bowl, whisk flour, baking powder
and salt. In a large bowl, beat butter and
sugar until smooth. Add eggs, vanilla and
¼ cup of the milk; beat 3 minutes, until
fluffy. In three additions, alternately beat in

flour mixture and remaining ½ cup milk.
Spoon scant ¼ cup into each liner.

③ Bake at 375° for 20 minutes or until
toothpick inserted in center comes out
clean. Cool on wire rack.

④ Blend whipped topping and pumpkin
pie filling. Spoon into a pastry bag fitted
with a medium-size round tip. Insert into
top of each cake, about ½ inch deep, and
squeeze until top starts to rise slightly.

⑤ **Frosting.** Microwave chocolate
and coffee for 30 seconds. Stir, then
microwave 15 more seconds. Stir until
smooth; add 4 pieces of butter at a time
and stir until smooth. Let stand until
spreadable consistency.

⑥ Frost cupcakes; chill until set.

PER CUPCAKE 280 calories; 14 g fat (9 g sat);
4 g protein; 37 g carbohydrate; 1 g fiber;
125 mg sodium; 52 mg cholesterol

To pipe in mousse, fill bag
half full; twist to close. Secure
with a storage bag tie.

Let's Bake!

Santa—and everyone else—will be sweet on these holiday cookies.

1. PEPPERMINT KISSES

MAKES about 4 dozen cookies **PREP** 20 minutes
BAKE at 375° for 12 minutes

1   cup blanched slivered almonds
3   tablespoons plus ½ cup (1 stick) unsalted butter, softened
1¾ cups all-purpose flour
1   teaspoon baking soda
½   teaspoon salt
1¼ cups granulated sugar
1   large egg
1   teaspoon vanilla extract
1   bag (1 pound) candy cane-flavor Hershey's Kisses, unwrapped

① Heat oven to 375°. In a mini chopper or food processor, pulse almonds until finely ground. Add 3 tablespoons of the butter. Pulse until combined and fairly smooth.

② In a medium bowl, combine flour, baking soda and salt. In a large bowl, beat the almond mixture and remaining ½ cup butter with an electric mixer. Add 1 cup of the sugar and beat until smooth. Add egg and vanilla and mix well. On low, beat in flour mixture.

③ Form a teaspoon of dough into a ball. Roll the ball in the remaining ¼ cup sugar and place on an ungreased baking sheet. Repeat with remaining dough and sugar.

④ Bake cookies at 375° for 12 minutes. Remove from oven; press a candy kiss into the center of each cookie. Cool 2 minutes on pans, then transfer to a rack to cool completely.

PER COOKIE 103 calories; 6 g fat (3 g sat); 2 g protein; 12 g carbohydrate; 0 g fiber; 59 mg sodium; 12 mg cholesterol

2. TRICOLOR MERINGUES

MAKES about 2 dozen cookies **PREP** 15 minutes
BAKE at 250° for 1 hour

2   large egg whites, at room temperature
¼   teaspoon cream of tartar
¼   teaspoon lemon juice
¼   teaspoon vanilla extract
    Pinch of salt
¾   cup superfine sugar
    Red food coloring
1   tablespoon unsweetened cocoa powder

① Heat oven to 250°. Line two large cookie sheets with nonstick foil.

② Using a mixer with the whisk attachment, whip egg whites until frothy. Add cream of tartar, lemon juice, vanilla and salt. A little at a time, add sugar while whisking on high speed. Whisk until all sugar is incorporated and stiff shiny peaks are formed. Transfer one-third into one bowl and one-third into a second bowl. Spoon remaining batter into a quart-size resealable plastic bag. Tint one bowl of batter pink with the food coloring. Sift cocoa over second bowl and fold into batter. Transfer both tinted batches of batter to two resealable plastic bags.

③ Snip a corner from all three bags and pipe dollops of batter onto foil-lined sheets. Bake at 250° for 1 hour, until dry to the touch. Remove to a wire rack to cool completely.

PER COOKIE 16 calories; 0 g fat (0 g sat); 1 g protein; 2 g carbohydrate; 0 g fiber; 5 mg sodium; 0 mg cholesterol

3. DOUBLE CHOCOLATE-MOCHA COOKIES

MAKES 4½ dozen cookies **PREP** 15 minutes
BAKE at 375° for 11 minutes

2½ cups all-purpose flour
¾   cup unsweetened cocoa powder
1   teaspoon baking powder
¼   teaspoon salt
1   cup (2 sticks) unsalted butter, at room temperature
¾   cup packed light-brown sugar
¾   cup granulated sugar
2   eggs
2   teaspoons vanilla
¼   cup hot coffee or water
1½ cups red, green and white M&M's candies

① Heat oven to 375°. Sift together flour, cocoa, baking powder and salt.

② Beat butter in a large bowl until smooth and creamy. Add brown and granulated sugars and beat until light and fluffy. Beat in eggs, one at a time. Add vanilla.

③ On low speed, beat flour mixture into butter mixture. Stir in hot coffee. Fold in M&M's.

④ Drop batter by heaping tablespoonfuls onto ungreased baking sheets.

⑤ Bake at 375° for 8 to 11 minutes or until set. Let cool slightly on baking sheets. Transfer cookies to wire racks to cool.

PER COOKIE 105 calories; 5 g fat (3 g sat); 1 g protein; 15 g carbohydrate; 1 g fiber; 28 mg sodium; 17 mg cholesterol

4. CANDY CANE TWISTS

MAKES 2½ dozen cookies **PREP** 20 minutes
REFRIGERATE 2 hours
BAKE at 350° for 10 minutes

2¼ cups all-purpose flour
½   teaspoon baking powder
½   teaspoon salt
½   cup (1 stick) unsalted butter, at room temperature
⅔   cup sugar
1   large egg
1   egg white, beaten
1   teaspoon peppermint extract
    Red and green liquid food coloring
1   egg white, lightly beaten

① In a small bowl, whisk 2 cups of the flour, the baking powder and salt. In a large bowl, beat butter and sugar until smooth, 1 minute. Beat in egg, egg white and peppermint. On low speed, beat in flour mixture. Remove half of dough to a bowl; tint dough dark pink/reddish with 6 to 8 drops red food coloring. Knead 4 drops green food coloring into second half of dough. Flatten each piece into an 8-inch disk; wrap each in plastic. Refrigerate 2 hours.

② Heat oven to 350°. On a floured surface, roll out dark pink dough to a 10 x 8-inch rectangle. Cut lengthwise into sixteen ½-inch-wide strips. Cut each strip in half crosswise; you will have 32 strips, each 5 x ½ inch. Roll with hands to make 6-inch ropes. Repeat with green dough.

③ Twist together one pink rope and one green rope. Curl one end of each twist into a "hook" to form a candy cane shape. Transfer to an ungreased baking sheet. Brush with beaten egg white. Repeat.

④ Bake cookies at 350° for 8 to 10 minutes, until firm and golden around edges. Remove promptly from baking sheets; transfer carefully to wire racks with a large spatula. Cool completely.

PER COOKIE 85 calories; 3 g fat (2 g sat); 2 g protein; 12 g carbohydrate; 1 g fiber; 52 mg sodium; 15 mg cholesterol

5. CRANBERRY BLONDIES

MAKES 32 blondie bars **PREP** 10 minutes
BAKE at 325° for 40 minutes
MICROWAVE 45 seconds

¾ cup (1½ sticks) unsalted butter, softened
1 cup packed light-brown sugar
1 egg
1 teaspoon vanilla extract
2 cups all-purpose flour
1¼ cups white chocolate chips
½ cup sweetened dried cranberries, chopped
½ teaspoon salt
¼ cup semisweet chocolate chips

① Heat oven to 325°. Coat an 8 x 8 x 2-inch baking pan with nonstick cooking spray.

② In a large bowl, beat butter and sugar together until smooth. Next, beat in egg and vanilla extract. On low speed, add in flour, 1 cup of the white chocolate chips, the dried cranberries and salt. Press evenly into bottom of prepared baking pan.

③ Bake at 325° for 40 minutes or until center is firm to the touch. Cool completely on a wire rack.

④ Place the remaining ¼ cup white chocolate chips in a small glass bowl. Microwave for 45 seconds. Stir until smooth. Transfer to a small resealable plastic bag. Repeat with the semisweet chocolate chips. Snip off a corner of each bag and drizzle chocolates over blondies. Cut into 16 squares, then cut each square in half, for a total of 32 bars.

PER BLONDIE 143 calories; 7 g fat (4 g sat); 1 g protein; 19 g carbohydrate; 0 g fiber; 48 mg sodium; 19 mg cholesterol

6. SNOWFLAKES

MAKES 20 cookies **PREP** 10 minutes
REFRIGERATE 2 hours
BAKE at 350° for 12 minutes

COOKIES
1¾ cups all-purpose flour
½ teaspoon baking powder
¼ teaspoon salt
½ cup (1 stick) unsalted butter, at room temperature
¾ cup granulated sugar
1 egg plus 1 egg yolk
1 teaspoon vanilla extract

ROYAL ICING
3 cups confectioners' sugar
2 tablespoons powdered egg whites (see note)
Sparkling sugar

① **Cookies.** Whisk flour, baking powder and salt in a small bowl. Beat butter, sugar, egg, egg yolk and vanilla in a large bowl until blended. Stir in flour mixture. Gather into a ball; wrap in plastic. Refrigerate 2 hours.

② Heat oven to 350°. Roll out dough with a lightly floured rolling pin on a floured surface to ⅜-inch thickness. Cut with 4-inch snowflake cookie cutter. Place 1½ inches apart on ungreased baking sheets. Bake at 350° for 10 to 12 minutes, until just browned at edges. Remove cookies to a wire rack to cool.

③ **Icing.** In a medium-size bowl, combine confectioners' sugar, powdered egg whites and 2 tablespoons cool water. Beat on high with an electric mixer for 5 minutes, adding more water as needed for good piping consistency. Divide in half; transfer one half to a pastry bag fitted with a small writing tip. Thin remaining half with a little bit of water (to make a base coat). Spread some of the cookies with thinned icing; let dry. Pipe decorations on cookies with thicker icing; sprinkle with sugar. Let icing dry 1 hour before stacking cookies.

Note: Look for powdered egg whites in your store's baking section or order meringue powder from wilton.com.

PER COOKIE 153 calories; 5 g fat (3 g sat); 2 g protein; 25 g carbohydrate; 0 g fiber; 48 mg sodium; 34 mg cholesterol

7. GINGERBREAD SNOWMEN

MAKES about 3½ dozen cookies **PREP** 15 minutes
REFRIGERATE 2 hours **BAKE** at 350° for 11 minutes

½ cup (1 stick) unsalted butter, softened
½ cup sugar
1 egg
¼ cup light molasses
2⅓ cups all-purpose flour
1 tablespoon cocoa powder
¾ teaspoon baking soda
1 tablespoon ground ginger
1 teaspoon ground white pepper
½ teaspoon ground cinnamon

Royal Icing (recipe, left)
Candy corn, halved lengthwise
Mini chocolate chips

① Beat together butter and sugar. Add egg and molasses and beat until smooth. Combine flour, cocoa, baking soda, ginger, pepper and cinnamon in another bowl. Stir into butter mixture. Divide dough in half. Wrap in plastic and refrigerate for 2 hours.

② Heat oven to 350°. Roll half of dough on a floured surface to ⅛ inch thick. Cut circles with a 3½-inch cutter; transfer to ungreased baking sheets. Reroll scraps; cut. Repeat with the remaining dough.

③ Bake at 350° for 11 minutes. Transfer to wire racks to cool. Spread with Royal Icing; decorate with candy corn and mini chips to resemble a face.

PER COOKIE 80 calories; 2 g fat (1 g sat); 1 g protein; 14 g carbohydrate; 0 g fiber; 29 mg sodium; 11 mg cholesterol

8. BUTTER-RUM RIBBONS

MAKES 5½ dozen cookies **PREP** 15 minutes
BAKE at 350° for 10 minutes

1 cup (2 sticks) unsalted butter, softened
¾ cup packed light-brown sugar
1 large egg
½ teaspoon salt
2½ cups all-purpose flour
½ cup ground pecans
2 teaspoons rum extract

CHOCOLATE-RUM GLAZE
4 squares (1 ounce each) white or semisweet chocolate, chopped
1 teaspoon rum extract
2 tablespoons heavy cream
¼ cup pecans, finely chopped

① Heat oven to 350°. In large bowl, beat butter, sugar, egg and salt until fluffy, 3 minutes. On low speed, beat in flour until smooth; stir in pecans and rum extract.

② Put dough into a cookie press fitted with a 1-inch sawtooth ribbon disc. Press out long strips on baking sheets. With floured knife, score strips crosswise every 1½ inches.

③ Bake at 350° until edges are light brown, 8 to 10 minutes. Cut cookies along score lines; let cool on rack.

④ **Glaze.** In small glass bowl, microwave chocolate at 100% power 1 to 1½ minutes; stir until smooth. Stir in extract and cream. Dip end of each cookie in chocolate; place on wax-paper-lined baking sheet. Sprinkle with pecans. Let stand at room temperature or refrigerate to set.

PER COOKIE 71 calories; 4 g fat (2 g sat); 1 g protein; 7 g carbohydrate; 1 g fiber; 20 mg sodium; 11 mg cholesterol

9. FESTIVE WREATHS

MAKES 6½ dozen cookies **PREP** 15 minutes
BAKE at 350° for 10 minutes

1 cup (2 sticks) unsalted butter, at room temperature
⅔ cup sugar
1 large egg
¼ teaspoon salt
2¼ cups all-purpose flour
    Green liquid food coloring
    Red Hots candies, edible confetti or mini red M&M's, to decorate

① Heat oven to 350°. In a large bowl, beat together butter, sugar, egg and salt until fluffy, 3 minutes. On low speed, beat in flour until smooth. Tint dough pale green with food coloring.

② Spoon dough into a cookie press fitted with a standard wreath disc, following manufacturer's directions. Press out wreaths onto large baking sheets, spacing cookies about ¾ inch apart. Before baking, press in candy "berries" or confetti.

③ Bake cookies at 350° for 8 to 10 minutes or until slightly puffed and set. Transfer cookies directly to wire racks to cool.

PER COOKIE 44 calories; 2 g fat (1 g sat); 0 g protein; 5 g carbohydrate; 0 g fiber; 9 mg sodium; 9 mg cholesterol

10. LINZER TREES

MAKES 24 filled sandwiches **PREP** 25 minutes
REFRIGERATE at least 2 hours **BAKE** at 350° for 11 minutes

3 cups all-purpose flour
1 cup pistachios, finely chopped
¼ teaspoon salt
14 tablespoons (1¾ sticks) unsalted butter, softened
1 cup confectioners' sugar, plus more for dusting

2 large eggs
1 teaspoon vanilla extract
¼ cup seedless raspberry jam

① Whisk together flour, pistachios and salt in a large bowl. Set aside.

② In another large bowl, beat butter and confectioners' sugar until smooth, about 3 minutes. Beat in eggs and vanilla. Mixture may look curdled. On low speed, beat in flour mixture. Divide dough in half; form into two disks. Wrap in plastic; refrigerate at least 2 hours.

③ Heat oven to 350°. Working with half of the dough at a time, roll out on a floured surface to ³/₁₆-inch thickness. Using a 3-inch tree cutter, cut out cookies and place on prepared baking sheets. Using a drinking straw, cut out "ornaments" from

half the cookies. Reroll scraps if necessary and repeat with remaining dough for a total of 48 cookies.

④ Bake at 350° for 11 minutes or until cookies just begin to turn golden. Remove from baking sheets to wire racks and let cool.

⑤ Dust half of the cutout cookies with confectioners' sugar. Spread ½ teaspoon raspberry jam on each remaining cookie. Place cutout cookies on top of jam-topped cookies. Let stand at room temperature until set.

PER COOKIE 179 calories; 10 g fat (5 g sat); 3 g protein; 21 g carbohydrate; 1 g fiber; 31 mg sodium; 35 mg cholesterol

Slow Cooker Suppers
Pot roast five ways.

YANKEE POT ROAST

One inexpensive cut of meat makes for many delicious dinners.

YANKEE POT ROAST

MAKES 8 servings **PREP** 15 minutes
SLOW COOK on HIGH for 6 hours or LOW for 8 hours

1	large onion, chopped
2	cloves garlic, chopped
1	beef chuck roast, about 3 pounds
½	teaspoon salt
¼	teaspoon black pepper
½	pound carrots, peeled and cut into 3 x ½-inch-thick sticks
1	pound small red-skinned potatoes, each about 1 inch in diameter, quartered
2	ribs celery, cut into 3 x ½-inch-thick sticks
1	cup reduced-sodium beef broth
2	tablespoons tomato paste
½	teaspoon dried thyme
2	tablespoons Worcestershire sauce
3	tablespoons cornstarch

① Coat slow cooker bowl with nonstick cooking spray.

② Place onion and garlic in slow cooker. Season beef with salt and pepper; place over onions. Arrange carrots, potatoes and celery around beef, in that order. Combine broth, tomato paste and thyme; pour over beef. Drizzle 1 tablespoon of the Worcestershire sauce over top.

③ Cover and cook on HIGH for 6 hours or LOW for 8 hours.

④ Remove beef from slow cooker and place on a serving platter. Spoon out vegetables with a slotted spoon and place around roast. Keep warm.

⑤ Strain cooking liquid into a medium-size saucepan; skim off excess fat. Bring to a simmer. Combine cornstarch with 3 tablespoons water and stir into saucepan. Simmer for 1 minute until thickened. Stir in remaining tablespoon Worcestershire sauce.

⑥ Slice beef and serve with vegetables and gravy.

PER SERVING 304 calories; 7 g fat (3 g sat); 38 g protein; 20 g carbohydrate; 2 g fiber; 337 mg sodium; 72 mg cholesterol

SAUERBRATEN

Eliminate carrots, potatoes and celery; reduce broth to ½ cup and add ½ cup distilled white vinegar. In place of tomato paste and Worcestershire add 3 tablespoons sugar. Serve with mashed potatoes and red cabbage.

**STROGANOFF-STYLE
POT ROAST**

Beef chuck roast is conveniently suited to slow cooking—it requires long cooking times to make it meltingly tender. It's the definition of comfort food, no matter how you spice it.

STROGANOFF-STYLE POT ROAST

Replace carrots, potatoes and celery with 3 cups sliced mushrooms and tomato paste with 1 tablespoon mustard. Eliminate Worcestershire sauce. Stir ½ cup sour cream and 2 tablespoons parsley into sauce. Cut roast into 2-inch pieces. Serve with cooked egg noodles and peas.

ROPA VIEJA

Try a Mexican spin by subbing 1 chopped green pepper for carrots, potatoes and celery; add 1 can (14½ ounces) fire-roasted diced tomatoes in place of broth and tomato paste. Eliminate thyme and Worcestershire sauce; add 1 teaspoon each ancho chile powder, cumin and dried oregano. Shred beef into sauce and stir in a 10-ounce package thawed frozen corn and 2 tablespoons chopped cilantro. Serve with corn tortillas.

COFFEE-BRAISED BEEF

Switch out carrots, potatoes and celery with 2 cups sliced mushrooms and 2 sliced scallions. Substitute 1½ cups brewed coffee and 2 teaspoons liquid smoke for broth and tomato paste. Use chili powder in place of thyme and eliminate Worcestershire sauce. Serve with cooked rice and a green vegetable.

ROPA VIEJA

COFFEE-BRAISED BEEF

CHOCOLATE-ALMOND BREAD,
PAGE 322

DECEMBER

313

316

321

Easy Does It

Weeknight recipes for the most wonderful time of the year.

**GNOCCHI WITH PINE NUTS
& BROCCOLI RABE**

GNOCCHI WITH PINE NUTS & BROCCOLI RABE

MAKES 4 servings   **PREP** 10 minutes
COOK 8 minutes

- 3   tablespoons olive oil
- 3   cloves garlic, thinly sliced
- 1   large bunch broccoli rabe, stems removed and discarded, cut into 2-inch pieces
- ¼   teaspoon salt
- ¼   teaspoon red pepper flakes
- 1   pound potato gnocchi (such as De Cecco)
- 2   tablespoons toasted pine nuts
- ⅓   cup shredded Asiago cheese

① Bring a large pot of water to a boil.

② In a large nonstick skillet, heat 2 tablespoons of the oil over medium-high heat; add garlic and cook 1 minute until golden. Add broccoli rabe, salt and red pepper flakes; stir-fry 4 to 5 minutes or until tender.

③ Cook gnocchi following package directions, about 2 minutes. Drain, reserving ½ cup cooking liquid.

④ In a large serving bowl, combine gnocchi and broccoli rabe. Add some of the reserved pasta water to create a sauce and sprinkle with pine nuts and cheese.

⑤ Drizzle remaining tablespoon oil over top and serve immediately.

PER SERVING 375 calories; 16 g fat (4 g sat); 12 g protein; 47 g carbohydrate; 2 g fiber; 757 mg sodium; 10 mg cholesterol

BLUE CHEESE-TOPPED TENDERLOIN WITH MUSHROOMS

MAKES 4 servings   **PREP** 20 minutes   **BAKE** at 400° for 60 minutes   **COOK** 11 minutes

- 2   large baking potatoes, about 1 pound, peeled and thinly sliced
- 1   medium onion, thinly sliced
- 2   cloves garlic, chopped
- 2   cups reduced-sodium beef broth
- ½   teaspoon salt
- ½   teaspoon black pepper
- 1   tablespoon plus 2 teaspoons olive oil
- 4   tenderloin steaks, about 1 inch thick, 4 ounces each
- ¼   cup crumbled blue cheese
- ½   pound sliced shiitake mushrooms
- 1   tablespoon sherry vinegar
     Steamed asparagus, optional

① Heat oven to 400°. Coat an 8 x 8-inch baking dish with nonstick cooking spray.

② Layer potatoes in prepared dish, in an overlapping fashion, alternating with onion slices. Sprinkle with garlic and spoon 1 cup of the broth over top. Season with ¼ teaspoon each salt and pepper. Cover with foil and bake at 400° for 40 minutes. Uncover and bake 20 minutes or until potatoes are tender. Keep warm.

③ In a large nonstick skillet, heat 1 tablespoon oil over medium-high heat. Season steaks with remaining ¼ teaspoon each salt and pepper. Cook for 3 minutes, turn and top each steak with 1 tablespoon cheese. Reduce heat to medium and cover. Cook 2 minutes or until internal temperature of steak registers 145°. Remove to a plate and loosely cover.

④ Add remaining 2 teaspoons oil and mushrooms to skillet; cook over medium-high heat 3 minutes. Stir in remaining cup broth and vinegar; cook 3 minutes, stirring occasionally.

⑤ Serve steaks with mushrooms, potatoes and asparagus, if desired.

PER SERVING 448 calories; 18 g fat (6 g sat); 40 g protein; 33 g carbohydrate; 4 g fiber; 731 mg sodium; 100 mg cholesterol

EASIEST-EVER CHOUCROUTE

MAKES 4 servings **PREP** 15 minutes **COOK** 16 minutes

1 tablespoon olive oil

1½ pounds thin boneless pork chops, cut into ½-inch slices

⅛ plus ½ teaspoon salt

¼ teaspoon black pepper

½ large onion, thinly sliced

2 apple-flavor fully cooked chicken sausages (such as Al Fresco), cut into ½-inch coins

1 bottle (12 ounces) dark beer

1 bag (16 ounces) coleslaw mix

¼ cup cider vinegar

2 tablespoons brown sugar

1 teaspoon caraway seeds

½ cup parsley leaves, chopped

① Heat oil in a large nonstick skillet over medium-high heat. Add pork and season with ⅛ teaspoon of the salt and the black pepper; cook 3 to 4 minutes until cooked through, turning once. Remove to a plate and set aside.

② Add onion and sausage to skillet and cook 5 minutes; add beer and scrape up any browned bits from pan. Stir in coleslaw mix, vinegar, brown sugar, caraway seeds and ½ teaspoon salt. Cook 7 minutes, stirring occasionally.

③ Add reserved pork to pan and heat through. Garnish with parsley and serve.

PER SERVING 458 calories; 18 g fat (5 g sat); 45 g protein; 23 g carbohydrate; 4 g fiber; 779 mg sodium; 143 mg cholesterol

SCALLOPS FRA DIAVOLO

MAKES 4 servings **PREP** 15 minutes
COOK 11 minutes

- 1 tablespoon olive oil
- ½ large onion, peeled and chopped
- 3 cloves garlic, finely chopped
- 1 can (28 ounces) crushed tomatoes
- 1 teaspoon sugar
- ½ teaspoon dried oregano
- ½ teaspoon red pepper flakes
- ¼ teaspoon salt
- 1½ pounds sea scallops
- 1 package (10 ounces) frozen peas, thawed
- 1 package (9 ounces) refrigerated fresh fettuccine
- ½ cup fresh basil leaves, torn

① Heat oil in a large nonstick skillet over medium-high heat. Add onion and garlic; cook 3 minutes, stirring occasionally.

② Stir in tomatoes, sugar, oregano, red pepper flakes and salt. Bring to a simmer. Add scallops and cook 5 minutes, turning once. Stir in peas and heat through.

③ Cook pasta following package directions, 2 to 3 minutes. Drain and place in a large serving bowl and toss with the scallops and sauce. Toss in the torn basil and serve immediately.

PER SERVING 488 calories; 7 g fat (1 g sat); 43 g protein; 63 g carbohydrate; 9 g fiber; 744 mg sodium; 89 mg cholesterol

PROVENÇAL PORK CHOPS

MAKES 4 servings **PREP** 10 minutes **COOK** 9 minutes **BROIL** 6 minutes

- 1 cup orzo
- 1 bag (6 ounces) baby spinach
- 2 scallions, trimmed and chopped
- 2 tablespoons olive oil
- 3 tablespoons lemon juice
- 2 teaspoons lemon zest
- ½ plus ⅛ teaspoon salt
- ½ teaspoon black pepper
- 4 pork rib chops, bone in (about 5 ounces each)
- 1 tablespoon Dijon mustard
- 2 teaspoons herbes de Provence seasoning

① Heat broiler. Coat a broiler pan with nonstick cooking spray.

② Cook orzo following package directions, about 9 minutes. Stir in spinach just before draining. Place in a large serving bowl. Stir in scallions, olive oil, lemon juice, zest, ½ teaspoon of the salt and the pepper. Cover with plastic wrap. Set aside.

③ Season pork chops with remaining ⅛ teaspoon salt. Spread mustard and evenly sprinkle herbes de Provence seasoning over both sides of chops. Broil for 3 minutes per side or until internal temperature registers 145°.

④ Serve pork chops with orzo and a green salad, if desired.

PER SERVING 437 calories; 16 g fat (4 g sat); 33 g protein; 39 g carbohydrate; 4 g fiber; 583 mg sodium; 73 mg cholesterol

CHICKEN-BACON BOW TIE BAKE

MAKES 6 servings **PREP** 15 minutes **BROIL** 17 minutes **COOK** 19 minutes

1   large boneless, skinless chicken breast (12 ounces)

4   slices turkey bacon

1   pound tomato and spinach farfalle

2   tablespoons all-purpose flour

2   cups fat-free milk

1   can (10¾ ounces) 98% fat-free condensed cream of chicken soup

½   teaspoon garlic salt

1¼   cups shredded reduced-fat Mexican cheese blend

① Heat broiler. Coat a 2-quart broilerproof baking dish with nonstick cooking spray.

② Place chicken breast on greased broiler pan and broil 4 inches from flame for 6 to 7 minutes per side until internal temperature registers 160°. Remove to plate and cut into ½-inch pieces. Keep warm.

③ In a large nonstick skillet over medium heat, cook bacon about 5 minutes until crisp. Chop and reserve.

④ Cook pasta following package directions, about 12 minutes. Drain.

⑤ Stir flour into milk and combine with soup and garlic salt in a medium-size saucepan. Simmer for 2 minutes until thickened; stir in ¾ cup of the cheese.

⑥ Return pasta to pot and stir in chicken and soup mixture. Spoon into prepared baking dish and top with bacon and remaining ½ cup cheese.

⑦ Broil 4 inches from flame for 2 to 3 minutes or until heated and lightly browned on top. Serve immediately.

PER SERVING 492 calories; 11 g fat (5 g sat); 33 g protein; 65 g carbohydrate; 3 g fiber; 782 mg sodium; 65 mg cholesterol

CHICKEN & BASMATI RICE CASSEROLE

MAKES 6 servings **PREP** 20 minutes **COOK** 14 minutes **BAKE** at 400° for 20 minutes

2   tablespoons canola oil

6   skinless chicken thighs (about 6 ounces each)

½   teaspoon black pepper

1   large onion, chopped

3   cloves garlic, finely chopped

2   tablespoons curry powder

1   tablespoon gingerroot, chopped

3   cups reduced-sodium chicken broth

1   can (15 ounces) chickpeas, drained and rinsed

1   can (14½ ounces) petite diced tomatoes

1   sweet red pepper, cored, seeded and chopped

½   teaspoon salt

1½   cups basmati rice

½   cup cilantro, chopped

① Heat oven to 400°.

② In a large lidded Dutch oven, heat oil over medium-high heat. Season chicken with ¼ teaspoon of the pepper. Cook 5 minutes per side. Remove to a plate.

③ Add onion to Dutch oven and cook 3 minutes over medium-high heat, stirring to loosen any browned bits from bottom of pot. Stir in garlic, curry and ginger; cook 1 minute. Stir in broth, chickpeas, tomatoes, red pepper, salt and remaining ¼ teaspoon pepper.

④ Bring to a simmer and stir in rice. Arrange chicken in rice mixture. Cover and place in oven; bake at 400° for 20 minutes until liquid is absorbed and rice is tender.

⑤ Sprinkle with cilantro and serve.

PER SERVING 485 calories; 16 g fat (3 g sat); 32 g protein; 51 g carbohydrate; 6 g fiber; 793 mg sodium; 86 mg cholesterol

CHICKEN & BASMATI RICE
CASSEROLE

In Good Company

Festive, delicious holiday classics for family and friends.

GLAZED HAM, PAGE 321

FRUIT-NUT PHYLLO CUPS

MAKES 30 appetizers **PREP** 15 minutes
BAKE at 350° for 10 minutes

2	packages (1.9 ounces each) mini phyllo shells
4	ounces Brie cheese, trimmed if desired, cut into ½-inch pieces
⅓	cup dried Mission figs, chopped (about 6)
¼	cup almonds, chopped
1	tablespoon honey
1	tablespoon white wine or cider vinegar
½	teaspoon fresh thyme leaves, chopped
	Pinch each of salt and pepper

① Heat oven to 350°. Spread phyllo cups over a large baking sheet. Bake at 350° for 5 minutes.

② In large bowl, combine Brie, figs and almonds. Toss to combine.

③ In a small bowl, whisk together honey, vinegar, thyme, salt and pepper. Pour over Brie mixture and toss to combine.

④ Spoon a small amount of Brie mixture into each cup, dividing equally among cups. Bake at 350° for an additional 5 minutes. Serve warm.

PER CUP 44 calories; 2 g fat (1 g sat); 2 g protein; 5 g carbohydrate; 1 g fiber; 32 mg sodium; 4 mg cholesterol

ARTICHOKE DIP

MAKES 4 cups (12 servings) **PREP** 15 minutes **COOK** 3 minutes **BAKE** at 350° for 30 minutes

2	tablespoons unsalted butter
2	tablespoons all-purpose flour
1	cup milk
¼	teaspoon each salt and pepper
⅛	teaspoon ground nutmeg
	Pinch cayenne pepper
1	cup shredded Swiss cheese
4	ounces cream cheese, cut up
2	cans (14 ounces each) artichoke hearts, drained
½	of a package (10 ounces) frozen chopped spinach, thawed and squeezed dry
2	cloves garlic, peeled
¼	cup grated Asiago or Parmesan cheese
	Endive leaves and crackers, for serving

① Heat oven to 350°. Coat a shallow 1½-quart baking dish with nonstick cooking spray.

② Melt butter in a medium saucepan over medium heat. Add flour and whisk until smooth. Whisk in milk, salt, pepper, nutmeg and cayenne. Bring to a simmer; cook, simmering, 3 minutes. Remove from heat and whisk in Swiss cheese and cream cheese until smooth.

③ Combine artichoke hearts, spinach and garlic in a food processor and process until evenly blended and chopped. Fold into cheese sauce and pour into prepared dish. Spread smooth and top with grated Asiago or Parmesan. Bake at 350° for 30 minutes, or until bubbly around edges. Serve warm with endive and crackers for scooping.

PER SERVING 148 calories; 8 g fat (5 g sat); 8 g protein; 12 g carbohydrate; 4 g fiber; 560 mg sodium; 24 mg cholesterol

ITALIAN BREAKFAST STRATA

MAKES 8 servings **PREP** 15 minutes **LET STAND** 10 minutes **COOK** 10 minutes **REFRIGERATE** overnight **BAKE** at 350° for 1 hour

- ½ cup sun-dried tomatoes
- ¾ pound sweet Italian sausage, casings removed
- 1 each green and red bell pepper, cored, seeded and diced
- 1 loaf Italian bread (14 ounces), cut into 1-inch cubes
- 8 large eggs
- 1 cup milk
- ⅓ cup packed basil leaves, chopped
- 2 cups shredded mozzarella

① Bring 1 cup water to a boil. Place sun-dried tomatoes in a bowl and add water. Let stand 10 minutes.

② Meanwhile, crumble sausage into a large nonstick skillet. Cook over medium to medium-high heat for 6 minutes. Add peppers and cook, stirring occasionally, 4 minutes. Remove from heat. Drain sun-dried tomatoes and chop. Stir into sausage mixture in skillet.

③ Place bread cubes in a very large bowl. In a medium bowl, whisk eggs, milk and chopped basil. Stir sausage mixture into bread along with 1 cup of the cheese. Pour egg mixture over bread mixture and stir to moisten all ingredients. Coat a 13 x 9 x 2-inch baking dish with nonstick cooking spray. Pour bread mixture into prepared dish. Cover with plastic wrap and refrigerate overnight.

④ Heat oven to 350°. Uncover dish and sprinkle with remaining 1 cup cheese. Cover dish with foil. Bake, covered, at 350° for 45 minutes. Uncover and bake 15 minutes. Cool slightly before serving.

PER SERVING 404 calories; 20 g fat (8 g sat); 23 g protein; 32 g carbohydrate; 3 g fiber; 814 mg sodium; 249 mg cholesterol

LATKES (POTATO PANCAKES)

MAKES 16 pancakes **PREP** 25 minutes
COOK 6 minutes per batch

2 pounds all-purpose potatoes, peeled
1 medium sweet onion, trimmed
2 tablespoons fresh lemon juice (from half of a lemon)
2 cloves garlic, minced
⅓ cup all-purpose flour
2 eggs, lightly beaten
1 teaspoon salt
½ teaspoon black pepper
½ cup vegetable oil
Sour cream and applesauce, for serving

① Heat oven to 200°. Coarsely shred potatoes and onion on a box grater or in a food processor. Combine in a colander or strainer and press out as much liquid as possible. Transfer to a large bowl and toss with lemon juice. Stir in garlic.

② Add flour, eggs, salt and pepper. Stir to combine. Heat ¼ cup of the oil in a 12-inch skillet over medium-high heat.

③ Scoop a scant ⅓ cup of the potato mixture into hot oil and press to flatten to ½ inch thick. Repeat, but do not crowd pan. Cook 2 to 3 minutes per side, until browned. Transfer latkes to a paper towel–lined baking sheet and keep warm in 200° oven. Repeat with all of the potato mixture, adding remaining ¼ cup oil to pan halfway through.

④ Serve latkes with sour cream and applesauce alongside.

PER LATKE 126 calories; 8 g fat (1 g sat); 2 g protein; 13 g carbohydrate; 1 g fiber; 155 mg sodium; 26 mg cholesterol

PEAR SALAD WITH SUGARED WALNUTS

MAKES 6 servings **PREP** 20 minutes
COOK 8 minutes

SALAD
2 cups walnut halves
⅔ cup sugar
1 package (5 ounces) arugula
1 small head butter or Bibb lettuce, cored, cleaned and torn into bite-size pieces
2 ripe pears, halved, cored and sliced
½ cup sweetened dried cranberries
½ cup crumbled blue cheese

DRESSING
3 tablespoons raspberry-flavor or traditional balsamic vinegar
2 teaspoons honey-Dijon mustard
⅛ teaspoon salt
⅛ teaspoon black pepper
⅓ cup extra virgin olive oil

① **Salad.** Combine nuts, sugar and ¼ cup water in a saucepan over medium heat. Cook 6 to 8 minutes, until almost all the liquid has cooked off, stirring constantly for the last 2 minutes. Pour nuts onto a foil-lined sheet and spread out. Let cool.

② In large bowl, combine arugula, butter lettuce, pears, cranberries and blue cheese. Set aside.

③ **Dressing.** In a medium-size bowl, whisk vinegar, mustard, salt and pepper. While whisking, add oil in a thin stream. Gently toss salad with half of the dressing; serve remainder on the side. Coarsely chop 1 cup of the nuts and sprinkle over salad. Reserve extra nuts for snacking or another meal.

PER SERVING 378 calories; 26 g fat (5 g sat); 6 g protein; 33 g carbohydrate; 4 g fiber; 239 mg sodium; 8 mg cholesterol

GLAZED HAM

MAKES 18 servings **PREP** 5 minutes
BAKE at 325° for 2 hours, 30 minutes

1 bone-in fully cooked ham (about 7½ pounds)
½ cup orange marmalade
½ cup orange juice
1 small can (8 ounces) jellied cranberry sauce
2 tablespoons Dijon mustard
¼ teaspoon ground ginger
⅛ teaspoon ground cloves

① Heat oven to 325°. Unwrap ham and place flat side down on a rack in a shallow baking pan. Cover with foil and bake at 325° for 2 hours.

② Meanwhile, combine marmalade, orange juice, cranberry sauce, mustard, ginger and cloves in a small saucepan. Cook over medium-low heat until cranberry sauce has melted and mixture is smooth, about 5 minutes.

③ Uncover ham and turn upright. Brush about one-third of the glaze over ham. Return to oven, uncovered, and bake at 325° for 30 minutes more, brushing with glaze once more during bake time. Serve with remaining glaze alongside.

PER SERVING 202 calories; 11 g fat (4 g sat); 13 g protein; 14 g carbohydrate; 0 g fiber; 1,003 mg sodium; 53 mg cholesterol

In-a-Pinch Substitutions

It can happen to the best of us: Halfway through a recipe,
you find you're completely out of a key ingredient. Here's what to do:

Recipe Calls For:	You May Substitute:
1 square unsweetened chocolate	3 tbsp. unsweetened cocoa powder + 1 tbsp. butter/margarine
1 cup cake flour	1 cup less 2 tbsp. all-purpose flour
2 tbsp. flour (for thickening)	1 tbsp. cornstarch
1 tsp. baking powder	¼ tsp. baking soda + ½ tsp. cream of tartar + ¼ tsp. cornstarch
1 cup corn syrup	1 cup sugar + ¼ cup additional liquid used in recipe
1 cup milk	½ cup evaporated milk + ½ cup water
1 cup buttermilk or sour milk	1 tbsp. vinegar or lemon juice + enough milk to make 1 cup
1 cup sour cream (for baking)	1 cup plain yogurt
1 cup firmly packed brown sugar	1 cup sugar + 2 tbsp. molasses
1 tsp. lemon juice	¼ tsp. vinegar (not balsamic)
¼ cup chopped onion	1 tbsp. instant minced
1 clove garlic	¼ tsp. garlic powder
2 cups tomato sauce	¾ cup tomato paste + 1 cup water
1 tbsp. prepared mustard	1 tsp. dry mustard + 1 tbsp. water

How to Know What You Need

Making a shopping list based on a recipe can be tricky if you don't know
how many tomatoes yields 3 cups chopped. Our handy translations:

When the Recipe Calls For:	You Need:
4 cups shredded cabbage	1 small cabbage
1 cup grated raw carrot	1 large carrot
2½ cups sliced carrots	1 pound raw carrots
4 cups cooked cut fresh green beans	1 pound beans
1 cup chopped onion	1 large onion
4 cups sliced raw potatoes	4 medium-size potatoes
1 cup chopped sweet pepper	1 large pepper
1 cup chopped tomato	1 large tomato
2 cups canned tomatoes	16-oz. can
4 cups sliced apples	4 medium-size apples
1 cup mashed banana	3 medium-size bananas
1 tsp. grated lemon rind	1 medium-size lemon
2 tbsp. lemon juice	1 medium-size lemon
4 tsp. grated orange rind	1 medium-size orange
1 cup orange juice	3 medium-size oranges
4 cups sliced peaches	8 medium-size peaches
2 cups sliced strawberries	1 pint
1 cup soft bread crumbs	2 slices fresh bread
1 cup bread cubes	2 slices fresh bread
2 cups shredded Swiss or cheddar cheese	8 oz. cheese
1 cup egg whites	6 or 7 large eggs
1 egg white	2 tsp. egg white powder + 2 tbsp. water
4 cups chopped walnuts or pecans	1 pound shelled